THE SEXUAL WORLD OF THE ARABIAN NIGHTS

From the stories of wives and their lovers to those of kings and their conquests, to the overarching story of Shahrazad and Shahryar, the tales of the Arabian Nights have offered countless audiences entertainment and enjoyment as well as serving as cautionary stories. An outstanding piece of world literature, the Arabian Nights provide a lively and interesting way of exploring aspects of sexuality, romance, gender, culture, wealth, and politics.

Examining a wide range of the tales with an extensive comparative perspective, David Ghanim offers a rigorous exploration of their profound sexuality: looking at both the context in which they were written and organized, as well as their legacy. By including accounts of heterosexuality, homosexuality, cuckoldry, insatiable lust, promiscuity, rape, incest, bestiality, demonic sexuality, and erotica, Ghanim highlights the complexity and dynamism of medieval sexuality, the active role of women in sexual activities, and the prevailing positive outlook on sexual liaison and gender mixing.

Born in Baghdad, David Ghanim, Ph.D., is a senior scholar of Middle East and gender studies whose previous books include *The Virginity Trap in the Middle East* (2015), *Iraq's Dysfunctional Democracy* (2011), and *Gender and Violence in the Middle East* (2009).

D1715463

THE SEXUAL WORLD OF THE ARABIAN NIGHTS

DAVID GHANIM

CAMBRIDGE
UNIVERSITY PRESS

University Printing House, Cambridge CB2 8BS, United Kingdom

One Liberty Plaza, 20th Floor, New York, NY 10006, USA

477 Williamstown Road, Port Melbourne, VIC 3207, Australia

314–321, 3rd Floor, Plot 3, Splendor Forum, Jasola District Centre, New Delhi – 110025, India

79 Anson Road, #06-04/06, Singapore 079906

Cambridge University Press is part of the University of Cambridge.

It furthers the University's mission by disseminating knowledge in the pursuit of education, learning, and research at the highest international levels of excellence.

www.cambridge.org
Information on this title: www.cambridge.org/9781108442251
DOI: 10.1017/9781108675277

First published 2018

Printed in the United States of America by Sheridan Books, Inc.

A catalogue record for this publication is available from the British Library.

Library of Congress Cataloging-in-Publication Data
Names: Ghanim, David, author.
Title: The sexual world of the Arabian Nights / David Ghanim.
Description: Cambridge; New York, NY: Cambridge University Press, 2018. |
Includes bibliographical references and index.
Identifiers: LCCN 2017057292 | ISBN 9781108425360 (hardback) |
ISBN 9781108442251 (paperback)
Subjects: LCSH: Arabian nights. | Sex in literature. |
BISAC: HISTORY / Middle East / General.
Classification: LCC PJ7737.G48 2019 | DDC 398.22–dc23
LC record available at https://lccn.loc.gov/2017057292

ISBN 978-1-108-42536-0 Hardback
ISBN 978-1-108-44225-1 Paperback

You have created beauty as a temptation to us

And said, O my servants fear me and abstain

Behold, you are beautiful and love beauty

How, then, your creatures from loving refrain

The Arabian Nights

CONTENTS

Preface   *page* ix

   Introduction   1
1 Alluring Sexuality   10
2 Inexorable Sexuality   23
3 Insatiable Lust   37
4 Demonic Sexuality   52
5 Rape and Incest   65
6 Promiscuous Life   77
7 Transgressive Adultery   88
8 Sexual Perfidy   98
9 Tales of Cuckoldry   111
10 Lesbian Encounter   125
11 Tempting Pederasty   138
12 Hedonistic Narrative   152
   Conclusion   167

Select Bibliography   173
Index   183

PREFACE

My personal journey with the tales of the Thousand and One Nights, also known as the Arabian Nights or the Arabic Alf Layla wa Layla, is a long and interesting voyage. We share the same place of birth, Baghdad, the legendary medieval city where these tales were first narrated and written. In my childhood, many tales of this collection gave me immense pleasure and stimulated my wild imagination. Later on, when I became a scholar of Middle Eastern studies, I had a pleasant and surprising thought-provoking re-encounter with the Arabian Nights. While I was at the University of London conducting research, I had access to the original Arabic Bulaq edition of these tales. I borrowed the two volumes from the university library for bedtime reading. Surely, the narrative gave me a tremendous pleasure every night, but it has also introduced me to a new world of the Arabian Nights; an adult world that was very different from the world I accessed in my childhood. When gender studies became my main research focus, I started to use some aspects of these tales in my work, particularly the agency of Shahrazad symbolizing gender resistance to an authoritarian, patriarchal order. In the end, I was so totally intrigued by the strong appeal and significance of these splendid tales that I undertook a comprehensive and systematic reading of the entire collection in all its forms and editions, both original and translations, and both expurgated and unexpurgated. I have a great pleasure in establishing the study of the Arabian Nights as a strong area of research in my academic life extending to lecturing, research, and writing. While my reading of these tales proves that the Arabian Nights is a valuable treasure for studying gender and sexuality, it is regrettable to say that in the Middle East this narrative is still disparaged as either bawdy tales or silly tales for children. Yet, the way a culture treats its literature is a function of the nature of society. It is time to re-internalize and appreciate this collection of tales celebrated as one of the outstanding world literatures. After all, these tales are a cultural and literary product of the same region.

I would like to extend my thanks to Maria Marsh, the commissioning editor at Cambridge University Press, for taking a keen interest in this work and supporting its publication. Thanks also to the three anonymous readers for their positive engagement with the text and for their valuable comments, particularly the reader who was involved in the review process twice.

INTRODUCTION

THE COLLECTION OF TALES OF ALF LAYLA WA LAYLA, LITERALLY translated as 'A Thousand Nights and a Night', or 'The Thousand and One Nights', also known as 'The Arabian Nights', is one of the great and most celebrated world literatures. The *Arabian Nights Encyclopedia* (Marzolph and Leeuwen 2004 I: xxiii) states that no other work of fiction of non-Western origin has had a greater impact on Western culture than the Arabian Nights. Irwin (1994: 290–1) comments that it is perhaps easier to name the few writers who have not been influenced by the Arabian Nights in Western literature than the ones who have; because the list is almost all. In fact, this literature was an inspiration to Goethe in his conceptualization of world literature. Measured by its ability to move beyond its culture of origin, across time and space, the Thousand and One Nights is one of the quintessential examples of world literature, by becoming one of the most globalized and circulated literary texts. Stories from this work have influenced medieval European literature, long before its first translation into French in 1704 by Galland (Amer 2008; Marzolph 2007).

The success of Alf Layla wa Layla as a world literature rests on at least two criteria: the orientalist adoption of the narrative and the greatness of the literary text itself. Malti-Douglas (1997: 41) affirms that 'It can justifiably be said that the Thousand and One Nights to be as much a part of Western literary and cultural traditions as it is of the Eastern ones. The European language translations helped provide the *Nights* with a permanent position in world literature.' The orientalist enterprise in this regard is hardly surprising, considering that the text itself is a product of several literary and cultural interactions and, therefore, the European interest in these tales signifies a natural continuity to an inevitable, and quite desirable, intertextuality and interculturality. These modes of literary interactions are better represented by popular culture and literature than by canonical literature that often put resistance to foreign influences.

Moreover, the Thousand and One Nights is fortunate that the European literary elites are working in an environment with an increasingly global and cross-cultural curiosity, outlook, and perceptions. Within this context, and in a process of establishing a more inclusive canonical literature, space is created for folk tales, not only for the Western but also non-Western traditions. Hence, the concept of world literature is born and established. Yet, Alf Layla wa Layla did not benefit from similar orientations by the established elites of the medieval Middle East. Perhaps one should not expect a contrary outcome here, considering the differences in outlooks between modern and medieval society.

Discernibly, the elites of the modern Middle East who live in a modern and global world do not necessarily benefit from any historical gap of outlook. The region continues to disregard this literature either as a collection of trivial stories for children, or an obscene text disseminating pornography that should be banned. Apart from the literary disdain, either this work is banned or constantly confronting attempts of banning it with excuses of being 'offensive to public decency' or destroying the youth and spreading vice. Ironically, the region is forbidding a literary text that has been produced by the same culture and widely considered as an important part of world literature. Yet, this is hardly surprising considering that how a society or a culture regards, appreciates, and interacts with its literature is a function of whether democratic and inclusive social values are cherished or affronted. Hence, the destiny of the Thousand and One Nights is contingent on the road the Middle East is taking. Appreciating this literary work would undoubtedly be an indication of the right direction.

However, the European adoption of the Arabian Nights has proved to be mutually beneficial. Apart from enriching literary achievements and influencing almost all writers in the Western world, this literature has made a valuable contribution to advancing issues of gender and sexuality in the West. The role of Shahrazad as a symbol of gender resistance to patriarchy has inspired women and feminist tendencies in the West. No similar impact has been witnessed in the Middle East where patriarchal values are still prevalent, yet with little resistance. The European translations, particularly the role of Burton and his unexpurgated version of the Arabian Nights, have contributed to the creation of a new and more inclusive sexual discourse, including homosexuality and pornography, against a Victorian background of social conservatism and sexual rigidity. Burton's translation of these tales and other sexual manuals was one the most visible and widely controversial forms of obscenity in the later nineteenth century because it was produced and consumed by the intellectual, economic, and political elites (Colligan 2006: 57). These translations were cultural magnets for early discussions on pornography and homosexuality (87). Burton's subversive use of the Arabian Nights against strict sexual morality could be an inspiration for Middle Easterners who still live in a sexual and gender reality not very different from nineteenth-century Europe.

The other benchmark for the popularity of this literature is the greatness of its literary styles and the variety of themes and motifs integrated into these tales. Obviously, the work must have appealed to the artistic sensibilities of medieval Arabs and modern Europeans to gain such wide circulation (Ghazoul 1996: 12). It is remarkable that a text, which is neither sacred nor canonical, can overpower and interpenetrate so many cultural and literary systems (150). The strength and spirit of this work is the constant reversion from myth to the real and from the real to myth (Matarasso 1982: 28). Originating during the Islamic Golden Age, this work was second to the Qur'an in being the most influential body of work in the Islamic world (Damrosch 2011: 606).

One of the great merits of this literature is that it reflected its social environment visibly. These fascinating, powerful, and complex tales address questions of social existence in its complexity. Miquel (1997: 6) contends that the Arabian Nights shows a glimpse of culture and society in the medieval Arab world. All social classes are represented, from the Bedouin to the caliph, including scholars, poets, merchants, fishermen, bandits, and the idle. It is a witness, a reflection of its society and not a deliberate act of the storyteller (10). Naithani (2004: 278) concurs by saying that these are tales of human characters and society – be they king or beggar, master or slave, man or woman, virtuous or vile, realistic or magical, thief or saint. They are stories about human beings and their relationships, their capabilities, their desires, their true and false sense of value, their power, and their weaknesses. Abbott (1949: 133) affirms that the narrative eloquently expresses the complexity of the human character and the dynamism of social life and its diluted, fluid, mercurial boundaries between different opposites and orientations. Indeed, Dunyazad tells her sister Shahrazad, 'If you are not asleep, relate to me the tale which you promised me and quote striking examples of the excellencies and shortcomings, the cunning and stupidity, the generosity and avarice, and the courage and cowardice that are in man, instinctive or acquired or pertaining to his distinctive characteristics or to courtly manners.'

Finke (1996: 353) debates that literary texts, like any other ideological texts, exist in a complex relation both to other texts and to the social conditions of their creation. They reflect, but also in turn shape, those social conditions in a process that is, finally, dialogic. The Thousand and One Nights is indeed a mirror that reflects the social aspects of the Middle Ages (Farag 1976: 202). The tales are a testimony to the movement and navigation among religious, regions, ethnicities, and nations, demonstrating its universal appeal (Musawi 2009: 21). Grossman (1980: 114) argues that the story of Shahryar and Shahrazad presents in an early form the problem that the recognition of female subjectivity has set for male-dominated cultures. While the *Arabian Nights Encyclopedia* (Marzolph and Leeuwen 2004 II: 535) states that this work is among the most important texts for our knowledge about jinn.

One of the many merits of this literature is that it captures the dynamism of social changes as society develops. The Arabian Nights is a product of the Golden Age of Arabic and Islamic civilization, witnessing great territorial expansions, expanding trade, economic prosperity, higher wealth and incomes, impressive process of urbanization, intellectual refinement, and scholarship. Grossman (1980: 114–15) establishes, 'It has been widely recognized that prose fiction as a genre is historically associated with the development and fortunes of the differentiated (or detribalized) individual consciousness. Typically, fiction has first risen in urban environments where individual mobility and social freedom were expanded and where interchange between different cultures enabled a new perspective on traditional cultural imperatives.' Irwin (1994: 121) specifies that the Arabian Nights are urban stories, written for the most part by people in the cities about people in the cities for people in the cities.

One of the great emerging and rapidly developing urban centres was Baghdad, the capital of the Islamic civilization in its apogee, where Alf Layla wa Layla was born. Founded in 762, it rapidly became a big, prosperous, and cosmopolitan city. It became one of the largest and most prosperous cities in the world (Lapidus 2002: 56). The seat of the great Abbasid empire, it developed into a centre of politics and international trade accompanied by an advanced banking system, and extensive systems of hospitals, schools, libraries, and a thriving scholarship and religious, intellectual, and literary expressions. Urban expansion and the influx of people increased its population to reach a level of one million in the ninth century (Clot 1986: 152). It is suggested that Baghdad contained 60,000 mosques, where the storytellers, *qasass*, who played an important role in medieval life, practised their skills in their courtyards. It also contained 60,000 bathhouses, *hammam*, playing an important social role (168). Baghdad, the centre of the vast Muslim empire, is 'mythical in its very reality' (Bencheikh 1997: 24). The *Arabian Nights Encyclopedia* (Marzolph and Leeuwen 2004 II: 486) mentions that Baghdad is among the most characteristic settings for the stories of the Arabian Nights, particularly the anecdotes about the Abbasid caliphs and their boon companions, giving a vivid picture of the life and manners of the capital's elite. They show a sophisticated court culture that is supported by wealthy patrons fostering literature, learning, and music, and dedicated to luxurious pastimes. In these stories, the depiction of Baghdad is sufficiently detailed to suggest that the stories originated in Baghdad itself. Other great urban cities appearing in the narrative include Basra, Cairo, and Damascus.

Opulence connected to expanding empire and trade has resulted in a rich intellectual life in the urban centres of the Middle East, particularly the capital of the empire. The golden age was characterized by the expansion of higher learning and intellectual culture, and the caliphs often relied on and sought the counsel of men of science and arts. This wonderful age is often associated with the legendary Caliph Harun al-Rashid (ruled 786–809), who is often mentioned in the Arabian Nights as a good and enlightened ruler. His equally open-minded son Caliph al-Ma'mun (ruled 813–33), who was a great patron of philosophy and science, established an academy in Baghdad, *Bayt al-Hikma*, House of Wisdom, a library and translation centre, employing many scholars. Scholars enjoyed a privileged status, and many rulers fostered in their courts circles of scholars who assembled occasionally to hold debates and discussions (Talmon 1999: 120). Not only had the caliphs been patronizing learned men but also the notables and viziers, like the Barmakides family (Clot 1986: 140; Lane 1987: 115). A distinctive court culture in Baghdad emerged in the ninth century (H. Kennedy 2008: 176). This development has led to a flourishing and refined urban culture, fostering the development of arts, literature, the sciences, theology, and other intellectual pursuits (Marzolph and Leeuwen 2004 II: 466). Libraries and bookshops were important intellectual meeting-places, for residents and travellers. The bookdealers' market, *Suq al-Warraqin*, in tenth-century Baghdad contained 100 booksellers. Some of these shops doubled as subscription libraries or as literary salons and many branched out into the manufacture of paper and the copying of manuscripts. Literary salons flourished, playing a crucial role in the transmission of literary and historical knowledge (Irwin 1999: 150).

It is this intellectual environment that has produced the Alf Layla wa Layla as well as other literary literature. Much of this literature falls under the category of erotica, addressing various sexual issues. During the medieval period, two quite distinct types of texts about sexuality flourished in the Arabo-Islamic textual tradition: anecdotal collections containing sections about sexual activities, and erotic manuals replete with sexual information (Malti-Douglas 2001: 125). Apart from mentioning the work of the Thousand and

One Nights, the tenth-century bookseller and cataloguist Ibn al-Nadim (d. 990) also mentions in his Catalogue of Books, *kitab al-fihrist*, several eroto-logical literary sources. This catalogue reveals a remarkable interest in all aspects of sexual activity in earliest Arabic writings. Al-Saymari and al-Tahiri wrote treatises about different sexual matters (Roth 1996: 320).

Flourishing medieval erotic literature included works by Nasr al-Katib, al-Tusi, al-Tifashi, al-Nafzawi, ibn Fatila, and ibn Kamal-Pasha (Reynolds 2006b: 252). Ibn Daniyal wrote a shadow play discussing sex, drinking, and hashish (Rowson 2008: 215). Erotic literature also included works by al-Suyuti, ibn Tayfur, al-Qazwini, and al-Sanaw'al al-Maghribi (Hämeen-Anttila 2014). The Abbasid secretary Rashid al-Katib wrote his poetry of *ayriyat*, a collection of poems on the penis, in the early ninth century (Papoutsakis 2014: 101). Most of ibn Tayfur's ninth-century treatise on wom-en's eloquence is devoted to what women have had to say in prose or verse about the merits and inadequacies of their husbands, containing either the erotic or the obscene (Hammond 2014: 255). Al-Baghdadi wrote an erotic treatise exclusively regarding women (Irwin 1994: 165). Another collection of anecdotes with a strong sexual content and highly erotic tales appeared in the tenth century, *al-Hikayat al-Ajiba*, Tales of the Marvellous (163). Thus, the Arabian Nights had to compete with books dedicated to pornography, in the form either of sex manuals or of collections of exclusively erotic tales (164). It is a truism that sex usually makes a good story, particularly when the sexual encounter is illicit (Marzolph 2015: 190).

During the medieval time, erotic themes were discussed with ease and erotic anecdotes were told in respectable, learned sources. Likewise, man-uals of Islamic law seem to discuss sexual behaviour as dispassionately as any other subject (Hämeen-Anttila 2014: 14). Medieval Arabic erotic man-uals remained within the sphere of court literature and were written by competent authors and read by cultured readers (21). The *Arabian Nights Encyclopedia* (Marzolph and Leeuwen 2004 II: 700) mentions that the aim of this genre of books is to stimulate a healthy sexual life between part-ners that will secure matrimonial harmony and regulate passions and desires. The texts contain information on the physical aspects of the sexual organs, coitus, pregnancy, instruction for sexual satisfaction, aphrodisiacs, cosmetics, and methods of abortion. They discuss homosexuality, prostitution, and the respective advantages of young men and women. This permissiveness reflects the life of the urban elite under the Abbasid caliphs, whose luxury, refine-ment, and pleasures are elaborately described in literary sources.

It is this medieval libertine environment where the Thousand and One Nights was born. The narrative went into an extensive literary interaction and intertextuality with a flourishing erotic literature, in both directions. There is an overlap in content in anecdotes included in erotic literature and the Arabian Nights (Marzolph and Leeuwen 2004 II: 468). There is a great deal of borrowing between the Thousand and One Nights and Arabic folk romances (Irwin 1994: 88–9). The Thousand and One Nights may be viewed as a microcosm of medieval Arabic and, to some degree, Islamic popular literature (Heath 1987–8 I: 4).

The magnificent and outstanding medieval Islamic-Arabic literature of the wonderful tales collection of the Thousand and One Nights did not attain the academic attention that it indubitably deserves. The 300 years anniversary of the first European translation of this work has triggered some academic interest in this collection. However, most of the research on this narrative has focused on the genesis, sources of these tales, and the merit or demerit of its translations to other languages. Undoubtedly, these issues are important, yet it is time to take a further step into studying other, equally important aspects of the narrative. A profound and comprehensive exploration of the complexity of sexual life and the intricacies of gender relations, roles, and constructs is utterly lacking in the literature. This is a hapless outcome considering that sexual and gender topics are overwhelmingly dominant in the entire collection of tales. The narrative is a treasure for studies of sexuality and gender and an excellent text for exploring various facets of perceptions of sexual and gender interactions as well as the relationship between literature and gender. While the narrative is about medieval sexual life, many of the themes and motifs addressed are stupendously pertinent to modern society. Sexuality and gender in the Arabian Nights is highly relevant to the Middle East, a region still struggling with violent and unpleasant gender construct, engulfed in many sexual taboos and a culture of the forbidden.

By consciously circumventing engaging in the contentious and still unsettled debate about the genesis of the stories, which story originally belongs, or does not belong, to the Arabian Nights and the merit of their various translations, this work provides a comprehensive mapping of the entire sexual narrative in this collection of tales. It delivers a thorough exploration of the rich, dynamic, and complex sexual life in the medieval Middle East as represented in the marvellous tales of the Thousand and One Nights. This examination is enriched by employing a comparative perspective with medieval canonical and folktale literature from the Middle East, Europe, and Africa.

Studying sexuality, a fundamental facet of human existence, furnishes knowledge about cultural and social beliefs and outlooks. This narrative communicates a rather rich sexual life in the medieval era and more relaxed and open-minded sexual and gender outlooks and perceptions where sexual pleasure is highly cherished and coveted. Perceptibly, this sexual awareness and attitude are what the modern Middle East needs to re-indigenize, or re-internalize in an overdue drive to humanize and normalize sexual life and to enjoy sexual pleasure like the people of the Alf Layla wa Layla once did.

Structure of the Book

This book contains twelve chapters in addition to an introduction and a conclusion. Chapter 1, 'Alluring Sexuality', highlights the significance of sexuality in social life and how curiosity, positive outlook, and active participation of women are pertinent to sexuality. It looks at various sources of sexual outlet, including gender mixing, slave-girls, eunuchs, and prostitution. It also pinpoints risks associated with sexual life. Chapter 2, 'Inexorable Sexuality', illustrates how enthralling sexuality is destined to be inescapable in social life, and that to fulfil their sexual desires, people overcome many obstacles, including distance, gender tension, and various barriers.

Chapter 3, 'Insatiable Lust', discusses the perceived unquenchable and voracious sexual yearning of women, extending to promiscuity, desire for large penises, and practices of bestiality, and how this perception is related to concerns about male sexuality. Chapter 4, 'Demonic Sexuality', sketches the sexual and romantic interaction between humans and jinn in both its forms of voluntary and violent relations, and the contrast between the bad and good jinn, as well as the rationalization of the world of jinn. Chapter 5, 'Rape and Incest', describes violent and taboo aspects of sexuality, including cases of rape, rape as politics, and incestuous relationships.

Chapter 6, 'Promiscuous Life', maps the promiscuity of sexual life in forms of both polygamy and polyandry, including multiple sexual bonding, the harem, and having intermediary husbands. Chapter 7, 'Transgressive Adultery', observes the misdemeanours of attempts of adultery, including royal adulteries, in conjunction with a culture of suspicion of women and hasty accusations of women. Chapter 8, 'Sexual Perfidy', scans various modalities of punishing sexual transgression, including femicide. It elucidates that infidelity is also linked to fortune as well as the significance of testing fidelity in amorous and sexual liaisons. Chapter 9, 'Tales of Cuckoldry', examines the intricate duplicity life of having husbands and lovers simultaneously, and the sophisticated levels of cunning and deceitfulness used in treacherous affairs.

Chapter 10, 'Lesbian Encounter', scrutinizes lesbian experiences and their relatedness to heterosexuality, stigmatization of lesbian tendencies particularly in a context of otherness, transsexuality and cross-gender dressing and their relationship to homosexual intimacy. Chapter 11, 'Tempting Pederasty', investigates the complex world of pederasty, its distinction from male homosexuality, its relative excellence compared to heterosexuality, and the involvement of women in pederastic tendencies. It considers pederasty in relation to the economic activity of trade, and the admiration of male beauty in conjunction with Sufi mysticism, wine drinking, and obscene poetry, particularly the influential role of Abu Nuwas. Chapter 12, 'Hedonistic Narrative', presents the unequivocally explicit sexual accounts involving homoerotic games, sexual verbal games, and stories of sexual intercourse, fun, and pleasure.

I

ALLURING SEXUALITY

D ELINEATING MEDIEVAL SEXUALITY, THE THOUSAND AND ONE NIGHTS presents sexuality as a significant aspect of social life. The narrative underscores the role of sexuality in people's lives and a predominately relaxed attitude to a sexual encounter in socializing. Many stories depict love and sexual intimacies between unmarried couples. Sexual curiosity motives people to seek sensual pleasure and to maintain a healthy and positive outlook on sexuality. This curiosity and outlook are channelled within obtainable sexual activities through access to gender mixing, slave-girls, male slaves and eunuchs, and prostitution. However, sexuality is occasionally associated with risks and dangers.

Curiosity and Sexuality

Curiosity, coupled with a positive outlook toward sexuality, often leads to sexual encounters. In *Man Who Never Laughed*, a young man reaches a magnificent house where eleven old men spend their days mourning. They die one after the other, and when the last man is about to die, he asks him about the secret of the house. He is told not to open a certain door. Unable to control his curiosity, however, he opens the door and reaches the shore of a vast ocean. An eagle lifts him into the air and puts him down on an island, from where he is carried away by a ship full of maidens. He encounters an Amazon tribe, marries the queen, and for some time lives a life of luxury and delights. In the royal palace, he is allowed to open every door but one. One day, he opens that particular door out of curiosity. Suddenly, the very same eagle that brought him to the Amazons lifts him up. The eagle returns him to his former house, where, just like the old men before him, he starts mourning his ill fortune. Curiosity in this tale has the double function of opening the door to happiness, marriage, and sexuality, yet on the other hand, it also leads to misery and ill fortune. Hence, curiosity seems to be ambiguous with a two-sided outcome like a double-edged sword, *sayf dhu hadayn*. Remarkably, the life of happiness that all these men in the tale regret to miss is associated with a life of sexuality. Its absence signifies mourning and death. Conceding to temptation and opening a forbidden door leading to sexuality and happy life, albeit only shortly as this is usually followed by difficulties and calamities, is a motif narrated in *Third Qalandar, Janshah*, and *Hasan of Basra*.

Curiosity about an image leading to sexuality and marriage is narrated in *Zayn al-Asnam*. A prince in Basra discovers an underground chamber containing gold, eight statues made of precious stones, and a message to visit a slave in Cairo to find the ninth statue. The prince travels there and the slave summons the jinn-king by means of fumigations. The king tells him that he is prepared to give him the ninth image, on condition that he brings him a fifteen-year-old virgin of unsurpassed beauty. After passing several adventures while searching in vain for some time, the prince finds out that the vizier of Baghdad's daughter corresponds to the description. He marries her, but then he remembers that he would have to deliver her to the jinn-king untouched. Although he has failed to meet the condition, the jinn-king forgives his broken promise. Sexuality in this tale is so alluring that he forgets his pledge, an outcome that could have led to the wrath, not the forgiveness, of the jinni.

Curiosity about a dream brings potential lovers together. In *Masrur and Zayn al-Mawsif*, an unrelated man and woman have overlapping dreams in their sleep, and they accidentally meet the following day to start an amorous and adulterous affair. In *Qamar al-Zaman and Budur*, a young female shows a strong lust and sexual curiosity in exploring the beauty of the young male, and she is impressed by his penis that she herself is lacking. This initial curiosity eventually leads to love and marriage. Curiosity contributes to the build-up of sexual knowledge even by very young women. Before consenting to reconciliation with her husband, in *Second Captain's Tale*, a wife asks the judge to answer a riddle about sexuality. When he fails, his fourteen-year-old daughter comes to the rescue, proving an excellent knowledge of the physiology and function of the penis. Scholars examine a fourteen-year-old slave-girl, in *Tawaddud*, to verify her knowledge of various matters. Asked about the benefits of fornication, she replies that it tranquilizes the heat of love, brings affection and joy to the heart, dispels worries and obsessions, and calms anger. Asked when it is the best time for having sexual intercourse, she replies that it is after digesting the food during night-time and after lunch during the daytime. The scholars ask her about the pleasure of an hour and she replies that it is sexual intercourse. However, curiosity is not the only

trigger to sexual knowledge in this tale. The functioning of the slave-girls
in society is closely related to accessing their sexuality and, therefore, sexual
knowledge inevitably becomes part of their training as slave-girls and of how
they are socially situated in society. An anecdote reminiscent of this tale is
found in the biographical dictionary 'Ta'rikh [History of] Baghdad' (Talmon
1999: 124).

Positive Outlook on Sexuality

In the narrative of Alf Layla wa Layla, people accept sexual activities and
encounters with ease and enthusiasm. Women are heavily represented in
projecting a positive stance on sexuality. The Arabian Nights Encyclopedia
(Marzolph and Leeuwen 2004 II: 701) mentions that it is remarkable that
many stories depict sexuality as a domain controlled by women. In Third
Qalandar's Tale, forty young women welcome a mendicant to their palace,
taking sexual initiative and all become sexually intimate with him for a
whole year. Tales of erotica, adultery, and insatiable sexuality clearly illustrate
an active female sexuality. In Singer and the Druggist, the wife is happy to have
a lover to come to her every day, paying him money for pleasing her sexually,
and outsmarting her suspecting husband in finding a new hiding place for
her lover. In Wife's Device to Cheat Her Husband, an old woman tries to make
a chaste wife consent to adultery, by using the trick that a particular dog has
actually been an enchanted girl who once rejected a man who loved her.
Consequently, the wife consents to the illicit sexuality. This story illustrates
the menace and vulnerability that are associated with rejecting sexuality. A
similar anecdote appears in the medieval literature about the cunning of
women (Jins-al 'inda al-arab 1997 I: 94–5).

   In Woman Who Had a Boy and the Other Who Had a Man as Lover, two
women argue about the more appropriate sexual partner for satisfying sexual
desires. While the two women debate the merit of having a young boy versus a man as a sexual partner and discuss the advantages and disadvantages of
each, it is apparent that sexuality as such is appreciated and enjoyed. In Mus'ab
ibn al-Zubayr and A'isha bint Talha, the beautiful wife is actively involved in
a tense and active sexuality with her husband. Rather than feeling embar-
rassed by the explicit marital sexuality, she considers it normal, expected, and
desirable. A profligate man who is addicted to sex, in Debauchee and the Three-
Year-Old Child, hears about a beautiful woman in another town and travels
to meet her. He wants to make love to her, but the woman refuses because
her three-year-old son is watching. While sexual debauchery is negatively
presented in this tale, the woman's positive attitude to sexuality is evident.

She does not reject engaging in sexual liaison per se but only because her child is present and watching.

One day in Baghdad, in *Di'bil al-Khuza'i with the Lady and Muslim ibn al-Walid*, a man and a woman are attracted to each other and she agrees to go with him. Having a modest house, however, he takes her to the house of his friend. The friend gives him some money to buy food. When he returns to the house, he finds that the friend has locked himself up with the woman. He just grabs the food and closes the door. When the man becomes furious, the friend says that he has no right to have her, since she was in his house and the food has been bought with his money. The patriarchal male approach to a woman and her sexuality is unmistakable in this tale where men are in a contest to possess and enjoy a female. Yet, this outlook is reinforced by the conduct of the female herself who switches partners so easily and promptly. On the other hand, sexuality is so alluring that the woman consents to be a sexual partner to a man yet ends up making love to another man. Apart from the issue of wealth and material comfort, a woman regards sexuality per se as an enthralling experience regardless of who the male partner is. It makes no difference to her who to have sex with as long as the alluring sex is ensured in the end. Who would be the sexual partner is of less importance than the preponderant satisfaction of sexual desires.

However, the indifferent identity of the male partner does not always make sense to a woman, particularly when romance is animated. The king of al-Hira in Iraq, in *Fatima and the Poet Muraqqish*, keeps his beautiful daughter, Fatima, locked up in a remote place because of her dangerous temperament. As she desires the poet Muraqqish as a lover, a servant smuggles him into her palace and he starts visiting her. One day, the poet allows a friend to take his place in secret. When Fatima discovers the deceit, she is so angry that she refuses to see Muraqqish anymore. Thus, the same patriarchal male outlook to a female is presented, yet the female agency is different. Moreover, female positive outlook to romance and sexuality is clearly exhibited in this story despite a life of enforced seclusion.

Adi ibn Zayd and the Princess Hind portrays two women approaching sexuality in a very positive way. During the festive time of Easter, Maria, the slave-girl of Princess Hind, notices the young man Adi, is impressed by his beauty, and becomes infatuated with him. She attracts the attention of Hind to his beauty, and Hind and Adi fall in love at first sight. The next day, Maria goes to his house telling him that she is in love with him and desires to have sexual intercourse. He complies on the condition of helping him to be united with Hind. After their sexual contact, Maria arranges for Hind to have a look at Adi from her palace. When the princess sees him, she almost falls down from the top of the palace, and tells Maria, 'If you do not bring him to me tonight, I will die,' and faints. Maria tells the king about this love story, suggesting that he should bless their marriage. They spend three years of happy married life, until one day the king wraths with Adi and kills him. Hind mourns him greatly and builds a convent, where she retires and devotes herself to religious affairs, weeping and bemoaning her husband until she dies.

In *Taj al-Muluk and Princess Dunya*, even an old woman shows sexual lust and interest when seeing a beautiful young man. Impressed by his beauty, she is rubbing between her thighs while looking at him and talking to him: 'Blessed she who sleeps in your lap, embraces your body, and enjoys your youth, especially if she has beauty and grace like you.' The old woman goes to Princess Dunya to show her the textile she bought from him, telling her that the owner of the material is even better than the clothes, as if paradise has opened its gates and this young man came out. She tells her that she wishes that tonight this man slept with the princess, lying between her breasts. Later on, when the princess sees him, noting his beauty and symmetry, she lustfully tells the old woman where this handsome young man comes from. The princess falls passionately in love with him and she is dazed by his beauty and elegance, promising the old woman 1,000 dinars and a dress worth as much if she helps her meeting him.

Thus, women have a positive outlook to, and a great enjoyment of, sexuality. In *Barber's Tale of His Second Brother*, sexuality becomes the subject of fun and delight in female gatherings. Amusement associated with sexuality is a repeated motif in the homoerotic game played by Budur, in *Qamar al-Zaman and Budur*, and by Zumurrud, in *Ali Shar and Zumurrud*, on their lovers. In these tales, sexuality becomes a joke and these women meant to create a hilarious situation derived from sexual imagination. By taking the full initiative in these humorous games, these women also show that women are resourceful and actively participate in sexuality.

One restless night, the legendary Caliph Harun al-Rashid, in *Al-Asma'i and the Girls of Basra*, asks the famous poet al-Asma'i (d. 828) to tell him the best of what he has heard of women and their verses. The poet says that he has heard many verses but none pleased him save three lines he once heard from three girls, and he starts telling the anecdote. He once took a walk in Basra and sat down in front of a house to take a rest. Through the open window, he overheard three young women agree to a poetry contest. The eldest recites,

> I delight in him if he visits my bed in dreams
> But it would be even more marvellous if he visits me on wake

The second girl recites,

> No one visits me in my dreams except his image
> And I said to him, welcome

The youngest recites,

> With my soul and my folk, I ransom my bedfellow,
>   whom I see each night
> And whose scent is pleasanter than the scent of musk to me

When the poet wanted to leave, the three girls stopped him and asked him to judge which verse is the best and the most agreeable. He composed a poem indicating that the youngest is the winner for her verse was nearest to the truth. The caliph asks him why he has decided in favour of the youngest girl. He replies that the eldest said if he visits her bed in sleep, and this is restricted and conditional, it might happen and it might not. The second said that his image came to her in her dreams, but the youngest said that she actually sleeps with him, smells his breath, and ransoms him with her soul and folk, and no one is ransomed with soul if he is not dearer than the soul itself. Thus, the winner of this contest is the one who is getting closer to the lover, and the one who has a more positive, welcoming, and daring attitude to sexuality. This tale depicts sexuality and the sexual perception of women in a positive outlook. Many medieval erotic treatises include an anecdote about three unmarried daughters reciting verses where the last verse reads, 'Oh Humam ibn Murra [her father], I long for a cock to stick into where I pee from' (Hämeen-Anttila 2014: 19).

Gender Mixing and Sexuality

One of the most important and natural sources of sexuality is the gender mixing and the relaxed way of social interaction between the sexes. On the way back from Caliph al-Ma'mun, the famous musician Ishaq, in *Ishaq of Mosul*, goes home and sees a large basket hanging from a wall in an alley. As he steps inside, he is drawn up. He enters a magnificent hall where a gorgeous woman appears. They spend the evening together reciting poems, telling stories, and playing music. After two similar nights, he asks whether he is allowed to bring along a cousin, and he takes the caliph along. The woman turns out to be the daughter of one of the emirs. She is later married to the caliph. Thus, gender mixing opens the door for women to have access to power and authority. This tale depicts gender mixing as ordinary and expected social convention. It is natural for a woman to receive men in her house while preserving her reputation and respectability. The narrative about respectable, independent, and confident women receiving men in their house appears in other stories too, such as *Porter and the Three Ladies of Baghdad*.

In *Christian Broker's Story*, a rich merchant from Baghdad travels to Egypt. In the market, he meets a beautiful and rich woman of a stately figure, *mayasat al-qwam*, and promptly falls in love with her, and she reciprocates. She tells him if she should come to him or he should come to her. They start a passionate and sexual liaison where she plays an active part. She not only takes the initiative of proposing marriage but also offers her wealth for the matrimonial union. An old woman takes a woman to meet a young man with the purpose of marriage, in *Portress's Tale*. The woman sees a handsome young man, elegantly dressed, and perfect in beauty, symmetry, and grace, with eyebrows like a bent bow and eyes that ravish hearts with lawful enchantments, and she recites verses flattering his beauty. They get married instantly, enjoy an amorous and sexy night until morning, and they continue in this harmony for a month. In the market, in *Ali ibn Bakkar and Shams al-Nahar*, a woman notices a young man of perfect beauty, falls in love with him, and invites him to the palace, to enjoy an amorous relationship. In *Jewish Doctor's Tale*, a young man from Mosul travels to Damascus where he meets a beautiful woman. They spend ardent nights of eating, drinking, and making love.

However, gender mixing sometimes comes into tension with the coercive enforcement of sexual morality on society. One day a constable, in *Second Constable's History*, hears rumours that a woman intends to invite a man to her house. After seeing the man enter, the police force their way inside, finding the two together. The woman acts in a friendly way, supplying the uninvited guests with food and drink and even offering her jewels. Meanwhile, she sends the man away. Once she knows him to be safe, however, she takes her jewels back while telling the police to leave immediately or she would scream and accuse them of improper behaviour. The woman in this tale finds it an ordinary thing to invite a man to her house. While gender mixing is officially condemned and prohibited, the agency of the woman twists the notion of improper behaviour to the disadvantage of the police. The intrusion of the enforcers of the law into the private life of citizens becomes the improper conduct rather than the mixing of young men and women. This narrative is unmistakable in depicting the creativity and cunning of women and their agency in outsmarting the law enforcement. A man displays a similar agency and conviction regarding the legitimacy of receiving a lover at home, in *Sixth Constable's History*. Some people warn a constable that a man is entertaining a woman in his house in an illegal way. When the police arrive, the man claims that the woman is his legal wife. He provides some forged documents to this effect, and a lawyer who is his friend corroborates his claim. While this action involves forging legal documents, yet the individual free will and the legitimacy of amorous and sexual attachment are reinforced in the tale. Sexuality is so important in people's lives that they turn to forgery to outsmart a discouraging legal code. Sexual pleasure triumphs in this tale despite contrary cultural social expectations.

Slavery, Prostitution, and Sexuality

Gender mixing is not the only way to fulfil sexual gratification in the narrative of the Thousand and One Nights. The alternative, or complementary, access to sexuality is ensured through the existence and proliferation of several sexual objects. Often, this sexual objectification is intersected with amorous attachments and admiration of beauty, both female and male. Slave-girls, *jawari*, play a prominent role within this sexuality, but also prostitutes and eunuchs, not to mention beardless boys. Medieval classical Arabic literature, *adab*, is full of anecdotes about these sources of sexual interaction. The Arabian Nights seems to be a clear reflection of this literature through the literary device of intertextuality. Within this collection of tales, slave-girls are presented as instrumental in the world of sexuality. H. Kennedy (2008: 178) emphasizes that slave-girls were a major feature of the court life of the Abbasid period. They were often highly educated and were important bearers of the musical and poetic culture in the court. They were always of modest social backgrounds chosen for beauty and talent rather than social status. However, Guthrie (2001: 208) comments that despite the huge prices paid for slave-girls in the context of nobility, the reality was that household slaves were commonplace in town and country and within the financial scope of many ordinary householders even those in the most frugal circumstances.

In *Mahmud and His Three Sons*, the vizier's son in the City of Lovers invites a man to a social evening where ten female singers are to talk about their sexual adventures. It is remarkable that talking about sex publicly is considered a normal thing and part of the social gathering and partying. Six slave-girls debate their merit, in *Man of Yemen and His Six Slave-Girls*. The slim slave-girl tells the fat one, 'A man lying with you is at no ease and cannot find a way to take pleasure of you, because the bigness of your belly holds him off from fornicating with you, and the grossness of your thighs hinders him from coming at your pussy.' In this debate, the girls make reference that the wise says that pleasure is in three things, eating flesh, riding on flesh, and inserting flesh into flesh. Once Caliph al-Mutawakkil was sick and had to take medicines, in *Al-Fath ibn Khaqan and al-Mutawakkil*. For this purpose, he received all kinds of presents. Among the gifts was a slave-girl sent to him by his vizier. The donor had also added a poem in which wine and sex were lauded as the ultimate prescription against illness. In another story, when the poet and musician Ibn Abi 'Atiq of Damascus visits the caliph, in *Two Dancers*, he is seated between two beautiful slave-girls, and the poet falls in love with them. Instead of receiving the expected money after he has shown his eloquence, he is presented with the two slave-girls.

A rich man from Baghdad, who later on becomes impoverished, in *Ruined Man of Baghdad and His Slave-Girl*, is forced to sell his slave-girl to a man from Basra. Because he loves her very much, he travels to search for her. Meanwhile, a man employs him in his shop, proposing to make him his partner if he marries his daughter, and he agrees. He regains his slave-girl in the end. Sexual interaction is irresistible when the son of the vizier and a slave-girl meet, in *Nur al-Din and the Damsel Anis al-Jalis*. The handmaid of the wife of the caliph, in *Reeve's Tale*, falls in love with a merchant in Baghdad and smuggles him into the harem in a trunk. After callously punishing him for his uncivilized eating manners, they marry and live together happily.

One night during wintertime, in *Ishaq of Mosul and His Mistress and the Devil*, the sky was cloudy and pouring with such heavy rain that people stayed indoors. Ishaq was alone in his house, thinking of a slave-girl who belongs to one of the sons of Caliph al-Mahdi, with whom he was infatuated, and who is skilled in singing and playing musical instruments. He thinks to himself that if this woman was with him tonight, his joy would be complete, and his night would be short of the restlessness that he suffers from. At this moment, someone knocks at the door, making him think to himself that perhaps the plant of his desire has fruited. Opening the door, the woman who was in his thoughts is standing in front of him, wrapped with a kerchief on her head to fend off the rain. She is covered with mud to her knees, and her clothes are wet. He asks her what brings her through all this mud, and she replies that his messenger came to her and described his love and longing to her and that she felt she had to answer him and come to him swiftly. Ishaq wonders at this, and he hated to tell her that he sent her no messenger. Instead, he says, 'Thank God for bringing us together.' Telepathy in this tale is instrumental in making alluring sexuality possible.

Slave-girls are often linked to prostitution. Not many female singers enjoyed distinguished careers and there was an overlap between the profession of singer and that of the prostitute (Irwin 1994: 174). There are two stories in the Arabian Nights that present prostitution as a way of engaging in sex. The story of *Harun al-Rashid and Abu Hasan the Merchant of Oman* gives a detailed description of a brothel in Baghdad. A rich Omani merchant sells his possessions, travels to Baghdad, and enters a brothel on the banks of Tigris. He tells the keeper of girls, an old man, that he desires to be a guest for the night. The old man replies that he has many damsels, some whose night is 10 dinars, some 20, some 40, others more, and asks him to choose the one he likes. The merchant chooses the one whose night is 10 dinars and pays the old man 300 dinars, the price of a month. A boy takes him to the bath, and then to a chamber to tell the girl that this man is her guest. The girl receives him with welcome and courtesy, laughing and rejoicing and lets him in her splendid room, decorated with gold. He looks at the girl to find her as beautiful as the moon at its fullest, having in attendance on her two slave-girls like stars. She makes him sit and seats herself by his side, and her maids set before them a table covered with delicious dishes of various kinds of meats, fowl, quails, grouse, and pigeons. Another table of wine, flowers, sweets, and fruits soon followed it. For a whole month, he lives in happiness with the girl.

When the month was over, he goes to the girls' keeper and requests to stay with a girl whose night is 20 dinars and pays for a whole month in advance. The same ritual of bathing and introduction to a girl, who has four *jawari* and who is good at playing the lute and singing, is repeated. Afterward, Abu Hasan spends another month with a girl whose night is 40 dinars, which has passed like one day for the beauty of the girl and the goodliness of her converse. One day, the merchant sees so lovely a young woman of stunning and dazzling beauty that she instantly captivates his heart and soul. He was told that this girl is the daughter of the brothel's owner and the price of her night is 500 dinars, for she is one for whom kings sigh in vain. He swears by Allah to spend all his wealth on this damsel. The next morning he requests to spend the night with the one whose night is 500 dinars and pays for one month in advance. He is taken to a saloon, of which his eyes never saw a prettier one on the face of the earth, where the young woman is seated. When he sees her, his reason is dazed with her beauty, for she is like the full moon on its fourteenth night, full of grace and symmetry and loveliness. Her speech puts to shame the tones of the lute, reciting the verses,

> The Compassionate did not create better sight
> Than two lovers on a single bed
> Embracing each other, clad with satisfaction
> Hand with hand and arm with arm

Another reference to prostitution is narrated in *Hireling and the Girl*. When a woman of an Arab tribe gives birth, a wise woman predicts that the new-born girl will have sex with a hundred men, a hireling will marry her, and a spider will slay her. Aiming to prevent this from happening, the woman's hireling slits the girl's throat and runs away. The girl survives and eventually becomes a prostitute. Later, the very same hireling marries her without knowing her identity. When they find out that two of the prophecies have already come true, they try to protect her from spiders by going to live in a secluded place that is kept neat and clean. When one day her husband sees a spider, she wants to kill it herself. As she is striking it with a piece of wood, a splinter enters her hand and gives her blood poisoning. In this story, fate plays a role in the death of the woman as she is destined to die in that particular way. However, fate is also linked to sexuality in this narrative. It dictates that prostitution is how the woman would access sexuality. While destiny brings together sexuality and death, it is plausible to consider that the death of the woman is a punishment for engaging in prostitution rather than in sexuality per se. Hence, prostitution, but not sexuality, is socially condemned in this story.

One of the sources of sexuality is the availability of the eunuchs. They are engaged in pederasty, mostly as the passive players, but also in various forms of heterosexuality with women, particularly in the harem institution. They are also involved in male prostitution. The sexuality of the eunuchs is narrated in *Three Eunuchs*. Kuefler (1996: 286, 291) asserts that institutional castration results in making eunuchs be an object of desire for men. However, in many cases, the sexuality of eunuchs continues even after castration. Women might also be attracted to eunuchs facilitated by their availability within the home. Their gender status is even less threatening than their sexual performance; they could associate with women and participate in feminine activities even in intimate surroundings.

Sexuality and Risk

Sexuality in the tales of the Thousand and One Nights is tempting even when it is coupled with risks and dangers. Three tales in the collection associate sexuality with death, a heavy price to pay for irresistible sexuality. In *Blue Salama the Singer*, a talented and beautiful student of singing tells her master that she once kissed a man in exchange for two pearls. Her master has the man whipped to death. After spending several amorous nights with her lover, in *Jewish Doctor's Tale*, the sexual outlook of the young woman takes a rather ambiguous turn. She decides to test their love by bringing her own sister to their amorous nights to see if any passionate bonding emerges between her lover and her sister. When the outcome of this testing disappoints her, she kills her sister in a sexual jealousy. Thus, this narrative associates sexuality with jealousy, compulsive testing, and death. In *Singer and the Druggist*, a woman desires a man who is tied to a tree as a punishment, rubbing his penis to an upright erection and starts playing an active part in making love. However, this agency and positive sexuality are punished as she is attacked and killed by a raging ram. Arrangements of the marriage of a prince and a princess are being made, in *Bihzad*. However, the impatient prince cannot resist looking into the bride's chamber, and the bride's mother gouges his eyes. While this tale depicts the context of gender segregation, it is nevertheless a narrative about longing, sexual yearning, and impatiently waiting for sexual union.

Third Constable's History is a story where sexuality is associated with crime. While a constable is walking along the street together with some mates, they meet a group of women. One of them, who is very beautiful, lingers behind. He makes advances to her, and together they go to an inn where they rent a room. Yet, when he washes in anticipation of what is to happen, she disappears with all his money and clothes. The housekeeper and the neighbours ridicule him. One day a merchant, in *Tailor's Tale*, sees the beautiful daughter of a judge, *qadi*, and immediately falls in love with her. With the help of an old woman, they arrange a secret meeting in the judge's house. However, the uninvited intervention of a barber causes confusion and disturbances to the meeting and a risk of punishment. A woman prospers as a merchant and wants to marry a young man, in *Woman Who Regained Her Loss*. She conceives a ruse to fulfil her wish. After agreeing that if the young man wins he will have to meet the conditions written down in a sealed document, they play a game of chess. During the game, however, his father secretly removes the condition stipulating that he should marry her. When she loses the game on purpose, she also loses the prospect of marriage as well as her wealth, reducing her to poverty. Thus, while her scheme has failed due to external intervention, yet the agency of the woman and her desire to be part of the world of marriage and sexuality is unmistakable.

While female positive attitude is associated with the free will of the women engaging in sexual activities, a female agency is also manifested in rejecting sexual advances, particularly when these advances are associated with taking advantage of women. *Blacksmith Who Could Handle Fire* is a story where sexuality is exploited in difficult situations. A blacksmith is in love with a girl, who always resists his sexual advances. When famine breaks out, she is forced to beg for food at his door. Twice he offers to feed her if she yields herself to him, and twice she refuses, saying that she would prefer death to dishonour. When she begs for the third time, he repents his selfishness and feeds her. In *al-Hajjaj and the Young Sayyid*, a strange young man steps forward in an assembly of notables held by al-Hajjaj (d. 714), the governor of Kufa, in Iraq. The governor is impressed by his knowledge to such an extent that he offers him one of three presents: 10,000 dirhams, a noble horse, or a handsome slave-girl. Secretly, the governor has made up his mind that he will kill him because of his preference for mundane items if he chooses the money, and for his lasciviousness if he chooses the woman. Only by choosing the horse would he prove to be brave and deserving not to be slain. The young man makes the right choice, however, and ends up receiving all three presents. While this tale condemns and punishes tempting sexual lust, yet a woman and the ensuing sexuality is present as a reward right from the beginning, as a possible choice, and eventually as a prize, ironically, for denying sexuality, at least tentatively. Thus, sexuality is so enthralling that people are motivated to defeat the many hurdles preventing them from realizing their sexual desires and dreams.

2

INEXORABLE SEXUALITY

E XPOUNDING MEDIEVAL SEXUALITY, THE THOUSAND AND ONE NIGHTS
makes a presentation of sexuality such an alluring aspect of social life
that it seems to be unstoppable. To engage in, and enjoy, romance and sexuality, people strive importunately to overcome various impediments in their
way. Apparently, sexuality becomes a fate and a stubborn destiny that is useless
to avoid or resist. Distance is no obstacle because sexuality is migratory, fluid,
mobile, and transportable. Fate and ingenuity ensure that various modes of
gender tensions and gender segregation are defeated. When it comes to their
sexual lust and desire, people break many barriers, permitting the dictates of
the inevitable fortune that their happiness depends on.

Wandering Sexuality

The narrative of the Alf Layla wa Layla presents distance as no obstacle
hindering the fulfillment of sexual desires and dreams. Sexuality is fluid and
travelling, and men and women embark on long journeys to search for love
and intimacy. By taking these trips, they enter into new and different worlds,
and yet boundaries do not discourage them from relentlessly pursuing their
dreams and lusts. The *Arabian Nights Encyclopedia* (Marzolph and Leeuwen
2004 II: 610) states that one of the most remarkable characteristics of the
heroes in this narrative is their mobility, whether in search of their beloved,
fleeing their enemies, or exploring strange worlds. The quintessential function of the journey in fictional narrative is to indicate boundaries. These
boundaries can be traversed, both on the practical and on the metaphoric
level. Journeys imply the crossing of boundaries between different worlds.

Many stories of the Arabian Nights portray travelling as sexuality. Travelling
is an opportunity for sexual intimacy that often leads to amorous attachments and marriages. The wandering of Judar, in *Judar and the Moor Mahmud*,

takes him to an underground building where he finds Princess Hayfa who
was abducted by a mighty sorcerer because she refused to marry him. Judar
falls in love with her and marries her in the end. Prince Qamar al-Aqmar of
Persia, in *Ebony Horse*, tries the ebony horse that can fly and cover the distance of one year in a single day. He alights on the roof of a palace in the city
of San'a'. As he sneaks inside, he encounters Princess Shams al-Nahar, who
is favourably inclined to his advances. When he visits her a second time, he
takes her with him on his horse. After some adventures, the lovers get married, and the prince succeeds his father as king of Persia. Travelling sexuality
is also narrated in *Mahmud and His Three Sons.*

Travelling not only leads to monogamy, but also to polygamy and promiscuity. Even though Hasan is in love and married a princess in Egypt, in
Hasan the King of Egypt, he hears about the wonders of the Maghreb and
decides to make a visit. While there, he marries another woman who accompanies him back home. The son of the king of Yemen, in *King of Yemen and
His Three Sons*, ends up marrying three women in his travels and adventures.
A man loves his slave-girl, in *Ruined Man of Baghdad and His Slave-Girl*, but
he was separated from her. In his search for her in another town, he marries
another woman. Yusuf is married with four children living in Cairo, in *Yusuf
and the Indian Merchant*. Because he has become impoverished, he decides
to find his luck elsewhere. His travels take him to Mecca, where he marries a rich widow, taking care of her possessions, and eventually becomes a
wealthy merchant, and even richer when she dies and he acquires her wealth.
In India, he marries the daughter of an old man and inherits his wealth
when he dies. His journey back home reunites him with his original family.
Interestingly, travelling in this narrative is leading not only to marriage and
sexuality but also wealth.

Many voyages in this narrative are related to seeing a portrait or hearing about the beauty of a woman, falling in love, and travelling to pursue
union. After seeing a portrait of a beautiful singing girl owned by a vizier in
Kashmir and falling in love with her, in *Goldsmith and the Cashmere Singing-
girl*, a goldsmith in Persia travels to seek union with her. He conceives an
extraordinary ruse enabling him to be united with his beloved and taking
her home with him. This story about migratory sexuality displays the cunning and agency of the male only. Another story demonstrating the agency
of both sexes is narrated in *Ibrahim and Jamila*. Ibrahim is the son of the
governor of Egypt, falling in love with a portrait of a beautiful woman, who
happens to live in Basra. He travels first to Baghdad and then to Basra and
manages to meet the woman, who happens to have heard about him and has
already fallen in love with him. They eventually marry after overpowering

numerous difficulties. Love by way of a portrait is also present in *Prince Who Fell in Love with the Picture*, but the prince fails to win the heart of the princess. Some highwaymen kill the prince on his second journey to the town of his beloved, and the princess, finding him dead, mourns him.

Hearing about the charm of the opposite sex is also a motif for travelling. Prince al-'Abbas of Yemen, in *Ins ibn Qays and His Daughter*, hears about Maria, the beautiful and well-educated daughter of the king of Baghdad and falls in love with her. She happens to reject all her rich and royal suitors but this did not discourage the prince from travelling to Baghdad to meet her. Because of his heroic fighting in battles, he wins the reward of the king and the marriage acceptance of the princess after initial rejection of his advances. A dervish tells Prince Yasamin about Princess Almond, in *Yasamin and Princess Almond*. He travels to her town and meets her in the palace garden. Her brothers, however, reject their marriage because they insist on enforcing her marriage to the son of their uncle. The lovers find no other solution but to elope together.

It is not only men that travel to seek out sexuality but also women. Sitt al-Husn is the daughter of the sultan of Iraq, in *Zunnar and the King of Iraq's Daughter*. Her father embarks on a military campaign and asks her what he should bring for her if he returns triumphant. After hearing about Zunnar, a proud king living a secluded life, she tells him to bring Zunnar to her. However, the gratified king rejects her request. Enraged by this reaction, she disguises herself as a slave and travels to his town. There she arranges to be presented to him as a slave-girl, but she refuses to be touched by him. As he is filled with desires, she escapes from the palace while leaving a note. Zunnar now regrets his initial rebuttal, follows her to Iraq and marries her. This tale presents the triumph of sexuality over seclusion and pride. Female agency pertinent to sexuality is clearly manifested, acknowledged, and rewarded.

If distance separating would-be lovers is a colossal and formidable challenge, sexuality becomes transportable with the help of the jinn. Jinn playing an active role in uniting lovers despite living separately and remotely are narrated in *Nur al-Din and His Son Badr al-Din Hasan*. Mesmerized by their beauty and aiming at uniting them for one night, the jinn transport Badr al-Din from Basra to meet Sitt al-Husin in Egypt on her wedding night of a forced marriage to a repugnant hunchback groom. The jinn intervene to lock the bridegroom in the bathroom the whole night, leaving Badr al-Din alone with the bride, who tells him that she had wished that he would be her husband, or at least that he and the bridegroom would share her. He assures her that he is her bridegroom and they spend a splendid and very erotic night, where she positively takes part. The intervention of the jinn to unite would-be lovers also appears in *Qamar al-Zaman and Budur*. The jinn transport Princess Budur and place her beside Prince Qamar al-Zaman, admiring and comparing their beauty. Despite their initial aversion to the opposite sex, they are captivated by the beauty of each other, falling in love, and eventually concluding a matrimonial union. A magician helps a cook to unite with his beloved, the caliph's daughter, in *Warlock and the Young Cook of Baghdad*. With his help, they spend happy nights together and contract a marriage in the end.

Many long wanderings and journeys initially start with a hunting game. *Diamond* is a story of a prince who loses his way during a hunting trip and meets an old man who tells him that all his seven sons were killed for failing to solve a riddle that Princess Muhra in the land of Chin and Machin puts up as a trial for her marriage. The prince travels and the couple meet and fall in love. To solve the riddle, he travels to another town, facing many difficulties. A woman bewitches him into a deer when he rejects her advances, while another woman restores him to his human form. The prince then defeats two giants and releases their captive woman. He marries all the three women he encounters in his adventures and returns to solve the riddle, marries the princess, and her servant who advised him how to solve the riddle. Thus, the sexual reward of this voyaging and adventure is indeed incredible. Prince Muhammad, in *Sultan of India and His Son Muhammad*, goes hunting one day and sees a beautiful green bird. An old man tells him that there are more birds of this kind on the Camphor Islands, inducing the prince to travel there. The king allows him to take some birds if he brings him some branches of grapes made of diamonds and emeralds from the isles of the Sudan. He travels there and vanquishes a lion that comes every year to devour some of the inhabitants. The daughter of the sultan happens to watch his stout fight and falls in love with him. He marries the princess and returns to the Camphor Islands with the grapes, where he marries the king's daughter and then returns to his hometown with his two wives.

One day, two princes go hunting but separate to chase some wild beasts, in *Faris al-Khayl and al-Badr al-Fayiq*. One of them loses his way and finally finds a palace without a gate, where the daughter of the Indian King Sabur is imprisoned. She falls in love with him and asks a jinni to locate his brother, who happens to be imprisoned by the king of Persia but gets the help and sympathy of the king's daughter who falls in love with him and converts to Islam for his sake. They instruct a jinni to abduct the brother with his beloved, and finally, the two couples are happily married. Travelling is associated with not only marriage and sexuality but also with discovering the illicit sexuality of related people. The journey of King Shahzaman to visit his brother, in *Shahryar and His Brother*, is associated with the promiscuous sexuality of his wife and the discovery of the adulterous act. The hunting trip of King Shahryar is also associated with the sexual orgy of his wife and the discovery of it, and when the brothers travel and meet the kidnapped bride, in *Ifrit's Mistress*, they discover the illicit and treacherous sexuality of all women.

Overcoming Gender Tensions

Many stories in the Thousand and One Nights portray various modalities of gender tensions and animosities between the sexes. These acrimonies, however, are no hindrance to sexuality in the narrative. Lovers always end up finding harmony, love, and sexual intimacy despite the initial sexual rigidities. A couple of stories depict gender misconception and the ingenuity of solving the difficulty. When they are in love, Princess Hayat al-Nufus, in *Ardashir and Hayat al-Nufus*, and Princess Dunya, in *Taj al-Muluk and the Princess Dunya*, do not hesitate to smuggle their lovers to the palace to enjoy their romantic bonding. However, smuggling lovers into the palace is not the only obstacle facing this bonding. Both princesses once had a dream, in which a female pigeon is caught in the net of a fowler, but her mate did not come to her rescue and the bird was consequently abandoned to her fate. This dream has caused the princesses to develop a strong loathing and distrust of men. To overcome the patriarchal tension and mistrust between the sexes, the lovers in both stories have to find a way to change this aversion to men by the princesses. They order a painter to paint images of a fowler catching a female bird, while a bird of prey holds the male bird in its claws, thereby explaining what has prevented him from coming to her rescue. When the princesses see the images they understand the full complexity of the situation that the two birds actually share the same fate and being united in death, they fall in love with the princes.

Detesting the other sex is also a motif in *Qamar al-Zaman and Budur*. When Prince Qamar al-Zaman has come of age, his father wants him to marry to secure the future of the dynasty, but the young man refuses because he detests women. After a year, the king again urges his son to marry, but again he does not comply. When, one year later, he is still unwilling, his father has him locked up in an old tower. There, two jinn find the young man and both admire his beauty while he is asleep. One of the jinn says that he has just come from the Islands of China, where he saw Princess Budur, who is as beautiful as this young man is. The king has built seven palaces for her and has repeatedly asked her to marry, but she has refused since she has no desire to be ruled by a man. Enraged by her obstinate behaviour, her father has her locked up in a remote palace. The jinn unite the two symmetrically beautiful youth who fall in love with each other and their mutual admiration eventually culminates in marriage. When beautiful young men and women meet, sexual interaction becomes irresistible, as is also confirmed in *Nur al-Din and the Damsel Anis al-Jalis*. The son of the vizier and the slave-girl become enamoured, leading to sexual intercourse, even when his father warns her that his son is a womanizer and even when she knew that the vizier has actually bought her for the king, not for her son.

One day a young woman comes to the shop of a merchant and hands him a love letter, in *Second Lunatic's Story*. In return, he gives her a beating and refuses to respond to her advances. After some time, a beautiful young woman comes to his shop to buy jewellery, telling him that she is the daughter of Shaykh al-Islam, the highest religious authority. When he proposes to marry her, she agrees but warns him that her father will attempt to ward him off by pretending that she is crippled and deformed. The young man nevertheless manages to conclude the marriage. As his bride is revealed, he notices that she is not the one he intended, but someone else who is ugly and hideous. Soon the young woman who tricked him into this situation visits him again to tell him that she has deceived him to punish him for his insulting conduct. She now instructs him how to dissolve his marriage, and when the divorce is arranged, the merchant marries the beautiful woman. Thus, the initial rejection of sexual advances proved to be ephemeral and indecisive. Sexuality ultimately triumphs, with the imaginative cunning of the woman who displays a great will and agency to get what she wants in the end. Thus, despite hesitation and rejection, sexuality demonstrates its inevitability. In fact, resisting unavoidable sexuality is an insulting comportment within the context of gender interaction.

Cryptic sign language needs not be an obstacle for sexual interaction. *Aziz and Aziza* is a story depicting two impediments to the enjoyment of sexual bonding, namely, the use of sign language, which is unintelligible to one partner, and the enticement of sleeping before the arrival of the lover on a date. One day Aziz is overwhelmed by the heat of the day and sits down to rest in an alley. Suddenly, a white kerchief falls into his lap. As he looks up, he sees a beautiful woman making a sign for him. Aziz immediately falls in love with her. His female cousin explains to him the meaning of the signs made by the strange woman. He returns to the alley three times and each time the young woman makes new signs, and his cousin always clarifies them for him. Finally, the lovers arrange a meeting in a garden, but three times Aziz falls asleep before the arrival of the woman because he feels hungry and eats from the rich dishes prepared for their meeting. When he wakes, he finds that the woman has left some objects as a message to him and each time his cousin decodes the messages. However, on the fourth meeting, he manages to stay awake until the woman arrives, and the two lovers spend a delicious and sexual night. From then on, he frequents the garden and relishes the joys of love and sexual intimacy.

The narrative of the Arabian Nights contains three stories revealing dangerous prophecies in relation to sexuality. Princess Hayfa' grows up to be an intelligent and beautiful young woman, in *Al-Hayfa' and Yusuf*. One night, her father in his dream hears a voice telling him that he will be killed because of her, and he secludes her in a remote palace. One day the wandering handsome Prince Yusuf arrives there and spends a blissful time with the princess. Finally, Yusuf kills her father in a duel, and the empire's notables acknowledge him as their new ruler, while the lovers get married.

When a daughter is born to a rich merchant, in *Merchant's Daughter and the Prince of Iraq*, he hears a voice telling him that the prince of Iraq will illicitly make her pregnant. Anxious to preserve his daughter's honour, he brings her to a remote cave. Meanwhile, in Iraq, a prince is born and when he becomes a young man, he goes out hunting one day, and when the horse goes wild, he reaches the young woman's cave. They fall in love, and the prince stays for seven months in the cave and then returns home, leaving the girl pregnant. Her father takes her home, and on the way, she gives birth to a son, who is left behind in the desert. The lovers are finally reunited and get married. Meanwhile, the leader of a caravan finds the baby and raises him as his own son. One day, the son goes hunting but loses his way and arrives at a certain city. There he overhears that every man who has so far been married to the king's daughter has died the next morning. In spite of her father's warning, the young man marries the princess. At night, the wall suddenly splits open, and a voracious basilisk appears ready to devour him. He slays the monster with a magic sword, and the young couple spend a blissful night together. The king offers him half of his empire, and when later the king dies, the young man inherits the throne. The son eventually reunites with both of his fathers. This story illustrates that sexual attraction could not be prevented no matter how stringent the precautions are. Virginity and illicit sexuality were no hindrances in this regard. The couple meet in the end and enjoy their sexual desires together. Likewise, sexuality for their son also triumphs despite the threat and the danger of the monster.

Sitt al-Banat, the daughter of a vizier in Andalusia, who knows how to predict the future, sees one day that she will become pregnant in an illicit way, in *Sitt al-Banat and the King of Iraq's Son*. She leaves the palace in disguise and arrives at a garden where she starts working as the gardener's assistant.

When she digs a hole to hide in the case of danger, she comes to a trap door
that gives access to a staircase leading to an underground corridor, where she
comes upon a handsome young man. They fall in love and spend the night
together. The following day, the young man disappears and, disappointed, she
returns home. It turns out that the young man is a son of the king of Iraq.
From his horoscope, it had become known that he would possess a girl in an
illicit way. To evade his fate, he had himself transported to the underground
chamber by a jinni. Sitt al-Banat now appears to be pregnant and travels to
Iraq to be united with her lover. Thus, the same hole that she digs to save
her from sexuality turns out to be a hole that inadvertently leads to the very
same thing. Sexuality is actually an irresistible fate. Fear of sexuality leads to
a sexual encounter.

The Arabian Nights contains many stories about defeating gender segregation. Hasan is the son of one of the wealthiest merchants of Syria, in
Zulaykha. He travels to Shiraz in Persia, where he is admitted to the royal
court and appointed chamberlain. One evening, he walks in the garden in
spite of the ban on doing so, because it was exclusive to women. A beautiful
woman surprises him but treats him very kindly, and they fall in love and
kiss. The couple elope to Damascus, where Hasan becomes the vizier. In
Jewish Doctor's Tale, a father narrates that he brought up his eldest daughter in
a very strict seclusion and when she became a woman, he sent her to Egypt
to marry her cousin. When her husband dies, she returns home, but she
has learned ugly sexual behaviours from the people of Egypt. The father is
referring to her sexual conduct of gender mixing and engaging in amorous
attachments with men.

Smuggling lovers to the women's quarters is a common trope in the narrative. A young man who becomes a servant to a learned man, in *Sage and
the Scholar*, hears people talk about the princess and he falls in love with her.
He desires to have a glance at her, and the sage helps him by applying some
powder to his eye so that the people see only half of his body and think him
a *nasnas*, a demon. Since everyone wants to have a look at him, he is even
allowed into the harem, thereby he sees the princess, and his love for her
grows stronger. The next time, the sage applies the powder to his other eye,
and so he becomes invisible. He enters the palace and cuddles the princess.
However, people think that a demon has entered the harem, and they fumi-
gate the rooms with the smoke of camel dung, making the young man cry,
so the powder is washed from his eyes and he becomes visible. He is captured and to be executed, but the vizier advises the king to consent to the
marriage. A similar motif of using magic to make the lover invisible appears
in *Hasan the King of Egypt*. Hasan falls in love with Princess Farhat in Egypt,

and the Moorish magician brings them together by moving the princess's bed to Hasan's chamber at night. As the princess desires to have Hasan come to the palace at least once, the magician renders him invisible by means of a magical inscription on his forehead. Because of the heat in her room, however, Hasan wipes his forehead and erases the inscription. He is now visible, and the king catches him. The magician holds the king prisoner and releases him only after he has agreed to marry the princess to Hasan.

Breaking Barriers

Many stories in the Thousand and One Nights depict people striving to overcome various hurdles obstructing them from fulfilling their sexual desires and aspirations. These impediments include jail and captivity, religion, virginity, difficult marriage conditions, parental objections, strict and complex rules of royal life, physical deformity, and poverty. In *Third Larrikin's History*, a larrikin was to deliver the dogs to their owners, but a dog that has only one eye lags behind. When he tries to catch it, it runs into the house of a woman who has a one-eyed lover. When the man asks for 'the one-eyed', she is afraid that he will betray her secret and offers him her bracelet. Thus, physical deformation is no hinder to engage in, and enjoy, sex in this tale. It is unclear if the woman is a wife, in which case the tale addresses adultery, or simply an unmarried woman who is merely enjoying sexuality. Disfigurement as no hindrance to sexuality also appears in *Barber's Tale of His Sixth Brother*.

The fact that the lover is in jail is not a deterrent to sexual attachment, particularly when female cunning is performed. The daughter of a merchant, who is often away on a journey, in *Lady and Her Five Suitors*, falls in love with a merchant's son. As the young man is in jail for fighting, she conceives a plan to release him. She visits the chief of police, the judge, the vizier, and the king, one after the other. They all admire her beauty and fall in love with her, and she invites them to her home. She then goes to a carpenter and orders him to make a cabinet with four compartments, one above the other, with locks. Since the carpenter asks her favours too, she asks him to add the fifth compartment. One after the other, all the five suitors come to see her and each guest that arrives is told to hide in the cabinet. Finally, they learn of each other's presence, and all are put to shame. She offers to relieve them of this situation on the condition of releasing her lover from prison.

An Arab of high rank, in *Man Who Was Lavish of His House*, intends to invite some friends to a party in his home. In the meantime, a poor merchant walks through town and notices a beautiful woman. She welcomes his advances, but since he has no place of his own, he breaks into the Arab's house. While they are enjoying themselves, the owner suddenly enters with his friends. Instead of accusing the trespassers, the generous owner sends his friends away and pretends to be the merchant's servant. He even gives the woman some money when she leaves. Later, the merchant and the Arab become close friends. This tale expresses an utmost respect for sexuality, where sexuality opens the way for a new friendship predicated on the appreciation of sexual desires. Being poor and not having a house, and breaking into a stranger's house are no hurdles to engaging in a sexual liaison.

The power of sexuality is so strong that the status of the royal family is not an impediment to engaging in a sexual attachment. In *Harun al-Rashid and the Barmakids*, the renowned Caliph Harun al-Rashid was very much attached to his vizier, Ja'far the Barmakid, yet he had him executed. The caliph had arranged for Ja'far's marriage to his sister Abbassa on the condition that the vizier would not touch her until marriage. Then Ja'far allegedly made love to her and she became pregnant. When the caliph discovered his unfaithfulness, he became furious and punished him. *Ja'far and the Barmakids* is another version of the story where Harun loved both his vizier and his sister. He arranged for the two to be married, on condition that they meet only in his presence and never consummate the marriage. This condition was eventually broken, and Abbassa gave birth to a son in secret. The secret was found out, and the caliph punished his sister and his vizier. This story reflects a true historical development in the Abbasid caliphate in Baghdad. There are many speculations as to the real reasons for the tragic end of the highly influential Barmakid family. The love affair of the couple in these stories seems to be one of the reasons for this debacle.

Engaging in intimate attachments is not confined to the caliph's sister but also his favourite concubine. In *Ghanim ibn Ayyub and Qut al-Qulub*, Ghanim travels from Damascus to Baghdad to establish himself as a merchant. One day he spends the night in the graveyard because the gates of the city have already been closed. He finds a young woman in a large trunk drugged with henbane. He takes her to his house and they live merrily together as a loving, yet chaste couple. At first, she is unwilling to comply with his longing, and after finding out about her status, he refuses to touch her. The woman tells him that she is the favourite concubine of the caliph, whose wife, Zubayda, became jealous of her and conceived this plan to get rid of her. One day the caliph learns the truth, marries the sister of the merchant, while the lovers are joined in marriage.

Having different religious affiliations does not necessarily discourage sexual attraction. The idol-worshipping queen Jan Shah, in *Gharib and His Brother Ajib*, makes advances on Gharib, even when he breaks the idols into pieces. She transforms him into a monkey, yet offers to release him on the condition of having sexual intercourse with her. Pretending to agree, he kills her. A Christian prince of Macedonia learns about the beauty of a princess in Baghdad, in *Zahr al-Rawd*. He travels in disguise, and when he sees her face, he falls desperately in love. He commissions a scout to kidnap her, but her brother manages to release her. The beautiful Prince Qamar al-Zaman, in *Qamar al-Zaman and Shams*, hears about the beauty of the daughter of the Magian king Bahram of Ghazna, but she refuses his request of marriage. The prince disguises himself as a merchant and travels to her city. When she sees him, she immediately falls in love and smuggles him into the palace where the lovers are united.

Women converting to Islam to pursue their sexual desire are a repeated motif in the narrative of the Arabian Nights. Religious conversion, always from non-Muslim to Muslim, seems to open avenues for love and sexual craving. A merchant from Upper Egypt, in *Man of Upper Egypt and His Frankish Wife*, travels from Damascus to Acre to sell his crop of flax. He sees a Frankish woman and falls in love with her. With the help of an old woman, he manages to meet her several times, but in his confusion and fear of God, he never touches her. He returns to Damascus and starts trading in captive slave-girls. One day, he notices the very same woman among the prisoners. He sets her free and marries her after converting to Islam. Thus, distance, captivity, religion, and fear of divine power do not prevent amorous bonding from realization in the end. The Christian warrior princess Abriza converts to Islam for the sake of her love for Prince Sharkan in *Umar ibn al-Nu'man*. A woman who converts to Islam because of love also features in *Faris al-Khayl and al-Badr al-Fayiq*.

Overcoming distance and the almost impossible marriage conditions to secure sexual union is a motif in *King's Son of Sind and the Lady Fatima*. To get rid of the prince who treats her badly, his stepmother tells him that he will remain a good-for-nothing until he has conquered Princess Fatima. The prince is intrigued and starts roaming the world until he meets an old man who tells him that the sultan assigns three tasks to his daughter's suitors. First, they have to pick out clover seed, sesame, and lentils from a large heap, then they must drink a cistern full of water, and finally, they have to produce 3,000 doors in a house in one night. On the way, he shows kindness by feeding the wild beasts, grasshoppers, and jinn. When he asks for the king's daughter in marriage, he is told to meet the three conditions. As he is facing the first task, sitting in despair before the heap of seeds, an army of grasshoppers helps him. Next, the wild beasts drink all the water in the cistern, and finally, the jinn produce the doors in a single night. Now the prince is given Fatima in marriage. Thus, in order for the stepmother to end the maltreatment of her stepson, she lures him by sharpening his interest in sexuality. Sexuality is so intriguing for the prince that he roams the world and takes the challenge of meeting difficult conditions to have access to sexuality and marriage.

Mercury Ali is a sharper in Cairo who travels to Baghdad and wants to marry Zaynab, in *Mercury Ali of Cairo*. Her uncle asks him to prove himself in trickery as a condition to agreeing to the marriage. After many tricks and counter-tricks, her uncle gives his permission to the marriage but asks him to present the magic robe of Qamar, the daughter of a sorcerer, as a dowry. Ali tries to kill her father, but the sorcerer at first turns him into stone, and then transforms him into a donkey, a bear, and a dog. Finally, Qamar releases him and becomes his co-wife together with Zaynab. Transportable sexuality and the condition of obtaining a magic robe for contracting marriage also appear in the story of *Sirkhab and Aftuna*. Prince Sinjar learns about beautiful Princess Aftuna in China, whose father puts the condition of defeating him first to give her in marriage. The prince travels and triumphs over the king and wounds him. He cures the king, who offers him his daughter in return, but Sirkhab prefers to fetch his family first. As his three brothers also want to marry Aftuna, her father tells them that he will give her in marriage to whoever will bring him the magic robe of Princess Taj Nas. He travels and with the help of a princess, he succeeds in his mission, marries both princesses and becomes a king. A difficult condition for marriage is also narrated in *Gharib and His Brother Ajib*.

The story of the *Two Viziers and Their Children* has multiple episodes of migratory sexuality. When al-Mahdi, son of a vizier, wanted to marry his cousin, the daughter of another vizier, her father objects because he promised her to a prince. Al-Mahdi challenges the prince and vanquishes him on the battlefield. After intercepting love letters between the cousins, her father takes her to Yemen, and her cousin secretly follows them. He manages to marry her disguised as a merchant, and eventually, they all return home. For all his merits, al-Mahdi is now appointed a third vizier, and the king sends him to the Safat Islands with troops. The army is vanquished, and the vizier is taken prisoner. It so happens that the princess sees him and falls in love with him, and releases him from prison on the condition that he should marry her and spare her father, to which he agrees. One day, he goes out hunting, loses his way, and encounters a Bedouin woman with two extremely beautiful daughters. Falling in love with the young daughter, he is allowed to marry her on the condition of herding the camels for eight years. In the meantime, his father departs to search for him and reaches the same place. The father marries the second girl, on the same condition. After some time, they secretly return to the Safat Islands. Now it is the turn of the two Bedouin women to travel, dressed as men, to search for their husbands, and they are finally reunited with them.

Overcoming a difficult riddle as a condition to marriage appears in *Diamond*. However, even if it is not a condition for marriage, solving riddles could inadvertently lead to marriage. In *Vizier's Clever Daughter*, female intelligence and agency not only save her father from death but she is also rewarded with a marriage to the handsome prince, who she unrequitedly loves. One day a woman with her grandson comes to a soothsayer's house to work for him, in *Soothsayer and His Apprentice*, and the soothsayer's daughter falls in love with the young man. Her father, however, rejects their marriage and expels the young man, who finds another job. Meanwhile, the young woman visits her lover secretly at night. Her parents find out about her adventures, become furious, but reluctantly agree to their marriage, after having the daughter examined to prove her virginity. If virginity was kept intact in this narrative, it is not always the case in other stories. The sultan wants to get rid of Muhammad, the beautiful son of a fisherman who has continuous rows with his ugly son, in *Fourth Captain's Tale*. He sends him to fetch the princess of the Green Country. When the princess enters his boat out of curiosity, he casts off. The princess is attracted to Muhammad and makes love to him right there. He returns home, marries the princess and becomes sultan. This tale presents women as having a positive outlook on sexuality even before marriage. She did not hesitate to instantly make love to the young man when she felt attracted to him.

In *Gharib and His Brother Ajib*, the handsome Gharib rescues Princess Fakhr Taj, from the jinn of the Mountain, and she becomes infatuated with him. Her father consents to their marriage, but even before the wedding night, she takes him to her bed and embraces him, and he feels a hot desire and deflowers her, spending the night together until morning. When her father finds out what has happened, he draws his sword and goes to his daughter to reprimand her for letting Gharib sleep with her without dowry or marriage. He asks her whether he had touched her, and she is silent lowering her head. Her father shouts at the slave-girls to bind the 'harlot' and inspect her vagina, which they do, telling the king that her virginity has gone. He intends to kill her, but her mother intervenes, telling the king not to kill her lest she will be dishonoured forever, suggesting instead that the king shuts her in a cell until she dies. At night-time, the king orders two of his officers to take the princess and cast her in the river without telling anyone and they implement the order. Thus, virginity does not prevent lovers from engaging and enjoying sexual intimacy and sexual pleasure. Yet, the princess pays with her life for acting upon her lust and feelings, being sexually active and infatuated with the young man who has rescued her from the jinn. She was so positive about her sexuality that she did not even care for the formalities of marriage and dowry, and did not even bother to wait for just a few days until the official wedding ceremony. Death as a price to pay for losing virginity and fulfilling sexual desire is a motif that appears in a folk tale from West Africa. A boy grows up with the prohibition that he must never make love with a woman, or he will die. Nevertheless, he meets a woman, loves her, and dies (Belcher 2007: 176).

3

INSATIABLE LUST

WOMEN ARE DEPICTED AS SEXUALLY INSATIABLE IN THE NARRATIVE of the Thousand and One Nights. Yet, these concerns are more to do with the sexual performance of men rather than a preoccupation with female sexuality per se. After all, the narrators and writers of these stories are mostly, if not exclusively, men. For men, satisfying rapacious female desires becomes the site of initiating and demonstrating their unfailing masculine power. In this sense, female sexuality is essential to male masculinity. Female sexuality, voracious or not, is important to men because they are dependent on women to perform sexually and to construct the patriarchal conditioning of their masculinities. It is interesting to explore the question of whether female sexuality is truly insatiable or whether it is only the imagination and exaggeration of men. But then why do men exaggerate the sexuality of women when they accordingly become full of worries about their ability or inability to satisfy this inflated sexuality? Why do men put themselves into this paradox when it is obvious that it is in their very interests to de-essentialize and normalize the female sexuality on which they are inevitably dependent? An exaggerated female sexuality is pertinent to the patriarchal social construction of masculinity. In fact, exaggerating the sexuality of women is one way for men to express their own inflated sexuality, as part of their inflated male ego and hegemonic masculinity. Men often need to reassure themselves about their virility and sexual ability and to convince themselves of their sexual potency. An overstated female sexuality that is naturally dependent on men for satisfaction is perceived to be an optimal way to reassure men about their socially constructed role in prevalent gender order. In the domain of sexuality, the patriarchal image of masculinity is always at stake. The Arabian Nights is not unique in presenting women with an unappeasable sexuality. A survey of medieval European literature shows that women were believed to be more sexually insatiable than men were.

The belief in women as sexually voracious became an accepted 'fact' shaping theological tracts and church law. This concept was linked to women as temptresses to become one of the defining elements of female sexuality in the Middle Ages (Salisbury 1996: 87).

Unquenchable Female Sexuality

Narrative of Alf Layla wa Layla repeatedly portrays female sexual lust and desire as not only far greater than that of men but also as insatiable. In testing the knowledge of his son, in *Jali'ad of Hind and His Vizier Shimas*, a king summons the greatest scholars of the empire to the palace. One scholar asks him what the four things in which all creatures concur are, and the prince answers that they are food and drink, the delight of sleep, the lust of women, and the agonies of death. A king, in *Sea Rose of the Girl of China*, narrates to his sons a story about a princess in India who changes sex with a jinni. When she later wanted to change it back the jinni refused, since he was now pregnant and he could tell out of experience that sex for a female is more intense than that for a male. One day, a man is showing his wife his garden, in *Man and His Wilful Wife*, when two young men who happen to be there spot them and suspect them of committing fornication, *zina*. Meanwhile, the wife invites her husband to have sex with her right away: 'I will not pray for you until you fulfil my desire of that which women usually seek from men.' However, the man protests, 'O woman, did not you have enough of me in the house; here, I fear scandal. Do not you fear that someone will see us?' She replies that they should not worry about it since they commit neither lewdness nor sin, and she rejects his excuses and insists on having sexual intercourse instantly. While they are having sex, the young men enter the garden, seize the couple, and say, 'We will not release you because you are adulterers and if we do not have sex with the woman, we will report you to the police.' The man says that the woman is his wife and he is the owner of this garden. They pay no heed to him and fall on the woman to rape her, who cries out to her husband for help, but one of them slays him with his dagger. They both rape the woman unimpeded.

Aziz is having an enjoyable sexual relationship with Dalila, in *Aziz and Aziza*. It happens that one evening an old woman lures him to a house. Next, a beautiful young woman grasps him and throws him on the floor. She forces him into sexual intercourse and marriage, seals the door and tells him that he is allowed to leave only once a year. After a year, Dalila is no longer interested in him because he is married, and orders her slave-girls to castrate him by cutting off his penis. Swooning from pain, he returns to the house, but he is thrown out since he is no longer a man. This story depicts three women in the life of Aziz. He has a platonic relationship with his cousin Aziza, a relationship of sexual love with Dalila, and a relationship grounded on lustful desires with a third woman, where sexual lust is notably separated from love, thereby projecting a negative perception of female sexual desires. The third woman is kept nameless in the narrative, in contrast to the other women, signalling a literary punishment and bad image of lustful and sexually active women. Narratives about the cunning of women in medieval literature mention a story about a woman who locked a man in her house for a whole week to have sex with her, reluctantly releasing him (*Jins-al 'inda al-arab* 1997 1: 97).

Prince Badr Basim reaches a white city, in *Jullanar the Sea-Born*, where the Queen Lab is a wicked, crafty, perfidious, and bewitching woman. She loves handsome young men and is in the habit of taking any attractive young man who enters the city to her palace to enjoy him for forty days and enchants him afterward. All the horses, mules, and asses in the city were once strange young men bewitched by her. She is impressed by his beauty and becomes passionately enamoured with him. She invites him to her palace, seating him beside her, kissing and embracing him. After spending an evening of singing, eating, and drinking, she lies on the bed, dismisses all the slaves, and orders him to fornicate with her, and they spend a lovely night together. One day he watches as a black bird descends into the garden and approaches a white she-bird. The black bird flies down upon the white bird and falls to billing her, after the manner of doves. Then he leaps on her and fornicates with her three times, after which she changes and becomes a woman, the queen herself. He finds out that the black bird is one of the many young men who Queen Lab loved and enchanted. When she discovered that he started to fancy one of her slave-girls, she killed the girl and enchanted him into a black bird. Because she is still infatuated with him, she transforms herself into a bird, so that he could fornicate with her when she lusts after him.

Impressed by the symmetrical beauty of the sleeping young boy and girl, the jinn dispute over who is the most beautiful, in *Qamar al-Zaman and Budur*. However, they agree on a wager considering that beauty should be measured by the desire it arouses. The bet is to wake them alternately and whoever is not moved to translate seeing into touching, contemplation into consummation, and the appreciation of physical beauty into a sexual act is the winner. 'The one who shows greater love and hotter passion for the other will be defeated in the test, by confessing that the charms of the other are more powerful.' While her beauty impresses the boy, he was restrained in his reaction because he thought that this is a test for him arranged by his father who is watching to see his response. When it was the turn of the girl, the outcome was different, proving that her lust is intense and her self-control is weak. In admiring and exploring the sleeping male beauty, her hand slips on his penis, giving her sexual sensation. She mounts him and showers him with kisses, 'for the physical desire of women is stronger than that of men'. Thus, this narrative not only indicates male beauty is the winner in this contest but is also irresistible for women. The patriarchal message in the gender divide concerning rationality, emotionality, and self-control is recognizable in this tale. Inasmuch as both Qamar and Budur had already professed to reject not only marriage but also any interest in the opposite sex, Qamar's self-control may be as consistent with his previously expressed penchant as Budur's lack of self-control is inconsistent with hers (Epps 2008: 119–20). Beaumont (2002: 73) argues that the lack of control and weakness of Budur in the test is proleptic, as it is intended to prepare us for her ultimate betrayal of Qamar al-Zaman by her incestuous desire for his son by his second wife.

The frame story with all the tales of infidelity and cuckoldry of the two royal wives and the kidnapped bride who copulates with the two kings clearly presents a perception of the sexuality of women as insatiable and uncontrollable. Insatiable female lust is also presented in the Arabian Nights as a revenge strategy in response to the female kidnapping. The bride who was kidnapped by a jinni, in *Ifrit's Mistress*, copulates with, if not forcing, any male she encounters, reaching a level of 570 men. The same motif is also repeated in *King's Son and the Ifrit's Mistress*.

Voracious Desire and Promiscuity

Tales of infidelity, which is a predominant motif in the Thousand and One Nights, are strongly connected to a male and patriarchal perception of an insatiable female sexuality. In this perception, all tales of sexual infidelity are in the end also tales of unquenchable female sexuality that function as a rationalization of an inescapable female sexual unfaithfulness. Because of a strong sexual desire, female treachery is essentialized and constantly expected, no matter how hard a woman tries to resist. Insatiable sexual desire makes it difficult for women to resist the temptation of adultery, leading to a life of promiscuity. Having husbands and multiple lovers is a common motif in the Arabian Nights. In *Coelebs the Droll Court's Jester*, when her husband is away, a woman receives four of her former lovers at home and hides them in a closet, one after the other. In *Wife Who Vaunted Her Virtue*, the husband discovers that his wife is cheating on him with three lovers. In *Wife and Her Two Lovers*, not only does a wife has two lovers but also makes love to each one of them in the presence of her husband. The same motif also occurs in other stories, such as *Simpleton Husband*. A married woman, in *Lady and Her Two Lovers*, has a lover and an extra affair with his young messenger. In *Singer and the Druggist*, the wife enjoys having a lover to come to her every day, paying him money for pleasing her sexually, and outsmarting her suspecting husband in finding a new hiding place for her lover every day. *As'ad and Amjad* is a story of a double and combined case of adultery and incest by the two co-wives of Qamar al-Zaman.

Insatiable female sexual desires induce women to have multiple conjugal partners, employing the use of resourcefulness to satisfy their cravings. In *Woman Who Has Two Husbands*, an imaginative woman in Egypt has two husbands who do not know about each other. One is a pickpocket who comes home only during the night, and the other is a robber who returns home only during the day. They discover the truth by coincidence while the wife tells them that she is unable to decide which one she prefers, and proposes to stay with the one who proves to be the more accomplished rogue. While this is still a roguery, the woman wishes for the most talented man as a partner. A deputy governor, in *Lady with the Two Coyntes*, neglects his beautiful wife and so she covets the horse-keeper. One day she tells her husband that her mother has died and asks for the company of the horse-keeper to attend the funeral. After spending a delightful time with her lover, she returns to tell her husband that she has inherited her mother's vulva, showing him her vagina from the back. For this, she needed an extra husband, and she has therefore married the horse-keeper. This is the only story in the Arabian Nights that makes an explicit correlation between a man neglecting his wife and her infidelity against him and, thereby, de-emphasizing the essentialized nature of female sexual perfidy that is heavily pronounced in other stories. However, the mentioning of the male neglect of his wife's sexuality could be interpreted in the context of affirming the perceived voracious lust of women. In this sense, the neglect of the sexual needs of the wife is not really the fault of the husband but because these needs are colossal and unquenchable. In medieval literature, there is a story narrated by al-Jahiz (d. 868) about a woman who recites verses wishing to be a lizardess and her husband to be a lizard. The narrator explains that the lizards have two sets of genitals and that the woman 'wished that she had two vaginas and he had two penises' (*Jins-al 'inda al-arab* 1997 II: 183).

A general travels in an official task, in *Admonished Adulteress*. He is married to a beautiful woman and is extremely worried about her chastity during his absence. He informs her that if one day she is unable to control her sexual desire, she should visit a certain friend of his and get what destiny has in store for her. Even though the woman initially took the position of categorically rejecting the suggestion, yet she is soon feeling strong fleshly yearnings and thus decides to visit the recommended man. The man appears to comply, but he wants to buy some food first. He returns with a recently slaughtered sheep and instructs her to suspend it from the ceiling. Then he stays away for seven days while the meat is rotting away. When the woman becomes resentful, he explains that had he agreed to her suggested adultery she would have become as rotten as the piece of meat. Informing her husband on what happened to her, he rewards his friend with a new robe. It is remarkable that the woman tells her husband about her attempt of the adulterous act and the woman is not punished for it. This story portrays that sexual needs are taken seriously, acknowledged, expected, and tolerated, even if not approved.

Some Bedouins attack a man and take him prisoner, in *Barber's Tale of His Sixth Brother*. Every day, his captor tortures him and demands that he ransom himself with money or he will kill him. Being poor and beggar, he is unable to provide money and his captor cuts his lips with a knife. The handsome wife of the Bedouin used to make advances to the captive, in her husband's absence, while he holds her off. One day, she tempts him and he starts to play with her, taking her on his knees. While they are in this position, her husband suddenly enters, cursing him for debauching his wife, and in rage, cuts off the captive's penis. What could be the explanation for the perfidy of the beautiful wife in making advances to a poor beggar, about whom the story is silent with regard to any beauty or physical attributes? She makes advances on him while the brutality of the husband makes him even less attractive with the physical disfiguration of his lips, an important part of the body when it comes to love and sexuality. The story does not furnish reasons to believe that the perfidy of the wife is taken as an act of revenge against her husband. While the narrative depicts him as a cruel man to his captive, there is no indication that he is equally cruel to his wife. With this in mind, it seems that the perfidy of the wife is safely explained by her insatiable lust, which is the essentialized attribute of many women in the Arabian Nights. Furthermore, this tale clearly shows that female sexuality could eventually lead to disaster and harm, illustrated by the excision of the penis. Dangerous female sexuality is a repeated motif in this collection of tales.

The Arabian Nights contains stories presenting not only female sexual insatiability and infidelity but also women who are punishing male sexual faithfulness to their partners when their sexual advances are rejected. In *Diamond*, Queen Latifa enchants the prince into a deer when he rejects her advances because he wanted to be faithful to his lover. In *Ali and Zahir from Damascus*, the jinn-queen Turaja desires young men and enchants them when they have satisfied her lust. Another queen wants to marry Ali but when he rejects the proposal because he wants to be faithful to his wife, she transforms him into a dog. The insatiable female sexuality is clearly illustrated in this story where the two queens crave for sexual intercourse with any young men who reach their islands. Queen Turaja has many lovers, both human and jinn, who continue to desire her, even though she is frequently changing partners.

Desire for a Large Penis

The collection of the tales of Thousand and One Nights contains many stories presenting women with insatiable sexual lust to the extent of essentialization. Essentializing female sexual desires reflects, subconsciously, strong concerns about the ability of men to satisfy the perceived rapacious desires of women. The concern of men about the size of their penis is professed to be very pertinent to their sexual performance in satisfying ravenous female sexual yearning and, therefore, becoming a serious preoccupation for men in the context of sexual encounters. Within this perception, the size of the penis is believed to be instrumental for virility. Believing in an exaggerated virility, in turn, necessitates a corresponding perception of an exaggerated female sexuality. Male narrators depict women believing that men with a large penis are more sexually satisfying. The search for a large penis and sexual lust tends to entice women to engage in bestiality and adultery. Within this context, the engagement of the wife in sexual adultery is only natural and inevitable. Adultery is bound to occur eventually, because women's resistance to the temptation of sexual seduction, concretized in a large penis, is extremely weak and unreliable. In his comments on the story of *Shahryar and His Brother*, Burton (2010) suggests that the reason, rather mythical, why the two royal wives commit adultery with black slaves is the size of their penises. Beaumont (2002: 50) also makes a similar remark. There are widespread fantasies on the part of medieval Arabs about the sexual powers of black men and their lusting after Arab women (Irwin 1994: 175).

The *Arabian Nights Encyclopedia* (Marzolph and Leeuwen 2004 1: 98) states that the male fantasy that the length of the penis decides whether a man is attractive to women is as old as it is ineradicable. A short anecdote in al-Jahiz's *Kitab al-Bighal* (*Book of the Mules*) satirizes this fantasy by having a witty person saying, 'If the length of the penis were a sign of honor, then the mule would belong to the Quraysh (the honorable tribe of Prophet Muhammad).' However, medieval erotic literature is saturated with anecdotes about insatiable female sexual lust and the relevance of a large penis to satisfy female desires. The erotic treatise of al-Tusi (d.1274) (2014: 117), *The Sultan's Sex Potion*, includes a recipe to double the length of the penis that lasts for twenty days. The famous pornographic manual, *rawd al-atir* (*Perfumed Garden*), by Sheik al-Nafzawi (*c.*1410), also includes advice on increasing the size of the penis (Irwin 1994: 165). Medieval literature narrates a story about two men living in the same place, one with a large penis and the other with a small one. The wife of the former is happy while the other is not and she uses cunning to have sex with the other man, for which she succeeds (al-jins 1997 I: 98–9). However, medieval Islamic literature is not unique in this regard. A survey of medieval European literature finds out that there was a perceived correlation between the size of the penis and virility. Men also appear to have boasted and told jokes and stories about penis size. These sources indicate that men experienced anxiety about penis size and women had certain expectations about the physical capacity of a large strong man. It was believed that there is a link between male virility and a sense of self-worth rooted in genital size and sexual prowess (Murray 1996a: 137).

Several tales of the narrative of the Arabian Nights make an explicit connection between the size of penis and sexuality. When the jinn admire and compare the beauty of the sleeping young boy and girl, in *Qamar al-Zaman and Budur*, one of the jinn notices the large penis of the boy: 'his waist sometimes complained of the weight that went below it'. A wife wishing her husband to have a large penis is narrated in *Three Wishes*. Seeing angels on the Night of Power, *laylat al-qadr*, a man is granted three wishes. When he consults his wife, she advises him to request that his penis is enlarged. He follows her advice, and his penis grows as large as a column. His second wish is to be relieved of this huge member, and his penis shrinks until it has completely disappeared. Now he is forced to use the third wish in order to restore his penis as it was. In this way, he lost his three wishes by a woman's ill advice, believing that a more enjoyable sexuality depends on the size of the penis. Naturally, calamities resulting from the ill advice of women make sense in a context of the patriarchal social construction of gender reality. While this story addresses the large penis within the context of marital sexuality, most of the tales in this regard are narrated within a context of adultery.

In *Ali with the Large Member*, two young men are hired as cattle-herders with different masters. While his master's wife moreover takes Ahmad as a lover, Ali is harassed by his master's wife and is extremely unhappy. Ahmad decides to help his friend. While he knows the wife of Ali's master to be listening, he calls him 'Ali with the two yards'. The woman takes Ali as her lover to satisfy her curiosity and sexual needs. A peasant, in *Peasant's Beautiful Wife*, sees his farmhand naked, and remarks to his beautiful wife about his large penis. The woman pretends to be offended but secretly desires sexual union. One day she instructs the farmhand to feign illness and stay at home while the peasant is away. As they are having lunch together with the couple's little daughter, the wife intentionally drops some of the melted butter. According to their previous arrangement, she is to be 'punished' by having sexual intercourse with him. Dropping the butter and the sexual punishment is repeated several times. When the farmer returns, his daughter warns him not to drop any of the butter lest the farmhand will punish him by pushing his 'snake' between his thighs. As the wife strongly condemns her daughter's talk, the husband sees no other solution but to disbelieve his daughter. The *Arabian Nights Encyclopedia* (Marzolph and Leeuwen 2004 I: 323) states that the motif of 'sexual intercourse as alleged punishment' is known from a unique Arabic collection of jocular tales dating from the tenth to eleventh centuries. In a relevant tale, a mule driver 'punishes' the woman riding the mule when she attempts to pick fruit from a garden. Having done so various times, in the end, he is not capable of responding to her further provocations. This tale illustrates the insatiable sexual lust of women.

One day a good-looking vizier's son, in *Vizier's Son and the Bath-keeper's Wife*, enters a public bath, *hammam*, and when he takes off his clothes, the bath-keeper notices that his penis is hidden between his thighs and appears as small as a hazelnut, because of the excess obesity of the young man. The bath-keeper feels sorrowful for the man because he is handsome, young, and wealthy yet he is lacking something of delight like other men. The young man agrees and gives him one dinar to fetch him a beautiful woman to prove himself on her. The bath-keeper, however, goes directly to his wife to suggest that no one is worthier of that money but his wife, telling her that she could spend one hour with the man, laugh at him and take the money. His wife takes the money, adorns herself, puts on her best clothes, and goes to the waiting man. She finds a handsome youth like the moon at its full, and he is impressed by her beauty. He takes the woman in his arms and presses her to his bosom, and they cuddle. His penis rises long, as it was that of an ass, and he mounts her breast and they engage in heated sexual intercourse, while she groans, sighs, and wriggles with pleasure under him. Her husband, who is waiting behind the door, starts to call her to come out, saying, 'Enough is enough', and that she should go to her suckling child. She answers him, 'If I go out, my soul will depart my body; so I must either leave the child to die of weeping or let him be reared an orphan, without a mother.' Thus, they continue to have sexual intercourse ten times, while her husband remains at the door, calling her, crying, and weeping. Full of despair, rage, and jealousy, he goes to the roof of the bathhouse, throws himself off, and dies. This is a funny, yet tragic, tale addressing the perceived connection between the size of the penis and sexuality, albeit from a different angle. The husband is convinced that the small size of the penis would not lead to sexual intercourse, thereby encouraging his wife to take the money and play the role. Thus, the story reinforces the belief that only a large penis could ensure a successful and enjoyable sexual interaction and, therefore, signifies virility. This is particularly so when the small penis is turned into a large one upon erection, resulting in an enormous sexual pleasure for the wife to the extent that she neglects her suckling child. Once a woman finds the large penis that ensures her sexual pleasure, she becomes very insensitive to the feelings of her husband or to the needs of her child.

Tales of Bestiality

Tales of bestiality in the Thousand and One Nights clearly illustrate the perceived insatiable female sexuality. Most of these tales involve women while men are present only marginally. The preponderance of women in tales of bestiality is also evident in the medieval mainstream erotic literature. This is interesting considering that experiences of bestiality, even today, are predominated by men. It seems that in narrating these erotic tales, men are projecting their own experiences of bestiality by extending it to women. This projection makes sense to men because men narrate it within a context of essentializing female sexuality as insatiable and unquenchable but also tinged with the insecurity and anxiety associated with their sexual performance. Stories about great sexual prowess and large penises would surely appeal to men who tend to worry constantly about their sexual performance vis-à-vis ravenous women.

Remarkably, tales of bestiality present women as the active partner enthusiastically seeking sex with animals, which are represented as passive and merely responding to women's initiatives. Tales of bestiality in the Arabian Nights show that it is the women who take the initiative in performing bestial encounters with animals, whereas European medieval literature, for instance, often narrates that it is the animals who take the initiative in bestial encounters, presenting more sexually active animals (Crispin 2008: 162). Additionally, the European literature depicts a more balanced presentation in terms of both sexes performing it, and also in a balanced mix of wild and domesticated animals involved in bestial sex. By contrast, most of the animals involved in the bestiality tales of Alf Layla wa Layla are wild animals. Understandably, depicting wild animals is perhaps a narrative strategy to make the tales more exciting and extraordinary. Yet it is also related to a gender perception that women are wild, irrational, and sexually voracious, like the animal world. Both belong to nature in contrast to the cultural and rational world of men. Pet animals, such as dogs, do not appear in these tales despite the fact that medieval erotic treatises narrate anecdotes in this regard (Borg 2000: 153; Munajjid 1958: 93–5; Nasr al-Katib 1977: 23).

Because of the disapproval of the parents, a couple decide to elope, in *Third Larrikin's Tale Concerning Himself*. When during their journey the man falls asleep for some time, an ape rapes his beloved. Later, they arrive at a certain town and become husband and wife. As his wife is about to die, a year later, she advises him to marry only a virgin, as the delight of having sexual intercourse with the monkey had never left her. The man starts roaming the world. Another story involving a woman having sex with an ape is *King's Daughter and the Ape*. A king has a daughter who, ever since having her first sexual experience with a black slave, has become nymphomaniac and passionately addicted to sexual intercourse, to the extent that she cannot abstain from it a single hour. The frustration of never feeling fully sexually satisfied induces her to ask the advice of older women in the palace. They advise her that there is no creature that makes love more than the monkey. It chances one day that an ape-dealer passes under her window with a great ape. She unveils her face and winks at the ape. The ape breaks his bonds and climbs up to the princess who hides him in her room to do nothing but eating, drinking, and fucking day and night. When her father eventually finds out about her bestial sexuality, he wants to kill her, but she disguises herself as a male slave and escapes with the monkey. Every afternoon she buys meat from a young butcher, who becomes suspicious and one day follows her. The woman and the monkey eat a meal, drink wine, and the ape then makes love to her ten times until she faints away. Thereupon, the butcher goes into the house and kills the monkey with his sharp knife. She implores him to kill her too, but he talks to her nicely to calm her down, promising that he would make love to her as much as the monkey used to do. She is finally persuaded, consenting to be his wife.

However, he soon finds out that he is no match for the monkey and his wife proves to be too sexually demanding for him. He seeks the assistance of an old woman who advises him to boil virgin vinegar and some pyrethrum and to fuck his wife until she passes out. The old woman then takes the woman and sets her vagina to the mouth of the cooking-pot. When the steam enters her vagina, two worms, one black and one yellow, fall down. The old woman explains that the black worm came from fucking the black slave and the yellow one is from fucking the ape. Muslims were far from free of fear and superstition regarding sexual matters, as it was believed that worms in the vagina caused nymphomania (Irwin 1994: 175). Consequently, she lives with her husband without asking for sex for a long period, and they live happily since she ceases demanding too much sex. Thus marital happiness and functionality are concomitant with reduced female sexuality and less insatiable women. Female sexuality is a serious problem for men, who are not only forced to compete with animals for the attention of women but also to subdue the excessive sexual nature of women. If the woman in this story is eventually cured of excessive sexual desires, the next story of bestiality leads to the tragic death of the woman involved. It is the story of the triumph of bestial sexuality over human sexuality and the conscious and active role a woman plays in this preference.

Every day, a woman buys meat from the butcher Wardan in Cairo, in *Wardan the Butcher with the Lady and the Bear*, and he becomes suspicious and follows her to a cave. The woman and a big bear eat food, drink wine, then the woman undresses and lies down, and the bear starts fucking her. She is very responsive and enjoys it very much and they repeat this ten times until they both fall down without a motion. Seizing the opportunity, the butcher then walks in and kills the bear. The astonished woman reprimands him, to which Wardan replies, 'Oh the enemy of herself, you slut! What made you do this terrible thing? Aren't there enough men for you to do this obnoxious deed?' She makes no answer but asks him to kill her as he has killed the bear and takes the treasure and leave. He tells her that he is better than the bear, asking her to repent and return to the path of God, and to marry him and live together happily with the treasure. She rejects his offer by replying that she could not live without the bear; 'this has been written down as my destiny! Since my time has come now, you must slit my throat too, just as you have killed this bear! After this has happened, there is no point for me to live on in this world!' Unable to convince her, Wardan slays the woman and takes the treasure.

This is a story about the risk and danger of an anomalous sexual contact and the deviation from the legitimate pattern of sexual relationship. It portrays the dangers pertinent to the insatiable female sexuality. This insatiable sexuality not only is feared and demonized but also severely punished. Extreme female sexuality leads to disaster and death and functions as an acceptable rationalization for femicide. Men are actually competing with animals, non-humans, to conquer the sexuality of women, which is utterly significant for the construction of the male hegemonic masculinity.

In the narrative of the bear and the woman, bestiality is normalized in the sense of not being an isolated incident but a daily sexual encounter where the participants are presented as a normal couple, eating, drinking, sleeping, per-forming sex, and both groaning and enjoying sex. Bestiality is habitualized here. It is the same in the affair with the monkey that started as strangers, but then the monkey actually stays in the princess's chamber, eating, drinking, and having sex, and they even flee together, like a couple who have to elope to overcome social barriers to their attachment. However, the story of the monkey ends with curing the princess of not only her bestial inclination but also of her voracious sexual appetite that drives her to be closer to nature and animals and causes her to engage in bestial activities. In this story, 'human nature' triumphs in the end as she settles in a marital and sexual relationship with a man, after normalizing her sexual drive and reducing it from a bestial state to a regular, human state. In contrast, the narrative of the bear and the woman shows the triumph of bestiality over regular heterosexual normativity showing not only a preference for bestial sex but also an intimacy and strong attachment to the animal partner.

Both of the animals involved in the narrative of bestiality show extraordi-nary sexual prowess, as both perform sexual intercourse ten times at one go. It seems that the number ten is a narrative fixation because it is also pertinent to human sexuality in the story about the wife of the bath-keeper. However, what distinguishes the bear in contrast to the monkey is the size of the sexual organ. A version of the story of the woman and the bear is included in a treatise on sexuality, *Ruju' al-shaykh ila sabahu* (*The Old Man's Return to His Youth*), authored by Ibn Kamal-Pasha (d.1533). In this version, the bear's sexual organ is described as being as large as that of a mule (Marzolph 2015: 199). Was this large penis a factor contributing to the outcome that the woman preferred being faithful to her animal partner, and thus death, over the human male? If that is the case, why are there no stories in the Arabian Nights about bestiality with a mule, or a horse for that matter, considering the sexual fixation on the size of the penis? Anecdotes about bestiality with the mule are narrated in medieval erotic literature. This literature reports men having sex with mules (Nasr al-Katib 1977: 93–5). The mystical poet Rumi (d.1273) tells a story about a woman and her donkey lover, who a servant girl tries to emulate, forgetting how deep a donkey may penetrate when not checked (Hämeen-Anttila 2014: 15).

In the Arabian Nights, however, there is one story only involving a man having sex with a mule. In *Mahmud and His Three Sons*, a woman surprises her male servant having sexual intercourse with a she-mule and invites him to have it with her instead. Once the act of bestiality is discovered, it is abruptly terminated and replaced by heterosexuality where a female is taking over.

Giving up the pleasure of bestiality is rewarded with an even more delightful pleasure of having sex with a woman. Even today, men or teenagers having sex with she-donkeys is quite common in many parts of the Middle East, particularly in rural areas. It has been reported that it exists in, for instance, present-day Morocco (Duran 1993: 185). However, it is important to mention that bestiality exists in all societies and in all historical epochs.

The destiny of a young princess in India is to marry an ugly he-goat, in *He-goat and the King's Daughter*. She is married to the beast, which in her bedroom changes into a handsome young man. He tells her not to disclose his secret to anyone, but she discloses the truth, and he disappears. The princess searches for him and reaches a palace in a cave, where there is a flock of he-goats, all of which turn into handsome young men. The couple is reunited. This story is bordering bestiality since she is having sexual intercourse with the beast only when he turns into a man. In the Middle Ages, the he-goat was thought to be a lascivious beast, which had a lusty and hot nature that could dissolve diamond. Literature from France in the late Middle Ages talks about sodomizing goats, depicting an image of an unending circle of anal sex performed by voracious goats with men (Crispin 2008: 162). However, this active and extraordinary sexual power of the he-goat would make a perfect match for the conceived insatiable sexual lust of women. The same trope is present in another Middle Eastern folklore tradition involving a story where a camel became a husband to a woman, whose father said, 'Nothing forbids the union as long as he can pay the princess's bride-money, which is her weight in gold' (Bushnaq 1986: 188).

Marriage to an animal but from the perspective of the other gender is narrated in the *Prince and the Tortoise*. The destiny of the youngest prince is to marry a tortoise. She excels in preparing tasty meals and finally changes into a beautiful young woman who is praised by everyone. However, changing into a beautiful woman would end the abnormal situation of bestiality. Thus, the narrative of the Arabian Nights insists on presenting bestiality as a temporal experience that would eventually cease to the advantage of human sexuality. In contrast to the permanent human sexuality, bestiality is tolerated as simply an ephemeral phenomenon. Heterosexuality is the reward for those who are willing to terminate their bestial encounter and relinquish the pleasure of bestial sex. Evidently, this applies to the slave man who had sex with a she-mule, the princess with the he-goat, the prince with the tortoise, and the princess who was obsessed with bestial sex with an ape. If bestiality is not terminated willingly, death takes care of it, as is the case of the woman with the bear. It is true that this story depicts a stubborn devotion to bestial sex at the expense of human sex, but death makes sure that this immersion in bestial sex is silenced forever. Death is also present in the case of the woman who elopes with her lover and a monkey rapes her. Death erases the delight of bestial sex that this woman could not forgo. Whether terminated by death or replaced by human sex, bestiality is presented as transient fantasy and experience, never enduring or autonomous.

4

DEMONIC SEXUALITY

The Jinn of the Arabian Nights

The world of the jinn is accorded an intense and passionate presentation in the collection of the Thousand and One Nights. This presence portrays the fairy tales aspect in the collection. Stories about the jinn and their sexual and amorous liaisons and marriages with humans strongly infiltrate this narrative. Not only do these worlds exist side by side, but they also interact and communicate. The recognition, acceptance, and tolerance of the existence of the world of jinn are so naturalized that sexual and romance attachments with them are also expected and accepted. The world of the jinn is rationalized by religion. The jinn are mentioned in the Qur'an, where a whole chapter, *sura*, is named after the jinn, stating that God has made his creatures of humans, from clay, and jinn, from smokeless fire (Koran 1974: 265). This religious rationalizing and backing of the existence of the jinn seem to have been extended to the interaction between humans and jinn. In the Arabian Nights, the question of whether someone is a human or jinn is often reiterated without causing astonishment; thereby the boundaries between these two worlds are shaky and shifting.

However, the inclusion of the world of the jinn into the literary narrative is not confined to the Arabian Nights only. Rather, it forms part of the canonical literature during the medieval period. The tenth-century authoritative catalogue of books, *Fihrist*, of Ibn al-Nadim included a section on humans who loved jinn and jinn who loved humans (Reynolds 2006b: 250; Roth 1996: 320). The *Arabian Nights Encyclopedia* (Marzolph and Leeuwen 2004 II: 534–5) states that the main source for the intervention of demons in the daily life of human beings remains the tradition of storytelling, and the Arabian Nights is among the most important texts for our knowledge about jinn. The jinn who are mentioned in the Qur'an as part of creation and belong to the realm of magic and supernatural powers are described in detail in zoological encyclopaedias, and legal handbooks contain speculations about the relationship between human beings and jinn. Remarkably, religious rationalization of the world of the jinn seems to feed an interest and belief in the existence of the jinn in even modern Middle East today.

While religion furnishes the foundation for rationalizing the interaction between humans and jinn, there are additional perspectives in contextualizing this interface. Sexual and love affairs with jinn in the narrative of Thousand and One Nights make sense within a context of the public recognition of the enthralling appeal of sexuality and its significance in social life, in addition to the consideration that female sexuality is intense and insatiable. This centrality and prominence of sexuality in medieval times tends to induce the narrators of these tales to externalize sexuality beyond the realm of the humans into the world of the jinn. In these tales, we find that the patriarchal code of honour is transported to the realm of the jinn, as is evident in the story of the *Second Qalandar's Tale*. Lesbian experience is alluded to in *Damir and al-Anqa'*, and transsexual experience is referred to in *Sea Rose of the Girl of China*, where a jinni changes sex with an Indian princess. The jinni finds female sexuality is so intense that he rejects to switch back gender. Both the lesbian and transsexual experiences are narrated within a context of human interaction with the jinn.

Furthermore, the narrative of the Arabian Nights portrays romance as an irrational experience, beyond the control of the individual. Consequently, love relationships with the jinn by themselves are not puzzling inasmuch as love itself is mysterious and unfathomable. Hence, the jinn are not to be blamed for falling in love with them, but the real culprit is love itself, which is uncontrollable and striking in strange ways. Just like love among humans, these stories narrate about princes who fall in love with jinn instantaneously, love attachments are ignited by seeing a portrait of a jinniyah, pining with grief when the beloved is far away, taking dangerous and long journeys in search of the beloved, and enduring hardships to be united with them.

The communication between the world of humans and the world of the jinn is so naturalized in the narrative of the Arabian Nights that foster-siblings become one of the outcomes of this interface. A jinniyah becomes a foster-sister to Hasan in *Hasan of Basra*, and when he misses her, he leaves his family to embark on a long journey visiting her. In *Sayf al-Muluk and Badi'at al-jamal* a human and a jinniyah become foster-sisters because the mother of the human female suckled the jinniyah infant. The jinn propagate their species, sometimes in conjunction with human beings; in which latter case, the offspring partakes of the nature of both parents (Lane 1987: 33). In a folkloric tale from Syria, a woman gets pregnant with an *ifrit* (Bushnaq 1986: 201).

Arabian demonology presented in the narrative of the Thousand and One Nights states that King Solomon rules the world of jinn and often punishes the jinn who disobey his orders. God has made the jinn subject to King Solomon for the duration of his life, placing their great strength and skills at his service (Bushnaq 1986: 67). There are good and friendly, often believing, jinn and there are evil and malicious jinn. *Ifrit* is a powerful evil jinn, and *Marid* is the most powerful, arrogant, and malicious kind of jinn. It is an evil jinni of the most powerful class (Lane 1987: 27). The *ifrits* are known as the snatchers of women. As mentioned in the Qur'an, an *ifrit* carried the throne of the Queen of Sheba from her kingdom in Yemen to Solomon in Jerusalem (Bushnaq 1986: 67). The *ghoul* belongs to an inferior order of the jinn, who lives a solitary existence in the deserts, burial grounds, and other isolated spots. It takes the forms of human or various animals and in many monstrous shapes. It kills and devours humans and often appears to people travelling alone in the night (41–2). The *ghoul* is similar to *Lamia*, a female or hermaphroditic demon who lives in caves and ventures forth to devour children or young men she has seduced and often appears in Greek mythology, arguably having its roots in ancient Mesopotamian demonology. It uses the pleasures of sex as a decoy for devouring humans. It also appears in Jewish tradition during the Middle Ages in the female demon *Lilith* (Resnick and Kitchell 2007: 82–3).

The Arabian Nights portrays and makes a distinction between the good jinn and the bad ones. There is harmony, love, sex, and marriage between humans and the good jinn, who are often happy to help the humans in their adventures and endeavours. In the story of *Sayf al-Muluk and Badi'at al-jamal*, even when the jinni abducts a princess, he does not harm her and does not enforce sexual intercourse on her and, therefore, she remains a virgin despite his love for her. In this narrative, humans often seek the help of the jinn who seem to be ready to assist and serve people. The positive depiction of the jinn and their help for the humans is also presented in other literary cultures. In Mande cultures in West Africa, there is a woman who tries desperately to have a child. She first approaches two human diviners for help yet they exploit the situation by having sexual intercourse with her. A jinni finally offers her the needed aid by helping her to conceive from her husband while refraining from engaging in surrogate activity with the woman (Belcher 2007: 176–7).

However, the world of the demons also includes bad jinn and, therefore, interaction with them becomes unavoidable; after all, they exist side by side with the humans. The bad jinn are unruly and violent. They often transgress the world of the humans by using violence, kidnapping, and enforcing sex and love on them. This behaviour of the jinn is understandable, if not expected because the jinn are considered inferiors to the humans. Fascinatingly, when it comes to kidnapping and violent interactions between jinn and humans, women appear often in these stories. This is hardly surprising considering that tales of jinn and magic are often narrated in the private domain of women and children. Bushnaq (1986: 65) states that while the Bedouin stories celebrate ideal conduct of noble men, tales of magic peopled with *ghouls* and *ifrits* are distinctly the entertainment of women; these are household proper. Having heard them as children, men also know these stories. However, a grown man's world is outside the house, while many great storytellers dwell within it. Demons kidnapping women is a trope found in other Middle Eastern folklore tradition as well (104).

However, the interaction between humans and jinn tends to reflect both hidden and overt tension between these two worlds. There is a clear competition between humans and jinn over access to love and sexuality. Many stories narrate about jinn who abduct human brides and keep them in secluded places, thus preventing them from having mutual access with humans. Many of these abductions occur during the wedding nights thus directly affecting human attachments and engagements. The *ifrits* who kidnap the brides in many stories, such as *Ifrit's Mistress*, *King's Son and the Ifrit's Mistress*, and *Second Qalandar's Tale*, are directly competing with the grooms over access to the brides. In this contest for intimacy and sexuality, the jinn are successful, sometimes temporarily but in other instances permanently. This direct competition between male jinn and male humans over access to virgins is clearly presented in *Zayn al-Asnam*. In this story, and in many stories, the jinni is presented as forgiving and tolerant, qualities that serve the interest of the human hero of the story. Thus, the good character of the jinn, clearly depicted in the narrative, seems to benefit humans in their interaction with the jinn. On the other hand, jinn are usually not very bright and this allows humans to outsmart them (Leeuwen 2014: 210; Marzolph and Leeuwen 2004 II: 535).

Regardless of the good or bad character of the jinn, all the jinn possess supernatural qualities that outstrip human capabilities. The possession of magic powers coupled with the ability to fly, and take on all kinds of shapes, tend to advantage them in their connection with the world of humans, and in winning the contest between these two worlds. However, these magical qualities seem to make sense in a narrative like Alf Layla wa Layla, a richly imaginative literary work. This collection of tales uses the character of the jinn as a narrative device to expand the horizon of human imagination in a literary work whose very existence is rationalized and predicated on pushing the boundaries of human intelligence and imagination far beyond the expected and known. Naithani (2004: 278–9) argues that the jinn and other creatures appear to regulate, change, and facilitate human affairs, but they either do not belong there, or they are not independent characters of a story. This is undoubtedly true, but the overall narrative strategy of using the jinn in the plots of these stories has unquestionably enriched the narrative tremendously. A careful reading of the Arabian Nights will establish that the world of the jinn in this narrative is natural, perhaps even indispensable. One of the pillars of the Shahrazad's sexual politics in this collection is the power, and the politics, of imagination, where the role of the jinn seems to be instrumental. The involvement of the jinn in the first story Shahrazad narrates, *Merchant and the Jinni*, is pivotal to her narrative strategy and to the very rationale of the Arabian Nights.

Thus, the world of the jinn is crucial in the collection of the Thousand and One Nights. The narrative successfully naturalizes the realm of the jinn and their coexistence with humans. Just like the case of the humans, there are good and bad jinn in these stories that portray a mix of social interactions between humans and jinn, including the voluntary and involuntary interface. Love and sexuality is an important realm of this interaction.

Jinn, Love, and Marriage

The adventures of Hasan take him to a palace inhabited by seven jinn-princesses, in *Hasan of Basra*. They allow him to stay in the palace and instruct him that he is allowed to open all rooms but one. Unable to control his curiosity, he eventually opens the prohibited door, leading to a roof terrace with a garden overlooking the sea, containing a magnificent pavilion and a water basin. While he is enjoying the scenery, ten birds suddenly descend on the terrace, take off their garment of feathers, and change into ten beautiful girls, who start swimming and playing in the basin. They are the daughters of a rich and mighty king of the jinn. Hasan falls in love with the most beautiful, and one of the princesses who became his foster-sister convinces her to marry Hasan. He takes the bride with him and returns to Basra to live with his mother. After moving to Baghdad, his wife bears him two sons and they live happily. Then Hasan feels the urge to visit his foster-sister, instructing his mother not to let his wife leave the house and telling her where he has hidden her vest of feathers. His wife, however, manages to persuade his mother to let her go to the bathhouse, where all the women, including a slave-girl from the royal palace, admire her beauty. Out of curiosity, the caliph's wife demands to see her. On hearing her story, Zubayda orders Hasan's mother to fetch the feather vest to see it on the female jinn, jinniyah. By using cunning, the wife manages to escape with her children and go home. This calls for another adventure for Hasan, who eventually succeeds in reuniting with his wife and sons and returning home with them.

A similar motif is narrated in *Janshah*. Prince Janshah arrives at a castle, is allowed to stay, and is warned not to enter a specific room. Nevertheless, he enters the forbidden room, leading to a garden and a lake. Three birds like doves precipitously land in the garden, take off their robes of feathers and change into three maidens, as beautiful as the moon. They plunge into the basin to bathe and to amuse themselves, and Janshah falls in love with the youngest damsel, Shamsa. He waits for her return after one year, confesses his love and she agrees to go home with him to get married. His father builds a palace for her, and Janshah hides the feather vest in the foundations. However, she smells the scent of her vest, puts it on, and flies to the roof of the palace, and cries, 'Oh my beloved, the solace of my eyes, and fruit of my heart. If you love me as I love you, come to me at the Castle of Jewels,' and she flies to her family, while Janshah falls down insentient. He sets out to search for the land of his beloved, and some jinn and birds help him to reach the castle. The lovers are reunited, and they initially stay there for two years, then decide to spend one year with their respective families alternately. They live happily for many years until on one occasion they descend on an island to rest. Shamsa goes swimming and a shark hits her in the leg and kills her. Janshah digs a tomb for her and one for himself next to it. Since then he has been mourning and awaiting his death next to her grave, reciting verses of agony and despair. Remarkably, the trick of hiding the feather vest did not work in the end in both stories. This narrative demonstrates that female agency is capable of outsmarting the imposed reality of denying the females an option of escape.

A man goes on a trip accompanied by his two brothers, in *Second Shaykh's Story*. He meets a beautiful young woman on the shore and takes her with him onto the ship. This has triggered the jealousy of his brothers who throw their brother and his woman overboard. They are saved, for the woman turned out to be a jinniyah, who transforms the wicked brothers into dogs. In *Diamond*, King Cypress falls in love with a jinn-princess and succeeds in marrying her after some difficulties. However, he notices that she goes out riding at night, so he follows her, witnessing her committing adultery with seven black men. He kills the men and punishes his wife. In *Zayn al-Asnam*, the jinn-king requests that the prince bring him a fifteen-year-old virgin of unsurpassed beauty. The son of the chieftain of an Arab tribe, in *Habib and Lady Durrat al-Ghawwas*, meets the jinniyah-queen of the Isles of the Sea, and they fall in love. He takes a long and adventurous journey to be reunited with her.

Three princes in India are in love with their niece, in *Ahmad and the Fairy Peri Banu*. To prevent jealousy, their father arranges an archery contest and the winner gets the cousin. While one of the princes wins the contest, the arrow of the youngest prince cannot be found. Looking for his arrow, the prince finds the place where it has landed, which was close to a pit giving access to an underground passage, leading to a spacious cave and a luxurious palace. There he meets the beautiful Peri Banu, the daughter of a jinn-king, who is in love with him and has lured him to this palace by deflecting his arrow. They marry and both enjoy a wonderful life together. In *Three Princes and the Daughters of Jinni Morhagian*, the jinni destroys the three palaces built by the Sultan of Samarkand for his sons because they were erected on top of the palaces of his daughters. The youngest prince descends into a well and arrives at the palaces of the jinn-princesses who treat him as a guest for forty days. He marries the most beautiful princess. A jinniyah of the jinn of China falls passionately in love with a man, in *Uns al-Wujud and al-Ward fi 'l-Akmam*. Being in fear of her family, she searches all the earth for a place where she might hide him from them until she finds a mountain on a faraway island in the Sea of Treasures, which is an isolated place and inaccessible both to men and jinn. She abducts her lover to this mountain and visits him furtively, and they remain in this situation for a long time until she bears him a number of children. This abduction is motivated by love for a shared life of affection and happiness. However, not all abductions by the jinn have the same motives and outcomes.

Jinn, Love, and Abductions

Relationships between humans and jinn are not only characterized by voluntary love and marriage but also by kidnapping and violence. The *Arabian Nights Encyclopedia* (Marzolph and Leeuwen 2004 II: 466) comments that abduction is a recurrent motif in the stories, especially the kidnapping of young women of a marriageable age.

When Prince Sayf al-Muluk, in *Sayf al-Muluk and Badi'at al-jamal*, sees the portrait of Badi'at al-Jamal, the daughter of a jinni-king, he instantaneously falls in love with her. His father tries to dissuade him: 'This girl is the daughter of the king of jinn and is difficult to obtain. Relinquish her, and I will bring you a hundred kings' daughters. We do not need the daughters of jinn, over whom we have no power and who are not of our kind.'Yet, the prince is not dissuaded and remains tenacious, deciding to set out in search of his beloved. He reaches a black palace inhabited by a beautiful woman who turns out to be the daughter of the king of Hind. One day when she and her slave-girls are playing naked in the pool in the garden of the castle, suddenly something like a cloud snatches her and puts her in this palace. The kidnapper transforms into a handsome young man who tells her that he is the son of the Blue King of the jinn and that he is in love with her. He comes to her once a week and stays with her three days. When he is with her, they eat, drink, cuddle, and kiss and nothing else, as she is still a virgin girl, the way God has created her. When the prince in his turn tells her his story, she reveals to him that his beloved is her foster-sister. Inquiring how it is possible that a human and a jinniyah are foster-sisters, she explains that her mother suckled her when she had just been born. She promises to help him unite with his beloved and instructs him how to free her from this place by killing the soul of the abductor jinni. They flee the place, and when they lie down to sleep, he sets her behind him and puts a naked sword between them to avoid any physical contact. They finally reach her father's kingdom. Badi'at al-Jamal visits her foster-sister and hears the story about the infatuated prince. On hearing this, she blushes and says that this will never happen, for humans do not match up well with the jinn. Her sister praises the man extensively and implores her to see him at least once until she finally consents. In the garden of the palace, her eyes fall on the prince and his beauty impresses her, while he faints upon seeing her. They are finally introduced, but she tells him that humans do not keep promises and do not know true love. They take an oath never to betray each other, neither with humans nor with jinn, and they are finally married.

In a dream, in *Ali and Zahir from Damascus*, Zahir, a rich official in Damascus, sees Farha, the daughter of King Mutaa of the Coral Islands, in India and falls in love with her. He travels to these islands and marries the princess. The next morning he wakes up in the desert and witnesses three jinn fighting one another to capture him. They kidnap him because he unwittingly interfered in their quest for the princess and thus became the object of their jealousy. His adventure takes him back to his hometown. Meanwhile, his wife gives birth to his son, Ali, who sets out to search for his father when he has grown up. His adventure takes him to the island of the jinn-queen Turaja, who desires young men and enchants them when they have satisfied her lust. The queen falls in love with him and marries him. He encounters a young man who is also in love with her and comes every day to see her in the form of a bird. Ali is then abducted by a jinni who is also in love with

Turaja, leaving him on a high mountain. However, the daughters of the Blue King of jinn rescue him, and while the princesses are quarrelling about him, he is again taken up into the air and falls into the sea. When he reaches an island, the queen wants to marry him, and he is transformed into a dog for rejecting her proposal. A helpful woman restores him to his human shape, and he is finally reunited with his wife and parents. A similar motif appears in *Diamond*. The prince arrives at the palace of Latifa, who changes him into a deer when he rejects her advances. He is able to escape and is restored to his human form by another woman. He eventually marries both, in addition to three other women.

The wife of a Persian king, in *Benasir*, is pregnant and having complications with her delivery. A jinni claims that he is capable of saving both mother and child on condition that he has the child upon reaching the age of eighteen. Devoid of choices, the king agrees and his son, Benasir, is born. To hide him, his father sends him to the king of China, who pretends that the child is his own son. As he grows up, Benasir falls in love with the princess. When he is eighteen, the jinni abducts the lovers and takes them to an underground mansion in Tunis. Benasir becomes a servant to an old man, the jinni's father, whose life can be prolonged only by human sacrifice. The princess pretends to accept the jinni's amorous advances and gets permission to move around the place. She finds books of magic and learns that the jinni's life is linked to a magic sword. The princess kills the magician, rescues her lover, and the couple return to Persia to be happily married. The Blue King of the jinn, in *Gharib and His Brother Ajib*, abducts the daughter of the king of China from her palace. The jinni deflowers her and she reproduces a daughter so beautiful that she is called *Kawkab al-Sabah*, the morning star. When she becomes a young woman, Gharib is impressed by her beauty and instantly falls in love with her. He decides to marry her, even though he is already infatuated with two other human females. He finds her a virgin and deflowers her. Afterward in the story, the ghouls of the Mountain attack a Persian army and takes a princess prisoner. Gharib eventually rescues her, and they fall in love.

Destiny dictates that a prince becomes a woodcutter to earn his living, in *Second Qalandar's Tale*. One day in a forest, he discovers an underground staircase, and descending the stairs, he encounters a young woman. She informs him that she is the daughter of the king of the Ebony Islands, abducted by a jinni on her wedding night, and kept imprisoned in that cave for twenty-five years. The jinni visits her once every ten days, but she can call him anytime by just touching a certain plate with a formula. The couple enjoy each other's company, making love every night and having fun. One night, the drunken prince suggests taking her from there, but she replies, 'You should be satisfied with nine days out of ten, leaving only one day for the jinni.' He insists on killing the jinni despite her protest. All of a sudden, the earth starts shaking. She says that the jinni is coming and he should escape immediately. He manages to escape but forgets his sandals and axe, enough for the jinni to discover that a human being was with her. The jinni brutally tortures the woman to confess the truth, but she is silent. The jinni, however, finds out where the intruder is, abducts him, and brings him to the cave. Finally, the jinni brutally cuts the body of the woman into pieces with the sword. He tells the man that in the traditions of the jinn, they kill the adulterous women, and therefore he acted upon their traditions. As a punishment for the man, the jinni transforms him into a monkey. Remarkably, the honour code in the world of the jinn has the same patriarchal dictate about the sexual conduct of the females. While the sexual act represents the agency of two participants, only the female is blamed and killed, even when she has been abducted.

In *Ifrit's Mistress*, the brother kings, Shahryar and Shahzaman, encounter a bride who was kidnapped by a jinni on her wedding night. The same motif is also present in *King's Son and the Ifrit's Mistress*. In *King's Son and the Ogress*, a prince on a hunting journey loses his way in the wilderness. He encounters a woman who tells him that she is the daughter of a king but an *ifrit* had kidnapped her three days ago. The demon was burned by a shooting star and was forced to put her down at this spot. While travelling together, the woman asks the prince's permission to follow a call of nature and returns in the shape of a hideous human-eating female ghoul, *ghouleh*. The prince prays to God to be delivered from danger, and hearing his prayers, the ogress leaves him unharmed. In the search for his missing brothers, in *Khudadad and His Brothers*, a prince reaches a castle where he finds a beautiful young woman who warns him of the ghoul holding her prisoner. He kills the demon, marries the woman, and frees his brothers who were also abducted by the ghoul. During a hunting party, in *Princess of Daryabar*, a king reaches a lonely hut in a forest where a ferocious ghoul is holding captive a young woman. The ghoul desires the woman, but she rejects his advances. The king kills him and marries the woman who tells him that the demon abducted her just before her marriage. The king's daughter is also abducted by a ghoul but is rescued. A sultan puts a difficult question as a condition for giving his beautiful daughter in marriage, in *Sixth Captain's Tale*. A handsome prince gives the right answer, marries the princess, and takes her home with him. He turns out to be a mischievous ghoul who wanted to devour her, but she offers to wash herself to be tastier. In the bathhouse, however, she changes clothes with an old woman and escapes. She arrives at a royal palace, where she marries the prince, but the ghoul appears at the wedding to gulp her. She prays and a friendly jinni saves her by destroying the ghoul.

In *Damir and al-Anqa'*, a jinniyah who hates men kidnaps al-Anqa' shortly before her marriage to her lover, insinuating lesbian desires in the world of jinn. The demonic abduction of women occurs on behalf of other women as well. In *Ala' al-Din Abu l-Shamat*, a princess orders the jinn to abduct the wife of Ala' al-Din, because the magic jewel predicted that the princess would marry her husband. Demons enter into romantic and sexual relations not only with humans but also with other creatures. The adventures of a prince, in *Prince of Khwarazm and the Princess of Georgia*, take him to an island inhabited by people without heads. When the prince distinguishes himself in a war against their bird-headed enemies, he is forced to marry their princess. As the princess is in love with a demon, she has her lover take him to another island, where he is finally united with his wife.

Bad versus Good Jinn

There are two stories in the narrative of the Arabian Nights about exorcism. In *Envier and the Envied*, the king's daughter is possessed by a jinni, and the envied overhears jinn discussing the appropriate remedy for her illness. He heals the princess, marries her, and becomes a vizier and eventually a king. In *Youth Behind Whom Indian and Chinese Aires Were Played*, an Indian princess and a Chinese princess are both possessed by a jinni. A man rescues them and marries them both.

One night, an old man comes to a slave-girl who sings and plays the lute in the palace of Caliph Harun al-Rashid, in *Tuhfat al-Qulub*, introducing himself as Iblis and inviting her to perform at his daughter's wedding. She is taken on the back of a flying horse to the palace of the jinn, and she performs for three festive days. On the fourth day, an evil jinni abducts her, but the other jinn rescue her. Iblis takes her back home, and she tells the caliph of her adventure. In *Sage and the Scholar*, a jinni abducts the princess on her wedding night. The king of the jinn helps to punish the kidnapper and return the princess to the palace.

The last will of the dying king, in *King of Kochinchin's Children*, is that his daughter should be married to the first stranger arriving in the city. The will is implemented and her husband disappears with her. After three years, her worried brother departs to search for her. An old man informs him that his sister's demon husband is holding her prisoner. The demon imprisons the brother and turns him into a dog. Meanwhile, the other brother also sets out to search for his siblings. His ship is wrecked and he is cast ashore on an island where he finds a stone with a ring. When he removes the stone, a giant jinni appears who had been imprisoned there. The jinni rewards him with a talisman with which he can destroy the demon holding his sister prisoner. By seizing the demon's external soul that is hidden inside a bird, he forces him to restore his brother to his human shape. When he then kills the bird, the palace disappears, and the demon takes the shape of a handsome man. He tells them that Solomon has transformed him from a kind jinni into an evil demon as a punishment for not obeying his orders.

In *Abu Muhammad the Lazy*, a man gives a merchant sailing for China little money to purchase something for him, and the merchant gets for him an ugly monkey who brings luck and wealth for him. Later on, the monkey reveals that he is a *marid*, and he encourages him to marry the daughter of a rich merchant. When the marriage is arranged, the jinni instructs him to destroy certain strange objects in a cabinet in the house of the bride, before deflowering the bride. When he did as instructed, he suddenly realizes that the monkey has abducted his bride, and what he has destroyed is a talisman to protect her from the *marid* who has been trying to kidnap the girl for years in vain. He sets out in search of his bride, and good, believing jinn help him to reach the place of her captivity, to find her being held captive by a talisman. She tells him that the *marid* out of love for her has revealed to her what benefits and what harms him and, therefore, she instructs him what to do next. By destroying the talisman, the giant jinn, *ifrits*, obey his order of capturing the *marid*, releasing his bride, and transporting him and his bride to his house, together with all the jewels of that place. A similar tale is narrated in *Muhammad of Cairo*. One day, a poor dervish buys a monkey who changes into a handsome young man and gives him money every day. One day the monkey tells him to ask for the sultan's daughter in marriage. The monkey procures the extraordinary jewels demanded by the sultan, and the marriage is agreed upon. The monkey instructs Muhammad not to touch the bride but to bring him her amulet bracelet first, which he does and then spends the night with the bride. When he wakes up, he finds himself in his old room and clad in rags. The person who sold him the monkey informs him that the monkey is actually a young jinni who has been in love with the princess for some time, but because the amulet protects her against him, he could gain her only with the help of the dervish's help. He sends a letter to the king of the jinn who executes the abductor jinni and returns his wife.

When Saba the king of Yemen, in *Saba*, failed to save his city from the flood, he used to take a virgin as his wife every week and then send her back to her family. When it is the turn of Belqis, the daughter of his vizier and a jinniyah, she kills the king and appropriates the throne. Thus, violence leads to more violence. One cannot help contrasting the conduct of Saba with that of Shahryar who used to deflower a virgin every night, not every week, and kill her in the morning, not returning her to her family. Still, Belqis was impatient with the relatively mild and less brutal conduct of the king. By contrast, Shahrazad exploits her cunning and narrative powers for three years in order to cure a much more ruthless and merciless king.

5

RAPE AND INCEST

RAPE AND INCEST FORM PART OF THE VIOLENT AND TABOO ASPECTS of sexuality narrated in the sophisticated sexual world of the Thousand and One Nights. Rape is also narrated in popular epics, as is the case with the hero Antara. Rape embodies a clear intersection and interrelation of sexuality and violence; it is a sexualized violence in the sense that violence takes the form of sex and sex is performed through violence. Enthrallingly, rape as violence resulting in violent vengeance is a theme that is clearly presented in these tales. Hence, rape becomes politics. The frame story evidently divulges that the motif of reprisal and rape furnishes the rationale for the entire narrative account. This narrative illustrates the complexity of family incestuous relationships, both coercive and consensual.

Tales of Rape

The Christian Princess Abriza meets Prince Sharkan and accompanies him to Baghdad, in *Umar ibn al-Nu'man*. When his father, King 'Umar, sees her face, his reason flees. Captivated by her beauty, he falls in love with her and makes sexual advances. The unyielding princess has only increased his passion and longing, and when he becomes weary of this, he decides to drug her with henbane and rape her, following the advice of his vizier. One night, the king visits her and they start drinking until drunkenness creeps into the princess's head. She unwittingly drinks the drug with her wine and falls asleep on her back. The air raises her dress enough for the king to see what is between her thighs under the light of a candle. Satan tempts him, and losing his senses, he is unable to control himself. He puts off his trousers, falls upon her, and takes away her virginity. Insulted by this act and now pregnant, Abriza eventually decides to leave the city and go back home. She asks a black slave, Ghadhban, to accompany her during the journey. The slave, who is impressed by her beauty, accepts the offer with the intention of making advances to her and taking her money if she refuses. As they travel through the desert and mountains, she stops to deliver the baby. When Ghadhban sees her on the ground, Satan enters into him and he draws his saber demanding to have sex with her. She not only rejects him but also insults him with remarks about his low social status by saying, 'How should I yield to a black slave, after having refused kings? How then should I let a son of a whore and a black slave have possession of me? How dare you demand this of me, son of shame and nursling of lewdness, do you think that folk are alike?' In a rage, he kills her and flees the place.

It is interesting to note that abusers often blame Satan for their reprehensible acts, thereby separating responsibility from the action. While the rapist is blaming the devil, the victim of rape is blaming herself, not the abuser. This story illustrates the perception of the victim of rape of what has happened, whose fault it is, and what are the consequences. Blaming is an interesting issue within the sexualized violence of rape. It is very often the case that victims of rape are blamed, even by the victims themselves who believe that they have brought shame on themselves and on their families. Princess Abriza tells her maid,

> Know that it is not the folk who have wronged me, but I who sinned against myself in that I left my father and mother and country. I abhor life, for my heart is broken and I have neither courage nor strength left. If I deliver the baby in this palace, I shall be dishonoured among my maids, and everyone in the palace knows that a rapper took my face and put me in shame; and if I return to my father, with what face shall I meet him.

When her father, King Hardub, finds out that his daughter was first raped and then killed, indignantly he says, 'King 'Umar ibn al-Nu'man dishonoured her by force and after this, one of his black slaves slew her. By the Messiah, I will be revenged for her and clear away the stain from my honour.' The patriarchal notion that honour is strongly related to the sexuality of the females of the family is clearly illustrated and stressed. The fact that dishonour is caused by a violent act of rape would make little difference to the predominant conceptualization of the relationship between honour and female sexual conduct. However, the rape and murder of Abriza eventually lead to revenge acts by her grandmother in a context of an interfaith tension.

In *Coward Belied by His Wife*, a man has a cudgel with an iron bludgeon at the end. He leaves every morning and comes back in the evening, telling his wife that he has killed two that day, sometimes even three, four, or ten. Accordingly, she supposes him to be a valiant fighter and wants to test him.

She pretends to be sick, and her only remedy is to lie in a field of beans. Arriving there, the owner shouts at the man and rapes the woman. When she later rebukes her husband for not having interfered, he tells her to shut up and listen to his valiant deed. While the man raped her, he flirted with his goat. His wife is so enraged by his cowardice that she leaves him. However, when two young men, in *Man and His Willful Wife*, wanted to rape a woman, her brave husband defended her, but they still raped the woman and killed the man. Rape is also mentioned in other stories. A handsome prince rapes one of his father's concubines, in *Al-Hayfa' and Yusuf*. His father wants to punish him, but he is warned, enabling him to escape. In *Mahmud and His Three Sons*, ten female singers narrate about their love adventures and joys of sex in a social gathering. The first woman used to be a lesbian and was initiated into sex by rape. The tenth singer used to be pious until one day a boatman noticed her beauty and raped her.

Attempts of rape are also present in many stories of the collection of Alf Layla wa Layla. In *Ali Shar and Zumurrud*, a villainous thief, Juan the Kurd of the gang of Ahmad al-Danaf, kidnaps Zumurrud. He threatens her: 'O whore, we are forty sharpers who will all slope in your womb, *yasfuqun fi rahmik*, this night, from dusk to dawn.' Zumurrud decides to make an escape this very night before the forty thieves come and 'Take their turns at me until they make me like a sinking boat in the sea'. She outsmarts the woman who is guarding her and makes her escape. On a pilgrimage, a woman with her newly born baby, in *Shipwrecked Woman and Her Child*, travel by ship that eventually wrecks and they are carried away on a raft of wooden planks. One of the sailors climbs onto the raft intending to rape her, and when she refuses him, he throws the child overboard. Through her devoted prayer, the sailor is miraculously devoured by a sea-monster. When another ship later saves her, she regains her child, as the sailors have seen the child safely riding on the back of a huge monster. In *Jullanar the Sea-Born*, the king buys a beautiful slave-girl who tells him that she met a man who tried to have forced sexual intercourse with her but she hit him on the head, almost causing his death.

In *Gharib and His Brother 'Ajib*, a prince is notorious for misbehaviour as he often raids neighbouring lands and carries off the daughters of kings and nobles. His father imprisons him for his misconduct but he is released after the intercession of the nobles. He kills his father and seizes the throne. To get rid of any potential rival to the throne, he examines the concubines of his father with the intention of killing any that are pregnant. He orders two slaves to drown the seven-month pregnant woman he finds among the harem of his father in the sea. Impressed by her surpassing beauty, the slaves take her to a forest to rape her, instead. Disagreeing on who will rape her first, they engage in an argument until they are attacked by some black people and are killed in the fighting. The pregnant concubine makes an escape unharmed. Another episode of this story presents rape to be part of the sexual world of the jinn as well. The Blue King of the jinn abducts the daughter of the king of China from her palace and rapes her. She delivers a beautiful daughter. Not only do humans and jinn rape but so do animals. Two lovers, in *Third Larrikin's Tale Concerning Himself*, elope together because her parents objected to their marriage. On the way, while the man falls asleep, an ape rapes his beloved.

Rape as Politics

Because it involves power relation, rape often signifies politics rather than sex per se. The intersection of rape and politics takes different modalities. In the narrative of the Thousand and One Nights, rape is presented either directly and deliberately as a political act or an act followed by a deliberate politics of retribution. In the context of rape as politics, false accusation of rape is also manifested in the narrative.

Rape as politics is an essential motif strongly related to the very rationale of the tales of the Arabian Nights. After being cuckolded by his adulterous wife, in *Shahryar and His Brother*, King Shahriyar embarks on a vengeful policy of marrying a virgin every night to send her to her death the following morning. Taking into consideration the circumstances, purpose, and outcome of these encounters, the one-night stand marriage is rather misleading because it conceals a ruthless serial rape and a sexual violence in the form of rape. Sexuality turns into a killing field, a scheme of elimination, and a site of ruthless vengeance. Thereby, rape becomes a deliberate politics of revenge against not only the cheating wife but also against all the women of the kingdom. Even Shahrazad was initially a project of rape, a delayed assignment due to her powerful cunning and narrative strategies every night.

However, sexuality as rape and rape as politics is not necessarily unilateral in this narrative. In *Ifrit's Mistress*, brothers Shahryar and Shahzaman were actually raped by the kidnapped bride when she forced them to copulate with her against their wills while her abductor jinni was asleep. By threatening to awaken the mighty jinni if they do not comply with her wishes, she actually raped not only the brothers but also 570 additional men, another case of serial rape. The same motif is also repeated in *King's Son and the Ifrit's Mistress*.

The very beautiful princess, al-Datma, is accomplished in horsemanship and the martial arts, in *Bahram and the Princess al-Datma*. Many kings' sons seek her in marriage, but she rejects them all. She proudly announces, 'None shall marry me except the one who vanquishes me in fighting. If any can do this, I will willingly wed him; otherwise, I will take his horse, clothes, and arms and write with fire upon his forehead, "This is the freedman of al-Datma."' In this way, she puts many challengers to shame. At last, a Persian prince, Bahram, wants to marry her and accepts the challenge. In their fierce fighting, she senses that he overpowers her and to avoid shame she resorts to cunning to win the fight. She opens her visor, and he is stunned and confounded by the beauty of her face, which is more radiant than the full moon, causing his strength to fail, thereby enabling her to defeat him. Consequently, she takes his horse and clothes and brands him with fire. Bahram stays several days without eating or drinking not only because of his sadness for being defeated but also because the love of the princess has taken hold upon his heart. He then designs a scheme to avenge his defeat and to win the heart of his beloved.

Disguising himself as an old man, he is hired as the palace gardener. When the princess accompanied by her slave-girls comes to the garden for a walk, they see an old man with many jewels, and they ask him what he does with all these jewels, to which he replies that he marries one of them. They laugh at him and say that if one of them would marry him, what would he do with her, to which he replies that he would only kiss her once and then let her go. The princess offers him one of her slaves as a wife, and he kisses her once and gives her jewels and ornaments, to which she rejoices and they leave, laughing at him. Next day, they find him with even more jewels than the day before, and he kisses another slave-girl and gives her the jewels. Now, the princess thinks to herself that she is in a better position to get these jewels than her slaves are, particularly when there is no harm done in this. The next day she offers herself to be kissed in exchange for the jewels and he grasps the unsuspecting princess and instantaneously rapes her and takes her virginity. He reveals his identity and the bewildered princess keeps silent. She elopes with him to his country and the two are married.

Al-Khansa is a daughter who grows up to be a famous warrior, in *Malik ibn Mirdas*. A king and his son covet her but they are both defeated. Her brother pardons them due to the intercession of the son's sister but he marks her arm to be able to prove his nobility later. This, however, infuriates the son who promises to afflict the transgressor with an even greater dishonour, and rapes al-Khansa. She seeks revenge but ends up marrying her rapist.

The narrative of Alf Layla wa Layla depicts the politics of rape as a motif involving the world of jinn as well. One day, Abdullah, in *Abdullah ibn Fadil and His Brothers*, climbs to the top of a mountain when he sees a frightful black viper chase a white snake. The viper seizes the snake by the head and coils his tail about hers, overpowering the snake who starts to cry out. Pitying her, Abdullah takes a heavy flint-stone and crushes the head of the viper. The snake surprisingly turns into a handsome young woman, kisses his hands, and thanks him for saving her honour, and is indebted to him. She opens the earth beneath her and descends into it, and the viper is kindled by fire. She tells him her story. She is the daughter of the Red King of the jinn. The viper who was fighting her and wanted to dishonour her was the ugly vizier of the Black King of the jinn who fell in love with her. He asked her father to marry her, but her father rejected him, saying, 'Who are you to seek the marriage of king's daughters, O scum of viziers?' Enraged by this rejection, he swore an oath to do away her honour, to spite her father. He engaged in fierce wars with her father, and he was tracking her steps. Every day she was forced to take a new shape but he sniffed her scent and pursued her, causing her great affliction. At last, she took the form of a snake, he took the form of a viper, and they fought until he overwhelmed her and mounted on her to dishonour her when Abdullah saved her. Presenting him to her family as the one who had saved her honour, her parents reward him generously. Rape as politics is strongly related to the social construction of honour, necessarily linked to the sexuality of women. Forced marriages reflect the power of the males in deciding marriages even when women reject their proposals. The vizier goes to great lengths to avenge the rejection of his marriage proposal and to dishonour the female in question by employing the sexual violence of rape. Rape is actively used as a political weapon to discredit opponents.

The Arabian Nights also narrates that acts of rape tend to result in deliberate acts of revenge. The *Concubine of al-Ma'mun* is a tale of cold-blooded murder because of a rape case, illustrating that violence often breeds more violence. A beautiful woman gives a merchant money and eventually asks him to build a pavilion at a certain place, to which he complies. One day she orders him to come to the pavilion, to find her in the company of a young man with whom she amuses herself for a while. After they have gotten drunk, she precipitously severs the young man's head, cuts his body into pieces, and then tells the merchant to throw it into the river. She explains that the young man had raped her a long time ago, and now had been the time to take revenge.

Even attempted rape could result in violent revenge. One day in Egypt, a rogue is brought home dead, in *Yasamin and Husayn the Butcher*. A young woman takes his brother to a palace and treats him extremely generously with food, entertainment, and a different maiden every night. After forty days, she asks him to help her, requesting him to befriend the guild of tailors, and invite them all one day. During the meal, the woman drugs them and cut their throats. She is the sultan's favourite concubine who bestows a favour on the chief of the textile merchants. One day, he had brought her to a garden outside the town, where the forty textile merchants assaulted her with the intention of raping her. She was saved only by the sudden arrival of his brother. Overhearing her story, the sultan offers her to the brother who is appointed as an emir.

Thus, rape attempts as sexual violence in this story end in a rancorous murder. Still, that the king rewards the vengeful murderer while assisting in a murder case results in unexpected fortune and prestige. Crime becomes intermingled with wealth, love, sex, and marriage. A mighty Persian king, in *Qayish and His Brother Ardashir*, receives a letter concerning a beautiful young woman who wanted to marry her cousin but is forbidden to do so by her people. The king gives orders to fetch her, but her lover rescues her. A second attempt succeeds in kidnapping the woman. The king falls in love with her, but she rejects his advances, and when he throws himself upon her, she stabs him to death.

False accusation of rape is also narrated in these tales. In *Craft and Malice of Women*, one of the favourite concubines of the king of China tries to seduce his son. When he rejects her advances, she accuses him of trying to rape her. His father sentences him to death, but the viziers intervene and save him. *As'ad and Amjad* is a tale where the interaction between incest, rape, and the female agency is pronounced. Each of the two wives of King Qamar al-Zaman makes incestuous advances against the son of the other co-wife. When the sons emphatically reject these advances, the wives make a false accusation of rape against their own sons. These two stories illustrate the important aspect of false accusation of rape, intersected with female agency taking the form of transgression and violence, and indicating the politicized aspect of rape.

Incestuous Relationships

There are several stories in the Arabian Nights depicting the taboo of incest. Incestuous relationships are regarded as a threat to the maintenance of the social structure and preservation of the sacral order. Any defiance of prohibitions stipulated in these orders is considered a grave transgression warranting severe punishment. The brother–sister relationship has a distinctive position within the taboo of incest. Studying sibling relationships in the Thousand and One Nights, Shamy (2004: 185) concludes, 'The brother–sister and brother–sister-like relationships are exclusively positive and may lead to sexual attraction'.

The motif of brother–sister incest is presented in the *First Qalandar's Tale*. One day a prince decides to visit his cousin who is also a prince in another city. The cousin asks him to go to the graveyard together with a veiled woman and wait for him at a certain tomb. The cousin joins them eventually, breaks open the tomb, descends a staircase leading downward together with the woman and asks him to close the tomb after them. After returning home to find out that the vizier has dethroned his father, he flees to his uncle's town. Meanwhile, his uncle is worried about the disappearance of his son. When he tells his uncle about the tomb, they go together in search of the missing cousin. They finally locate the tomb and upon opening it, they are met by a great smoke that blinds their eyes. They go inside to find the cousin and the woman are embracing each other on a bed but have turned into black coal as if they had been thrown into the fire to be completely burned. The uncle spits on the face of his son, takes off his shoe, and strikes him with it. He exclaims that this pig deserves what has happened to him and that this is the punishment of this world but he should await an even more terrible punishment in the world to come. He discloses to his nephew that his son was madly infatuated with his sister since childhood. He said to himself that they are but children, yet when they grew up, sin befell them, despite the warnings. The uncle rebuked his son for his ugly and dishonouring sin and enforced a total segregation regime between the enamoured siblings. His doomed sister loved him vehemently and the devil entered between them and beautified this sin in their eyes. Instead of heeding the warnings, he made this place of refuge to continue their sin but the wrath of God was great and the torture of hell even crueller.

While the tale condemns incestuous relationship, yet the mutual agency of both partners in this bonding is clearly illustrated. This agency is manifested in choosing a hard life in a cemetery to escape what the couple perceive to be an even harsher order of segregating them and condemning their union. The incestuous relationship is portrayed in a context of mutual romantic love and free will of both partners, where there is no force implicated in the attachment. However, this subjectivity is severely punished by a divine power. Moreover, this story divulges the common rationalization of pointing the finger at evil spirits for the socially unacceptable conduct, resulting in a dichotomy between culpability and deeds.

The inadvertent incestuous sibling relationship is narrated in *Umar ibn al-Nu'man*. Unwittingly, King Sharkan marries his half-sister, Nuzhat al-Zaman, who he had not seen since she was a child. The girl leaves the kingdom of her father and her adventures lead her to be sold to King Sharkan as a slave. When she impresses him with her beauty and knowledge, he buys her, releases her from slavery, and marries her. He deflowers her and she instantly becomes pregnant, and after nine months gives birth to a beautiful baby girl. One day she accidentally mentions that she is the daughter of King Umar ibn al-Nu'man, who also happens to be his father. Sharkan loses consciousness upon hearing the surprising fact. She also faints, in turn, when he tells her the truth, crying and saying that they have committed a great sin. They have agreed, however, that she should marry his grand vizier and not reveal their secret to anyone. They name their daughter *qadha fakan*, which means what has been ordained binds!

A brief depiction of sibling incest or extraordinary brother–sister love appears in other stories as well. In *Gharib and His Brother 'Ajib*, Gharib rescues his stepsister, who was kidnapped by a rival tribe. He falls in love with her and wants to marry her, but her father resents the idea and creates difficult conditions for him. He eventually manages to marry her. In *Sayf ibn Dhi Yazan*, Prince Sayf becomes enamoured with his foster-sister and succeeds in marrying her in the end. Brothers and sisters forming a social unit is presented in *Hammâd the Bedouin*. The love between them is so great that the sister kills herself after the death of her brother. In *Qamar al-Zaman and Budur*, Marzawan's love for his foster-sister Budur was more than the usual love between brothers and sisters, implying an incestuous tone. In *Salim and Salama*, the sibling love of Salama for her brother Salim makes her relinquish the throne that she gained because of her cross-gender dressing, to her brother.

Ameny is a story that historically makes little sense yet it also exposes sibling incest. As the custom in Pharaonic Egypt was to marry young women to their brothers, Princess Ameny is promised to one of her brother princes. She refuses to marry him, however, telling her father that she wants to be taught the martial arts first. When she is nevertheless tempted by the prince's beauty, she runs away to Baghdad dressed as a man. In *Buluqiya*, a Jinni narrates to a human an account for the origin of Iblis (Satan) in terms of his failure to comply with a paternal command for brothers to marry their sisters. *Three Eunuchs* and *Nu'mah and Nu'm* depict stories of children who were raised together like brother and sister, yet end up in love and sexual intimacy. In *Qamar al-Zaman and Budur*, the couple engages in an intense love affair after being presented mythically as 'twins', hidden brother and sister. In a later episode of the same story, after revealing her true identity following an emblematical wedding, Budur asks her 'bride' Hayat, 'Would you have been happy if I were your brother?' and Hayat answers, 'Ah! I would die of happiness.'

Incestuous advances against stepsons are unambiguously portrayed in *As'ad and Amjad*. The adventures of Prince Qamar al-Zaman lead him into polygamous marriages with Princesses Budur and Hayat al-Nufus, who both bear a son. As unalterable fate and foreordained destiny would have it, when the two boys have grown up, Budur falls in love with her co-wife's son As'ad, and Hayat al-Nufus with Burdur's son Amjad. Each of them used to play with the other's son, embracing him, kissing him intensely, sucking his lips and tongue, and pulling him to her breast, while each thought the other's behaviour was no more than motherly affection. Gradually, passion got the mastery of the two women's hearts and they became madly in love with the two youths so that when the other's son came to either of the women, they would press him to their bosoms and long for him never to be parted from them. When they could not find ways to copulate with the youths, they would refuse food and drink, and forgo the solace of sleep.

One day, Hayat al-Nufus wrote a letter to Amjad revealing her passion for him and that she would like to copulate, *wisal*, with him,

> From the wretched lover, the sorrowful severed one, whose youth is wasted in your love and whose torment is prolonged because of you. Were I to recount to you the extent of my affliction, the passion in my heart, the weeping and groaning of my sorrowful heart, my ceaseless grieves, no letter could contain. I have no hope and no trust but in you.

Then she folds the scroll together with tresses of her hair, wrapping it in a piece of rich silk, scented with musk and ambergris, lays it in a handkerchief, and orders a slave, who is oblivious of the content of the letter, to deliver it to the prince. When Amjad reads the letter, he is enraged to find out that his father's wife intends on adultery and treachery. He denounces the behaviour of women, saying, 'May God curse perfidious women who lack reason and religion!' Then he turns his wrath on the slave, yelling, 'How dare you, wicked slave, carry adulterous messages for the wife of your master; there is no good in you black slave, you are of an ugly face and a silly nature.' He kills the slave with his sword and immediately goes to his mother to inform her of what has happened and reproach her by saying that each one is worse than the other. He tells her that if he were not afraid to transgress against his father and brother, he would have beheaded her as he did with her eunuch. He passes the night sick with anger, unable to eat, drink, or sleep. Meanwhile, when Hayat al-Nufus finds out what has happened to her messenger, she curses him and plots perfidy against him.

The next morning, Budur entrusts a crafty old woman to send a love letter to As'ad for her, complaining of the excess of her love and longing for him,

From someone who perishes for passion and love-longing, from the despairing lover to Prince As'ad whose love consumes my body and tears my skin and my bones. Know that my patience fails me and I am at a loss what to do. Longing and sleeplessness weary me and desire and passion torment me. To you, O As'ad, I complain the pangs of passion; have pity on a slave of love who burns for longing pain.

Then she scents the letter with odoriferous musk and winds it in the tresses of her hair. Reading the letter, As'ad becomes furious, cursing treacherous women and beheading the old woman with his sword. He directly goes to his mother, railing at her and cursing her. He then goes straight to his brother to tell him what has happened and his brother tells him what has passed with him. They spend the night cursing traitorous women, deciding to keep the matter secret from their father lest he kills their mothers.

Meanwhile, the mothers, who fear to be at the mercy of their sons after making their advances, decide to plot against their sons and concert to do away with their lives. When the king returns, he finds his wives sick in bed and they tell him, 'Know, O king, that your sons who have been reared in your bounty, have betrayed you in the persons of your wives and brought dishonour to you.' When he hears this, the light in his eyes becomes dark and his reason flees due to the excess of his rage. Requesting explanation, Budur tells him that for many days his son As'ad was sending her letters and messages to solicit her to adultery. She forbade him until he rushed on her while drunk and with a drawn sword in his hand. He killed her slave, mounting on her breast while still holding the sword, and he took his will of her by force. She told the king that if he does not do her justice on him, she would slay herself with her own hand, for she does not need to live after this horrid deed. Choking with tears, Hayat al-Nufus tells him a similar story about the deed of Amjad, and then they both weep before their husband, who believes them after seeing their tears and hearing their words, deciding to put his sons to death. He orders his treasurer to bind the hands of his sons, put them in two chests, take them to the desert, slaughter them and fill two vessels with their blood. The sympathy of the treasurer eventually spares them the death sentence.

In an episode of the long story of *Umar ibn al-Nu'man*, there is a depiction of an incestuous lesbian relationship between the Christian princess warrior Abriza and her grandmother, where both lesbianism and incest are condemned. This politicized denunciation is narrated within a context of interfaith encounter and tension. The insinuation of incest is also narrated in a number of other stories. A mother accused of having an affair with her son whose identity is unknown to other people is narrated in *Azadbakht and His Son King of Abyssinia*, and *Sulayman Shah and His Niece*. A man is exiled because he pretends to be the father of his sister's child, in *Malik ibn Mirdas, Youth Who Would Futter His Father's Wives*, is a story of a son who has the habit of seducing the wives of his father, portraying an ethical rather than technical incest since there is no blood relationship involved in these interactions. Incest is also present in Arab folkloric tales. A story from Egypt narrates that after the death of his wife, a king wanted to marry his own daughter, after an old woman advises him, 'Why not marry the princess? Why give her to a stranger and deprive yourself?' (Bushnaq 1986: 193).

6

PROMISCUOUS LIFE

POLYGAMY AND POLYANDRY ARE EMBODIED IN THE NARRATIVE OF
the Thousand and One Nights that often presents a promiscuous
life where having more than one partner is frequently the case. The frame
story about the two kings and their wives is a tale about the promiscuity of
women, having husband and lover simultaneously. The same applies to the
story of the bride kidnapped by the demon and as a revenge copulating with
the two kings and with hundreds of other men as well, while she is in the
captivity of her abductor. In this respect, the frame story presents an essentialized perception of women as promiscuous by nature. The many tales of
adultery and cuckoldry in this collection tend to reinforce the perception
about the promiscuity of women. However, these tales make a clear and
unambiguous presentation of men engaging in polygamous relationships
involving several partners reaching the level of a harem. The promiscuous
life of the Arabian Nights is a true reflection of the medieval Islamic society
characterized by wealth, prosperity, and cultural refinement. Jayyusi (2006:
53) explains that a polygamous outlook on love and sexuality was the vogue
during that period, further complicated by widespread homosexual practices
since a profusion of slave-girls and boys furnished a great variety of choice;
the great influx of slave-girls and boys into cities facilitated access to sensual
pleasures, permitting, in effect, a legalized promiscuity (35).

Tales of Tripartite Relationships

Hasan falls in love with Princess Farhat in Egypt, in *Hasan the King of
Egypt*. A magician helps the lovers to meet every night, and to get married.
However, Hasan hears about the wonders of the Maghreb and decides to
make a visit. In his adventures, he marries al-Na'isa, the daughter of a Jewish
sorcerer, who hands him the riches accumulated by her father, and together

they return to Egypt. A man, in *First Shaykh's Story*, is married to a cousin who did not bear him any children. He takes a concubine, who bears him a son. The jealous wife uses her knowledge of magic to turn the son into a calf and his mother into a cow. The cow is slaughtered, but the calf is rescued and restored to his original shape, while the wife is punished by being turned into a gazelle. Two sisters who are married to the same man, in *Qadi and the Bhang-eater*, both gave birth to children on the very same night, a daughter and a son. Now they could not agree whose child the boy was and, therefore, approach the vizier to solve the problem. Believing that the milk of the boy's mother is heavier, he suggests weighing their milk. As this decision is not accepted, he offers to have the boy cut in two, in a Solomonic manner. The true mother refrains from claiming the child.

In *Ali Baba and the Forty Thieves*, the woodcutter Ali Baba is married to a poor woman. One day, while working in the forest, he notices a dust cloud approaching. As it turns out to be a group of robbers, he hides inside a tree and looks on while the robbers open a doorway in the rock by shouting, 'Open, O Sesame', and enter the cave. When they have left, he opens the cave by shouting the same words, finds a huge treasure, and takes some of the money. His brother, Qasim, who is married to a rich woman, finds out about the treasure, and Ali Baba shows him the cave. Inside the cave, Qasim forgets the magic formula and is locked in. The returning robbers find him and cut him into four parts. Ali Baba marries his brother's widow.

When his wife Zubayda mysteriously disappears one day, in *Ala' al-Din Abu 'l-Shamat*, Ala' al-Din assumes that she is dead, and so he goes to the slave market and buys a new concubine. However, some Christians kidnap him and take him to Genoa where he eventually meets his wife. He finds out that Princess Husn Maryam has ordered a jinni to abduct Zubayda because a magic jewel predicted a long time ago that she would marry him. The two women and Ala' al-Din travel back to Baghdad on a flying couch, and when they finally arrive in Cairo, he marries the princess as a second wife. Abdallah is a poor fisherman, married with a large family, in *Abdallah the Fisherman and Abdallah the Merman*. He becomes rich after trading goods with one of the people of the sea. The sultan admires his richness, appoints him vizier, and marries him to one of the princesses. Thus, richness brings more wives to the lucky man. King Hassan, in *Faris al-Khayl and al-Badr al-Fayiq*, has a son by each of his two wives.

In *Qamar al-Zaman and Budur*, the prince marries his beloved Princess Budur. After a long separation, the lovers reunite in the Ebony Islands where the prince also marries Princess Hayat al-Nufus and becomes a king. Prince Sirkhab of Babil, in *Sirkhab and Aftuna*, travels to China and ends up marrying

two princesses. In *Sultan of India and His Son Muhammad*, the adventures of
the prince in searching for the green bird results in his marriage to two
princesses. In *Mercury Ali of Cairo*, a sharper in Cairo travels to Baghdad and
ends up marrying two women. In *Ruined Man of Baghdad and His Slave-Girl*,
a man loves his slave-girl but he is separated from her. In his search for her
in another town, he accepts marriage to another woman. Showing his eloquence to the caliph, a poet musician, in *Two Dancers*, is rewarded with two
beautiful slave-girls, and he falls in love with both. In *Adi ibn Zayd and the
Princess Hind*, the young and handsome Adi is in love with Princess Hind.
Her slave-girl approaches him with the proposal that she helps him unite
with his beloved if he would consent to have sexual intercourse with her.
Adi accepts her offer and bonds with his lover after the sexual intimacy with
her slave-girl.

In *Satilatlas and Hamama Telliwa*, the son of a prominent merchant in Cairo
is very devoted to his wife. This devotion arouses the jealousy of his slave-girl
who makes him impotent with the help of a sorceress. His only remedy is to
travel to India and eat the blossoms of a certain tree, but he has to wait for
a year for the tree to blossom. Meanwhile, his wife is almost convinced that
he has died and allows another man into her company, agreeing to marry
him. After suffering shipwreck, he returns home just in time and spies on
the newly wed couple to see if her love for him has endured. When she
remembers his tenderness in contrast with the demanding ways of her new
husband, he reveals himself and is finally reunited with her. A jinni abducts
a man from a bathhouse, in *Tamim al-Dari*. After experiencing many adventures, he eventually manages to return home to find out that his wife has
married another man, but she agrees to return to him. In *Al-Mutalammis
and His Wife Umayma*, a poet has to leave the region to escape an enemy. His
wife refuses to remarry even when he is absent for a long time. As her people
put pressure on her, she finally concedes and arrangements for the wedding
are made. On the wedding day, her husband finally returns. Seated on the
bride's throne, she recites some verses, whereupon the poet answers with his
own verses. Deeply moved, the bridegroom relinquishes her for the poet. In
Contest in Generosity and *Thief Discovered by Storytelling*, the husband himself
consents that his new bride continues her relationship with her lover. In
Admonished Adulteress, the husband himself suggests to his wife to approach
his friend when he is travelling.

Impressed by his beauty, a bride on her wedding night, in *Nur al-Din
and His Son Badr al-Din Hasan*, wishes that Nur al-Din would be her
bridegroom, instead of the ugly hunchback groom. Nur al-Din tells her
that he is the real husband for her. Confused, she says, 'Who is my husband

then? He, you, or both?' She tells him that she wished he would be her husband, or that he and her bridegroom would share her as her partners. Thus, desperate to get the very handsome and young man, she would even willingly accept being shared by two men. A mendicant meets a woman abducted by a jinni, in *Second Qalandar's Tale*. They develop sexual intimacy and when he suggests helping her escape, she says, 'Be content and keep quiet, for, in every ten days, there is one day for the jinni and nine days for you.' Thus, not only is the princess positive toward sexuality and gender mixing but also positive to sexual multi-partners, by accepting being shared by two males.

Princess Dalal, in *Sixth Captain's Tale*, marries a handsome prince who turns out to be a ghoul. When he tries to devour her, she uses a ruse and escapes. She reaches a royal palace and marries the prince. When a sultan, later on, proposes to marry her, she professes to be married already, and he is satisfied with marrying her daughter. In *Dadbin and His Viziers*, a woman is married to the king but because of suspicion of adultery, she is left in the desert. She eventually marries another king. In *Di'bil al-Khuza'i with the Lady and Muslim ibn al-Walid*, a woman accepts having a sexual liaison with a man who takes her to the house of his friend because of the modesty of his own house. However, the woman ends up making love with the owner of the house rather than the man she originally went with. In *'Adila*, a demon restores the life of a woman but she chooses to go with a passing prince while her husband, who grieved her death, has gone home to fetch her decent clothes to take her from the graveyard. In *Ensorcelled Prince*, a woman has a husband and a lover at the same time.

The motif of women having multiple conjugal partners is also present in the Thousand and One Nights. An imaginative woman in Egypt has two husbands who do not know about each other, in *Woman Who Has Two Husbands*. When they discover that they share the same woman, she desires to keep the more talented of the two as a husband. In *Lady with the Two Coyntes*, a woman convinces her husband that she has married a second husband, who is actually her lover because she has attained an extra vagina. A life of promiscuity is also manifested in the many tales of adultery and cuckoldry in the narrative of the Arabian Nights where women actively participate. Finally, a funny story that reflects the extensive promiscuous life is presented in *Astute Qadi*. A pregnant woman in Cairo is accidentally pushed over causing her to lose her child. The *qadi* (judge) orders the woman to be given to the man who caused her abortion. The man should get her pregnant again and deliver her back to her husband when she is again six months pregnant, as she was before. She withdraws her case from the judge.

Bonding with Many Partners

Aziz has three female partners in the story of *Aziz and Aziza*. He enjoys the attention of his cousin, Aziza, who has an unrequited and platonic love for him. He, on the other hand, enjoys a reciprocated love and sexual attachment with another woman, Dalila. Moreover, one day yet another woman lures him to her house, forcing him into sex and marriage. After spending many amorous nights with her lover, in *Jewish Doctor's Tale*, a young woman brings her younger sister with her one day and urges him to sleep with her. The woman herself insists that her lover enjoys another partner, besides her. However, at the end of the story, the young man ends up marrying another woman, the virgin sister of the two girls. A married woman not only has a lover but she also makes love to his young messenger in *Lady and Her Two Lovers*. The son of a vizier in China, in *Two Viziers and Their Children*, is married to his cousin. When he becomes a vizier and his army is vanquished in a battle in another country, he is taken prisoner. The princess falls in love with him and releases him on the condition that he should marry her and spare her father, to which he agrees. However, his hunting adventure leads him to a Bedouin woman with two very beautiful daughters. He marries the youngest one, while his father who was searching for him marries the other daughter. Thus, he ends up marrying three women while his father is married to two wives.

The woodcutter Ahmad tricks his quarrelsome wife into having her lowered into a well and leaves her down there for two days, in *Youth Behind Whom Indian and Chinese Aires Were Played*. When he wants to pull her up again, a frightening jinni appears. The jinni used to live in the well but now wants to escape from the terrible woman. To reward Ahmad, the jinni promises to help him marry the daughter of the king of India. The jinni possesses the princess so that she will appear mad, and hands Ahmad some weeds with which to cure her. Ahmad cures the princess and marries her. Sometime later, he learns that the daughter of the king of China is suffering from a similar affliction. It appears that she is possessed by the very same jinni who refuses to leave her when Ahmad wants to cure her. Employing a ruse, Ahmad pretends that his former wife, who has escaped from the well, is pursuing him. When the jinni hears about the woman's imminent arrival he flees, and Ahmad marries the princess.

After rescuing his stepsister, Mahdiyya, from a kidnapping by a rival tribe, in *Gharib and His Brother 'Ajib*, Gharib falls in love with her and wants to marry her, but her father resents the idea and creates difficult conditions for him. During his adventures, he rescues the daughter of King Sabur of Persia,

Fakhr Taj, who was abducted by the jinn. They have intended to get married, but having intimate sexual intercourse before the wedding night has infuriated her father who consequently kills his daughter. His adventures take him to the Blue King's palace, where he falls in love with Kawkab al-Sabah, the daughter of a princess of China who was abducted by the jinn. He rejects the sexual advances of Queen Jan Shah, and after killing her, he is finally able to return to his beloved Kawkab al-Sabah and Mahdiyya.

On a hunting outing, a prince in Yemen, in *King of Yemen and His Three Sons*, finds a string of pearls and emeralds that belongs to a magic bird. He reaches a town in which a lion devours a young woman every year. He kills the lion and marries the king's daughter. During the night, he exchanges rings with her while she is asleep and writes into her hand that she should follow him to his hometown if she loves him. He continues his journey to a town terrorized by an elephant that kills a young woman every year. He kills the elephant, marries the princess, and leaves her after leaving the same message. Next, he reaches the city of the magic bird, where an old man tells him that the bird belongs to a princess and there are seven lions and forty slaves guarding it. He manages to overcome these obstacles, marries the princess, and leaves her after writing the same note. He returns to his hometown, and soon the three princesses follow him. He becomes sultan, living happily with his three wives. A merchant married with four children in Cairo, in *Yusuf and the Indian Merchant*, travels to seek his fortune elsewhere. In Mecca, he marries a rich widow, taking care of her possessions, and eventually becomes a wealthy merchant. He travels to India and marries the daughter of a rich old man. In the end, he returns to Cairo to be united with his original family.

Damir and al-Anqa' is a story of one man with four female partners. Damir is in love with a woman who was kidnapped by a jinniyah shortly before their proposed marriage. He sets out to search for her and eventually unites with her. However, he also marries another woman and her two sisters. Oddly, he marries three sisters, which is religiously inadmissible. In *Sayf al-Tijan*, the adventures of a prince lead him to meet a princess who is impressed by his beauty, and he marries her after fighting and killing another suitor. In his further adventures, he fights, imprisons, and marries another princess. In his subsequent fights, he rescues and marries two additional princesses. In *Coelebs the Droll Court's Jester*, a woman meets four of her former lovers when her husband is away. In the stories of *Ali and Zahir from Damascus* and *Diamond*, the jinn-queens Turaja and Latifa desire young men and often changes partners, enchanting them when they have satisfied their lust.

Diamond is a story of a prince who marries five women. He travels to remote places to find the answer to a question put by Princess Muhra as a trial for her marriage. During his adventure, he marries Aziza after releasing her from her two giant captors. He marries Latifa who initially changes him into a deer. He then marries Jamila who restores him to his human form. Diamond returns not only with three wives but also with the answer to the riddle to marry the princess and also her servant who advised him how to solve the riddle. In another episode of this tale, one night King Cypress discovers that his wife has seven sexual partners copulating with her. In *Mahmud and His Three Sons*, Husayn reaches the town of Turiz where he falls in love with and marries Princess Barq al-Thana', after defeating an enemy king. Later, he visits the country of the infidels, where he marries Princess Sabiha after she has converted to Islam. Next, he fights the Christians of the city of Turiz, falls in love with Princess Bughyat al-Qalb, and marries her after converting to Islam. A Christian magician kidnaps the new wife, yet he succeeds in freeing her with the help of the magician's daughter Shumus, who eventually joins him in marriage. When a dervish describes the Amazon princess Hayat al-Ruh to him, he sets out to meet her. He proposes to marry her yet she rejects his proposal and, therefore, he declares war. While they are fighting, the princess realizes him to be the stronger, but she manages to dumbfound him by showing him her beautiful face. She takes him prisoner but has meanwhile fallen in love with him, and soon she becomes his fifth wife.

Tales of Harem

In addition to the unlimited number of concubines and his wife and cousin, Zubayda, Caliph Harun al-Rashid contracts several marriages in the stories of the Arabian Nights. In *Al-Bunduqani*, the caliph and his vizier stroll around town in disguise. When the caliph sees a woman begging, he gives her a gold coin and asks her to marry him. She requests the annual revenue of Isfahan and Khorasan as dowry. The woman turns out to be a distant relative of the Persian King Kisra. As she is quite presumptuous about her origin, the caliph decides not to touch her for a whole year. A year later, the caliph and his entourage again tour the city in disguise. He observes an old woman reciting the Qur'an beautifully without receiving any money in compensation. He secretly follows her and sees that she has a very attractive daughter, who she wants to marry off to a young man who cannot afford the bride-price. The caliph then marries the daughter and gives orders to restore and redecorate the woman's house.

A woman who forces her lover to have another partner is narrated in
Al-Ma'mun and Zubayda. Zubayda, the wife of Caliph Harun al-Rashid, tells
Caliph al-Ma'mun that she once played chess against her husband. He won
and had her walk naked through the palace. Angry, she played again, and
this time she won. She retaliated by forcing him to sleep with Marajil, the
foulest domestic servant in the kitchen, who subsequently gave birth to
al-Ma'mun. Promiscuous life in the palace of Caliph Harun al-Rashid leads
to a strong jealousy from his wife, particularly when the slave-girl is beautiful
and accomplished. In *Ghanim ibn Ayyub and Qut al-Qulub*, the queen orders
some slaves to put the concubine in a trunk and leave it in a graveyard.
Ghanim of Damascus who establishes himself in Baghdad as a merchant
finds her, and an amorous attachment between them develops, eventually
leading to their marriage. In *Khalifa the Fisherman of Baghdad*, the jealous
Zubayda drugs the slave-girl with henbane, puts her in a trunk and orders
her slaves to sell the trunk at the market, without revealing its contents. A
fisherman buys the trunk to find the girl, still alive. She asks him to deliver
a letter to the caliph for her, who brings her back to the palace and rewards
the man. Additionally, jealousy and the conflict-ridden institution of polygamy are presented in *Woman Whose Hands Were Cut Off*. The polygamous
wives of the king are so jealous of the new wife, who bears the king a son,
that they accuse her of infidelity.

A caliph, in *Concubine and the Caliph*, spends each night with one of his
forty concubines. In return, all the concubines take lovers. In *King and His
Vizier's Wife*, a king has ninety concubines of various colours. King Sharman
has 100 slave-girls in *Jullanar*. A rich merchant has 100 concubines in
al-Hakim and the Merchant. King Shahriman of the Khalidan Islands has 300
concubines and 4 spouses, in *Qamar al-Zaman and Budur*. King al-Nu'man of
Baghdad has 360 concubines, in *'Umar ibn al-Nu'man*. In *Sayf ibn Dhi Yazan*,
the son of the king of Yemen supplements his marriage to his foster-sister
with several marriages to many princesses during his adventures, resulting in
having many sons. King and Prophet Solomon has 300 wives and 700 concubines, in *Solomon and the Queen of Sheba*. In the story of *Saba*, Solomon is
associated with 500 free women and 700 slave-girls. He decides to copulate
with 1,000 of them in a single night so that they will all become pregnant with
twins and thus provide an ample number of descendants. In accordance with
God's will, however, only one woman becomes pregnant, and she bears him
an incomplete child.

A mendicant, in *Third Qalandar's Tale*, reaches a palace inhabited by forty
young women who are like moons – one is never tired of gazing at them.
They all welcome him, praising God that he sent them someone who is

worthy of them and they of him. After eating, drinking, singing, and spending a merry time, they tell him to choose one of them to spend the night with him. He chooses a girl with a beautiful face and spends with her a most wonderful night. This situation continues for a whole year, and he spends every night with another woman, in rotation. *Abu Hasan the Old Man Who Bemoans Ja'far* is a story portraying both polygamy and polyandry experiences. A wealthy merchant in Basra buys a slave-girl but she refuses to give in to his advances because the vizier previously owned her. The vizier's jealous spouse expels her from the house. However, the merchant eventually marries her. Later, the governor of Basra attacks the house and takes the woman to Baghdad. Her husband complains to the vizier's father and gets his wife back.

Stories of Intermediary Husbands

There are several tales in the collection of the Arabian Nights where a woman has an interim husband, following some religious and legal prescriptions, stating that if a man divorces his wife and wants her back because of regretting his decision, the wife has to marry another man for one night and consummate the marriage. The intermediary husband is expected to divorce his wife the following morning making her free to remarry her previous husband. However, many complications occur during the process. The narrative shows that many women exploit this arrangement to fulfil their desires and dreams and to get rid of unwanted husbands or unpleasant matrimony.

In *Harun al-Rashid, the Slave-Girl and Abu Yusuf*, Caliph Harun al-Rashid and his vizier, Ja'far the Barmakid, argue about a slave-girl. The caliph neither donates nor sells her to his vizier, who insists on having her. Unable to resolve the conflict, they seek the advice of the judge Abu Yusuf, who proposes that the caliph presents his vizier with one-half of the slave-girl and sells him the other half. They do so, but as the caliph wants to have her back, she has to marry a man first. A slave marries her but is unwilling to divorce her. Now, the judge advises the caliph to declare the slave-girl the property of the slave, thereby invalidating the marriage. Thus, the cunning use of legal tricks seems to solve the problem for the caliph. Abu Yusuf was a famous legal scholar who lived in Kufa and was appointed by Harun as the chief qadi of Baghdad, to become one of the founders of the Hanafi school, one of the four orthodox law schools of Islam (Marzolph and Leeuwen 2004 II: 469).

In *Mahmud and His Three Sons*, Ali sails to India, where he is invited by a merchant to marry his wife to enable him to remarry her after a second divorce. Instead, the wife falls in love with Ali and instructs him not to divorce her. The merchant appeals to a judge to decide the case, but the judge's verdict comes in favour of Ali. It is remarkable in the story that even though the arrangement of the intermediary husband is legally prescribed, yet the judge decides against it. A young merchant in Damascus has a shop, in *Loser*. One day a beautiful woman passes by, and the following day she returns accompanied by a still more beautiful young woman. The merchant marries the young woman but soon finds her in bed with another man and, consequently, he divorces her. Only then, he finds out that the two women had made use of his assistance without letting him know. The young woman had needed him as an interim husband because her husband who now wanted her back has divorced her.

Ala' al-Din, in *Ala' al-Din Abu 'l-Shamat*, is the son of a merchant in Egypt who travels to Baghdad but loses all his possessions when Bedouins attack him during the journey. Taking refuge in a mosque, two men approach him to seek his help. One of them had married the young woman Zubayda. He divorced her but now regrets his decision and wants to have her back. They ask him to marry the woman and divorce her soon after. In case he refuses to divorce the woman, they agree that he will have to pay a fine of 10,000 dinars. He marries the woman but, after a delicious night, falls in love with her and refuses to set her free. The judge gives him three days to collect the fine. While the young couple is sitting at home in desperation, three dervishes, who are in fact Caliph Harun al-Rashid, his vizier, and his executioner in disguise, visit them. To solve their problem, the caliph arranges for a caravan with merchandise to be sent to them. Not only is the bridegroom able to pay the fine, but he is also appointed provost of the merchants of Baghdad.

Salim of Egypt is a story that starts with a woman having an interim husband but develops into a series of promiscuous life experiences for her. When his father dies and his brother inherits the throne in Egypt, Salim is afraid of him and leaves for Mecca. He finds a purse in the street and returns it to its owner, an old man, who takes him back to Baghdad and finds him a job. One day, his benefactor, who has divorced his wife and wants to marry her again, asks him to fulfil the legally required role of the intermediary husband. On the advice of the woman, who has taken a liking to him, Salim refuses to give her up after the wedding. The old man, however, forgives him and dies. One day, Salim's wife has disappeared with a lover, and he returns to Egypt to become the new ruler after his brother's death. One day, a case of three men accused of murder is presented to Salim. One of them denies any guilt but wants to be punished anyway. He turns out to be the former lover of Salim's wife. He then tells the ruler that when eloping together they had reached the palace of one of the princes of Basra. The woman had fallen in love with the prince and had tried to get rid of him by pretending he was her slave. Instead of killing him, the prince had only thrown him out. He had then travelled to Cairo, where he had been arrested by mistake together with the murderers. The man is released and Salim, now knowing for sure about his wife's unfaithfulness, marries another woman, who bears him a son, and they live happily.

One day, however, a woman asks for protection. She turns out to be his former wife, who has again taken a different lover and is now being chastised by the prince of Basra. As her treachery and unfaithfulness are proven beyond doubt, the ruler has her killed, while admitting the prince to his court. Understandably, the divorced woman takes the opportunity of the legal stipulation of divorcing her to get rid of her old husband to the advantage of having a younger one. Age differences and spousal incompatibility tend to rationalize this conduct. However, the agency of the wife goes much further by changing sexual partners too often and, therefore, paying with her life for living a life of promiscuity and debauchery. It is interesting, however, to note that male promiscuity goes unpunished in the narrative.

7

TRANSGRESSIVE ADULTERY

NARRATIVES OF ATTEMPTS AT ADULTERY AND UNFOUNDED AND hasty accusations of sexual perfidy are well represented in the Thousand and One Nights. Any perfidious act is the interaction of two agencies, male and female. Yet, adultery in this narrative is associated with women, focusing on them and their side of the deceitful act. The male part in perfidy is hurriedly mentioned, while the main narrative focus is on the female agency. Adultery is portrayed as an attribute of women's sexuality, in contrast to men's sexuality, which is not considered as an act of infidelity. Therefore, accusing women of committing adultery is prevalent in the narrative. Consequently, the Arabian Nights represents a discriminatory perception of adultery that tends to subscribe to a culture of suspicion of women. However, cunning and suspicion of women are mutually reinforcing: the more she is suspected, the more she resorts to cunning, and vice versa. Moreover, there is a link between the beauty of women and the probability of committing adultery. Tales of adultery are often about beautiful women. Any beautiful woman is considered an object for sexual advances and attempted adultery.

Stories of Adultery and Misdemeanour

The astrologists tell the king of China, in *Craft and Malice of Women*, that his son will die if he speaks a single word in seven days. The king orders him to remain silent and sends him to the harem. There, one of the king's favourite concubines becomes amorous with the prince and tries to seduce him. When he rejects her advances and threatens to tell his father, she accuses him of trying to rape her. She rushes to the king telling him that his son has made advances on her and wanted to kill her for rejecting him. In a rage, his father sentences him to death, but the viziers intervene by advising the king not to do something that he will eventually regret. They tell the king that his decision is based on a report of a woman who could be true or false, and it could be a trick by the woman against his son. The king now asks his viziers if they know anecdotes and tales about the cunning of women. Because the prince is unable to tell his version lest he will die, the viziers and the concubine engage for seven days in narrative and counter-narrative on whether men or women are more untrustworthy and deceitful. When the prince is finally allowed to speak, he eloquently tells the gathering the story of a slave-girl who buys a jar of clotted milk. While she is walking home, a kite with a serpent in its beak flies over and a drop of the serpent's poison falls into the jar, and everyone who drinks from the jar dies. The prince elaborates that the moral dilemma in this story is who is at fault. The answer is that nobody is at fault since God has decreed this mishap. The same female agency of false accusation of rape ensuing failed attempted adultery appears also in *As'ad and Amjad*.

A fisherman is married to a beautiful woman, in *Third Captain's Tale*. One day when he is too ill to go to work, he takes his wife to the shore to teach her how to fish. The sultan sees her, falls in love with her, and desperately wants to possess her. The vizier advises him not to have her husband executed without good reason and suggests ordering him to perform impossible tasks. Accordingly, the fisherman is asked on pain of death to procure a carpet in one piece that covers the whole hall of the palace, and a child of eight days that will tell a story beginning and ending with a lie. Advised by his wife, he procures the items from a magic creature inside a certain well. After narrating the required tale, the child then admonishes the sultan to quit longing for the wife of the angler. Even though she is assisted by magic, the wife demonstrates a high level of faithfulness to her husband by preferring her poor, and now even ill, husband to the richness and might of the sultan. Female agency associated with the motif of a wife sticking with a poor husband despite temptations of power and richness is also narrated in *Bedouin and His Wife*. In *Two Sharpers*, two sharpers meet in an inn, *khân*, and try to deceive each other. When they become aware of what they are doing, they decide to act as partners and conceive a plan. One of them will pretend to be dead, while the other will collect alms on his behalf. However, the sharper pretending to be dead noticed that his colleague had tried to make advances to his wife while he was performing the trick.

The following two stories illustrate a conflict between adultery and religious faith. In *Devout Tray-Maker and His Wife*, a pious man earns his living by making trays. One day he comes to the house of a wealthy merchant, and the wife desires him. One of the servants takes the man inside, and the woman insists on having sexual intercourse with him. The merchant's wife takes him by the gown, draws him to her, and tells him, 'The place is perfumed and the food is ready, the master of the house is absent this night, and I give myself to you.' The man does not raise his eyes from the ground and asks to be allowed to wash on the highest place of the house. He is taken to the roof terrace, where he first performs his prayer and then throws himself down. An angel catches him in mid-air and puts him on the ground. He returns to his home empty handed.

In *Water-Carrier and the Goldsmith's Wife*, a water carrier in Bukhara is used to bring water to the house of a goldsmith who has a very beautiful and pious wife. One day, inside the house, he comes closer to the woman. He takes her hand to stroke it and squeeze it, and then leaves the house. As the goldsmith returns home, his wife asks him what kind of reprehensible act he has done that day in the bazaar. The man first denies doing anything wrong but his wife insists that he did and threatens to leave the house. The goldsmith then confesses that he has pressed the beautiful hand of a woman who bought a bracelet. She tells him that the water carrier, who has entered their house for thirty years with no sign of treachery, squeezed her hand today. The man repents and asks God for forgiveness. When the next day the water carrier asks her forgiveness, the wife tells him that it was not his fault but her husband's, and God has punished him. She tells her husband that the water carrier has shown remorse for what he did. Her husband says, 'Tit for tat! If I had done more, the water-carrier had surely done more!' and this has become a current axiom among the folk. In these two stories, faith triumphs over sexuality and attempts at adultery. Notably, however, the woman becomes the object of divine retaliation and justice rather than the male transgressor. This reflects the patriarchal code of sexual honour and the way gender order is constructed within this code.

There are several stories in the Arabian Nights where adulterous advances are made yet receptions were not only negative but also retaliatory and punishing. A tailor, in *Tailor, the Lady, and the Captain*, sits in his shop, which is opposite the house of a beautiful woman. Since he desires her and always stares at her when she passes by, she decides to teach him a lesson. One day, she invites him to her house all by himself. While they are sharing a meal, her husband happens to return home. The woman hides the tailor in a closet while breaking a tooth of the key. Then she tells her husband aloud that she has hidden her lover in the closet. In vain, her husband tries to open the closet until she tells him that she was only joking. Now the two get together and make love. When the husband has left, she releases the tailor, who is now warned not to be impudent.

The hunchback brother of the barber, in *Barber's Tale of His First Brother*, is a tailor in Baghdad. One day, while sitting in his shop, he sees the landlord's wife and desires her. The woman orders some clothes but she does not pay him. Together with her husband, she mocks him and makes fun of him. They even trick him into pulling their mill instead of the bull and beat him. After a while, the woman pretends to agree to a meeting, but then she lets him be caught and brought before the police. He is subsequently flogged and sent out of town on a camel. He falls from the camel, breaks his leg, and becomes lame. Attempting adultery is turned into a lesson for the transgressor but in a cruel way concomitant with exploitation and making fun. This strong reaction is probably, partially at least, associated with the fact that the transgressor is deformed and poor, where chances of sexuality and adultery are slim.

A beautiful woman in Cairo, in *Goodwife of Cairo and Her Four Gallants*, is on her way to the public bath and passes by the qadi's house. As the qadi notices her, he admires her beauty and asks her to arrange a meeting. On her way back, she encounters the leader of the traders' guild and agrees on a meeting with him too. Likewise, a butcher and a trader have themselves invited to her house. One by one, the visitors come to the house and, as each one arrives, he is hidden in a closet after she has asked him to clothe himself in a caftan and a bonnet. When finally her husband returns home, she tells him that she has met four fools all clad in caftans and bonnets and that she has taken them home to have a laugh. One by one, the four enamoured fools come out of the closet, dance, and tell stories. Finally, the four intruders are released. Thus, attempted adultery becomes a joke, fun, and amusement for the wife and her husband, as well as a lesson for the entrapped suitors, all due to the crafty agency of the wife.

Ali the Fisherman is a story where no adulterous advances are made and the transgression is unrelated to sexuality, yet adultery is still implicated. A poor fisherman has a virtuous and beautiful wife. One day, a Turk takes his catch away from him. In order to teach him a lesson, the wife dresses as a frivolous woman and invites him to their home for dinner. As the guest is about to start his meal, her husband knocks on the door. The guest is forced to hide in a closet where they leave him all night long. Thus, adultery becomes a lesson for the transgressor, even when there are no sexual advances made. Hence, adultery, or the use of adultery, becomes instrumental in retaliating and reacting to actions performed outside the realm of sexuality.

Adultery attempts are part of the practices of other creatures as well. A tribe of black cannibal creatures capture Prince Sayf al-Muluk, in *Sayf al-Muluk and Badi'at al-jamal*. The king gives him to his married daughter as a present. This princess used to elevate to a high estate anyone she fancies and pleases her. She likes the beauty, grace, and symmetry of the prince and asks him to fornicate with her. He rejects her sexual advances by saying that he is passionately in love with someone else and that he will not consent to any sexual liaison, *wisal*, with anyone but her. She entices him to no avail and orders him to be her servant, fetching wood and water. His servitude continues for four years, until one day he decides to intercede with the princess again. She gives him no choice but to submit to her desires, upon which she promises to reward him by setting him free to leave. Once again, she tries to tempt him but he remains stubborn. However, he eventually manages to escape from the island and marry his beloved.

Stories of Adultery and Suspicions

Suspicion and false accusation of adultery are widespread in the collection of the Arabian Nights. In *Salim and His Sister Salma*, a rich merchant in Khorasan has a son and a daughter. One day they watch their mother embracing a strange man. They suspect her of an illicit relationship with the man and leave the house. After bearing the king a son, in *Woman Whose Hands Were Cut Off*, the jealous co-wives accuse the new wife of committing adultery, and so the king orders that the woman and her son should be banished to the desert. Two angels saved them because the woman used to give alms to the poor. In *Muhammad of Damascus and Sa'd of Baghdad*, Muhammad invites Sa'd for a visit. The wicked guest tells his host that all the women in Damascus are promiscuous, and wagers that he could even tell him the details of his wife's body. An old woman helps him to hide in a place where he can watch Muhammad's wife naked, and he tells his host about her body. This convinces the host of the unfaithfulness of his wife and, therefore, he deserts her. The cunning and agency of his wife, however, expose the malice of the imposter and save her marriage.

The portress, in *Portress's Tale*, is a rich widow. One day, an old woman comes to her house and invites her to attend the wedding of her daughter, who does not know anyone in town. The portress follows her out of pity but soon realizes that she has been tricked. The old woman is actually the sister of a young man who is deeply in love with her, and since he is handsome and well educated, the portress agrees to marry him. After staying with him for a whole month, she goes to the bazaar with the old woman to buy some textiles. The merchant refuses to accept her money, instead insisting on kissing her cheek. As she sees no harm in permitting him to do so, the portress agrees. However, to her dismay, the merchant bites her cheek. When she returns, her husband is furious about her apparent infidelity and has her whipped and tortured. Finally, he divorces her.

The risk that a wife becomes a target of sexual advances tends to increase when the husband is travelling, whether for pilgrimage or trade. The judge, *qadi*, of Baghdad, in *Oft-Proved Fidelity*, is married to a beautiful and chaste woman, to the envy of his brother. He goes on a pilgrimage and leaves his wife in his brother's care. The brother attempts to seduce her but she rejects his advances, and the brother in return accuses her of adultery. As the people believe him rather than her, the woman is flogged and chased away. She seeks refuge with some camel drivers, but one of them tries to seduce her, and when she resists him, he tries to kill her. Accidently, he kills the son of his host, but the woman is blamed for the killing and, therefore, she is once more chased away. Eventually, she saves a young man from the gallows, and when she rejects his advances, he sells her to a sea captain as a slave. The captain covets her as well, but again she refuses, and when the ship is sinking by a storm, she is saved by clasping onto a piece of wood. She is washed ashore and starts wandering. She arrives at a city and asks the sultan to build a palace for her outside the city gate, and he complies with her wishes, for he believes that she is a pious saint. One after the other, all the men who had previously coveted her, visit her to be cured of some diseases. She lets them confess their crimes and forgives them.

The same story appears in two other versions with slight changes. In *Jewish Qadi and His Pious Wife*, a Jewish qadi goes on pilgrimage and his brother makes advances to his wife. She is accused of adultery and is to be stoned, and suffers further injustice from other people as well. The other version appears in *Devotee Accused of Lewdness*. The brother and other men make advances on a married woman who is accused of adultery. She escapes and wanders through the land disguised as a man. Later, she becomes friends with the king's daughter, but when the king dies, the princess is accused of having an illicit sexual relationship. When it turns out that the supposed young man is, in fact, a woman, people repent. She not only forgives all the men who have wronged her but also cures their illness. Her husband returns and is invested with the kingship. In all versions of the story, false accusations and illicit sexual advances are punished by a divine power.

In *Devout Woman and the Two Wicked Elders*, a pious Israelite woman goes to a particular place to pray every day. Next to this place is a garden guarded by two men. They desire the woman but she rejects them. They tell her that if she does not comply they will accuse her of fornication. When she is still unwilling, they scream, telling the gathering crowd that they found this woman with a young man making love but the man has escaped. According to customs, the transgression of fornication is publicly announced for three days before stoning the accused to death. Every day the two men approach the woman to thank God for his wrath on her. When it is the time to stone her, Prophet Daniel, who is twelve years old at the time, advises the crowd not to rush things. Daniel interrogates the witnesses separately, which is the first miracle performed by the prophet since it is the first time that witnesses are separated for interrogation. He asks the first man where exactly in the garden this has happened and the man says in the eastern part of the garden under a pear tree. Asking the other man the same question, the man says it happened in the western part of the garden under an apple tree. Meanwhile, the accused woman is praying to God to save her, and God sends a thunder to burn the two men to death. The woman is acquitted of the false allegation.

In *Rake's Trick Against the Chaste Wife*, a man desires a beautiful but chaste woman who rejects his advances. One day he decides to play a trick on her. Without her knowing, he enters her house and spills the white of a raw egg onto the woman's bed. When the husband returns home and sees the stain on the bed, he thinks it is a man's semen and beats his wife. The neighbours intervene to prevent him from killing her. They fry the substance and find out that it is not semen but an egg, and the spouses are reconciled. A similar motif is narrated in *Harun al-Rashid, Queen Zubayda, and Abu Yusuf*. When Caliph Harun al-Rashid lies down to rest, he notices traces of semen on his bed sheet. He calls the judge Abu Yusuf to ask his advice, whether he should suspect his spouse, Zubayda, of deceiving him. The judge, however, notices a cleft in the ceiling and tells the caliph that it is the semen of a bat. He pokes into the hole and the bat falls down. The caliph is extremely pleased, and the queen promises the judge a lavish reward.

Accompanied by his vizier Ja'far and his executioner Masrur, the legendary Caliph Harun al-Rashid goes to town in disguise, in *Three Apples*. They see a fisherman on the shore of the river Tigris drawing a heavy trunk out of the water. On inspecting the trunk, they are shocked to find the mutilated body of a young woman. Enraged, the caliph says that he is responsible for the lives of the populace before God, and he gives his vizier three days to discover the murderer, otherwise, he will hang him and forty of his relatives. The vizier, however, fails to solve the mystery and prepares himself for the execution when all of a sudden, two men come forward, both claiming to be the killer. The old man is the father of the victim, but the real killer is the young man, her husband, and he starts to tell his story.

They are cousins, loved each other, and had three sons together. She was good to him and served his needs well, and they lived happily until one day she became ill. She desired an apple when apples were extremely hard to find at the time. He was told that the only place to find the apple was in the caliph's gardens in Basra. Out of love, he took the pain of spending two weeks going back and forth and finally managed to buy three apples for 3 dinars. However, when he offered the apples, his wife was not pleased as she had now lost interest in the apples. Afterward, while he was in his shop one day, a black slave holding a similar apple passed by. He asked him about the apple, and the slave replied that it was from his lover who was sick and her cuckolded, *maqrun*, husband went all the way to Basra to buy three apples for her. Feeling that life had darkened, he closed his shop and went home, brainless from excessive anger. He saw that there were only two apples on the table. He asked his wife about the third apple, but she replied that she did not know. He took a knife to slaughter and decapitate her, put the mutilated body in a trunk, and threw it in the Tigris River. When he came home, he saw his eldest son crying and saying that he took one of the apples and went into the street, but a black slave snatched it from him and when the slave asked him about the apple, the boy told him the story. The husband then realized the mistake he had just made because of the lies of the slave about his wife. He felt remorse for killing his wife unjustly.

Stories of Royal Adulteries

There are several stories in the Arabian Nights portraying kings attempting to commit adultery with beautiful wives in general and with the wives of their viziers in particular. In *King and the Virtuous Wife*, a king makes sexual advances to a beautiful married woman. She hands him a book containing pious warnings against adultery, and the king repents. In *King and His Chamberlain's Wife*, a king of Persia is addicted to the love of beautiful women, and one day he visits the beautiful wife of one of his chamberlains. She refuses to comply with his wishes, and the king leaves her house, forgetting his girdle. Her husband discovers the girdle and wants to divorce his wife on suspicion of adultery. When he informs the king of his intention, the king reassures him that 'the lion did not do harm to the garden'. Another version of the story, *Firuz and His Wife*, narrates that a king sits on the roof terrace in his palace and sees a beautiful woman on the roof of an adjacent house, who turns out to be his vizier's wife. He covets the woman, sends his vizier on an assignment, and enters the house. The woman greets him by asking whether he comes 'to a watering place from which a dog has drunk'. Ashamed at this admonishment, the king leaves the house in a rush, forgetting his sandal. As the vizier returns, he finds the king's sandal and suspects his wife of adultery, but the king assures him that 'no lion has trespassed in his garden'.

A more elaborate version of the same motif is presented in the *King and His Vizier's Wife*. A king is addicted to the love of women. One day, he sees the beautiful wife of one of his viziers and falls in love with her. He dispatches his vizier on an errand and visits his wife. He tells her that his love and longing for her have brought him to her, but she tells him to have patience, and because he is going to spend the whole day with her, she will cook something for him to eat. She gives him a book about the sin of adultery to read meanwhile. She offers him ninety dishes and the king starts to eat one spoonful to find out that even though the dishes are of a different variety, they taste the same. The woman explains that this is a parable to rebuke him because the king has ninety concubines of various colours yet their taste is the same. Feeling ashamed, the king leaves the house in haste, forgetting his ring under the cushion, to be discovered by the vizier upon his return. The vizier takes the matter to his heart, isolates himself from his wife, and does not speak to her for a whole year without explaining the reasons. She informs her father, who decides to make a complaint of the vizier to the king. Her father says that he planted the garden with his own hand and spent his money until it bore fruit. He offered it to the vizier who ate from it but he then forsook the garden and stopped watering it until its flowers withered and its beauty faded. The vizier says that he saw the track of a lion and therefore he deserted the garden. The king understands the parable and tells his vizier to return to the garden for the lion did not come close to it.

Stories with the reverse situation are also narrated. When the king of Iraq one day goes hunting, in *Three Sisters and Their Mother*, his vizier covets the queen. The queen not only rejects his advances but also kills the slave-girl he sent to her. Later, when the king is away on the pilgrimage, the vizier resumes his efforts. When the queen continues to be unwilling to comply, the vizier accuses her of adultery. She is to be executed but manages to escape together with her three daughters. Eventually, the king finds out about his vizier's betrayal and has him executed by throwing him into a fire with a catapult. In *Dadbin and His Viziers*, a vizier makes advances on the queen and because she is unwilling, he denounces her to the king as having deceived him. She is left alone in the desert but eventually marries an even mightier king who punishes her husband. In *Aylan Shah and Abu Tammam*, a king sends a man as an envoy to ask the daughter of a notorious Turkish king for her hand in marriage. However, the viziers who want to get rid of the man accuse him of having illicit sexual relations with the bride, and he is subsequently executed. Later, however, the treachery of the viziers is revealed, and they are also executed. When the governor of Iraq, in *Khuzayma ibn Bishr and 'Ikrima al-Fayyad*, hears that a man who was famed for his wealth and generosity is in a financial trouble, he visits him at night to give him money. However, his wife is suspicious about her husband's night-time absence and accuses him of committing adultery. The truth is exposed in the end.

Accusations of adultery between mother and son also occur when people are oblivious to the true nature of the relationship. In *King of Abyssinia*, a king of Abyssinia marries a Persian princess. It turns out that the princess had a secret lover and already has a son, and she arranges to bring her son with her to Abyssinia without anybody knowing. One day, the king sees his wife kissing him and becomes enraged for thinking the young man to be her lover. Subsequently, he sentences her to death. However, an old woman hands the doubting king a talisman that will reveal anyone's deepest secrets, which the king applies to his wife, and the truth is revealed. In *Sulayman Shah and His Niece*, a prince is married to his cousin and they have a son together. Out of jealousy, his brother kills him. The widow eventually marries the king of Rum without informing him about her son. One day the son is caught while giving a kiss to his mother and he is jailed for transgressing into the king's harem. She tells her story to the king's nurse, who thinks of a ruse by which to let the king know. She makes the king believe that a hoopoe's heart would make the wife confess the truth while sleeping. The king follows her advice, and the identity of the son is disclosed.

A Persian king, in *Azadbakht and His Son*, marries the daughter of his vizier against the will of her father. The viziers start a rebellion, forcing the king and his new wife to leave the country. The king's wife is pregnant and on the way gives birth to a boy, who they leave behind along the road. The king of a neighbouring country helps them to defeat the viziers and restore the throne. Meanwhile, a band of highwaymen pick up the boy who ultimately becomes a robber. He is captured by the royal forces and is raised and educated by the king himself, who eventually appoints him keeper of the treasuries. One day the boy gets drunk and falls asleep in the queen's chamber. The furious king has him and the queen imprisoned, suspecting them of adultery. Suspecting sexual relationships between mother and son is present in Arab folklore as well. In a story from Iraq, a merchant goes on a very long journey, leaving his pregnant wife with his mother. Returning home after a long absence, he thinks the young man he sees with his wife to be her lover when he is actually his own son. Consequently, he kills his mother, wife, and son for the hasty suspicion of adultery (Bushnaq 1986: 94).

8

SEXUAL PERFIDY

A LLURING SEXUALITY LEADING TO ADULTEROUS AFFAIRS IS A universal aspect of sexuality in all cultures. Adultery is strongly represented in the collection of tales in the Thousand and One Nights. With an extensive and unambiguous presentation of sexual unfaithfulness, the motif of sexual perfidy appears to be predominant and relentless in this narrative. The fact that this collection is full of stories of adultery might support the hypothesis that the genesis of this collection is traced to literary India because Indian ancient literature abounds in tales of extramarital sexual activities (Marzolph 2015: 193). The Arabian Nights tales are about sexual infidelity and adultery, which is the overriding motive that initiates and rationalizes the entire collection of stories. Indeed, the frame story and the determining motif and rationale of the entire collection of tales are predicated on a double case of the sexual perfidy of the wives of the two brother kings, Shahzaman and Shahryar. The discovery of the unfaithfulness of their respective wives sets the frame and the social dynamics that rationalize the narratives of the Arabian Nights.

The transfixing motif of the sexual perfidy of the wives of the two kings tends to result in essentializing the infidelity of women and projecting their unfaithfulness as part of their nature. A merchant, in 'Adila, weeps on the grave of his wife who has just died. Precipitously, a demon appears and restores her to life. While the merchant goes home to fetch her decent clothes, the woman goes with a prince who happens to pass by to his palace. The husband begs the prince to return her to him, but the woman denies any relation to the man. Instead, she pretends that he is a robber who stole her possessions and wanted to bury her alive. Believing her story, the prince orders that the man should be hanged, but he is saved by a demon. This story essentializes the treacherous nature of women because the infidelity of the wife is indeed extraordinary considering the circumstances. The story

signals that women are not only perfidious in life but also when they are res-
urrected. It shows that it is not only men that falsely accuse women, causing
their death, but also vice versa. The woman not only displays an agency of
treachery but also almost causes the death of her husband.

Essentializing infidelity as a human feature is presented in *Sayf al-Muluk
and Badi'at al-jamal*. When a prince falls in love with a jinniyah-princess, she
hesitates by saying that humans do not keep promises and do not know true
love. In defending himself, he reassures her that treachery is not his trait and
that not all men are alike. Still unconvinced, she says that she is afraid that if
she agrees, 'she will find with him neither affection nor love, for the virtues
of men are few and their perfidy is great'. She illustrates her point by saying
that Solomon took Belqis by love but when he saw a more beautiful woman,
he deserted her. Peculiarly, this is the only narrative in the Arabian Nights
that addresses the infidelity of men. The rest of the narrative depicts only
women as the guilty party, while men are totally absent in cases of perfidy
except as victims of female cunning and treachery.

The presentation of the involvement of men in adulterous affairs is almost
absent, indicating that the male agency in sexual perfidy is taken for granted,
expected, tolerated, and lacks condemnation. While the sexual interaction
of adultery signifies the agency of two parties, the tales are mostly preoccupied with singling out and condemning only the female agency. However,
it is important to state that adultery is a multidimensional process involving
a complex interplay of various subjectivities. Subversion and resistance to
the patriarchal construction of gender realities are strongly implicated in
decisions and feelings associated with infidelity. When these gender realities
are relatively advantageous to men, women become involved in adultery as
resistance and vengeance, with the help of cunning. Still, these tales do not
present more details about marital life or the nature of conjugal attachments.

Testing Fidelity

Sexual and amorous liaisons in the tales of the Thousand and One Nights
entail testing and verifying the sincerity of the commitment to these
attachments. Testing is a normalized aspect of social life in this narrative,
whether in relation to faith, political loyalty, matrimony, or love. Testing love
is pertinent to many stories of romance in this collection. Fidelity is either
naturally tested by events or deliberately verified by any of the partners. In
Al-Mutalammis and His Wife Umayma, the wife remains faithful to her husband the poet even when he is forced to leave her for a long time to escape
an enemy and even when her people pressure her to marry someone else.

When she finally capitulates to the pressure, she nevertheless chooses her husband when he returns on her wedding night, rather than someone else.

One day, a very angry man approaches Caliph Mu'awiya in Damascus, in *Bedouin and His Wife*. He asks for protection against the governor of Medina, Marwan ibn al-Hakam. He tells the caliph that he is happily married to a very beautiful woman, Su'ad, who he loves dearly, but when he became impoverished, her father took her back. The governor became interested in the woman and put her husband in jail and tortured him to divorce his wife, paid her father an expensive bride-price, and married the woman. The caliph, however, orders the governor to divorce the woman and send her to him. Being himself very impressed by her beauty, the caliph offers the husband a compensation of three virgin slave-girls and 1,000 dinars with each of them, in addition to a yearly allowance from the treasury, in return for his wife. The man rejects the offer, saying that he would not replace his wife, 'Even if I get the entire treasury'. Finally, the caliph asks the woman to choose between the caliph with his honour, glory, palaces, power, and wealth; the governor with his injustice and abuse; or the Bedouin with his hunger and poverty. Su'ad chooses her husband, reciting the verses,

> This man even if he is in hunger and misfortune
> Is dearer to me than my folk and neighbours are
> Dearer to me than the one who wears the crown,
>   or Marwan his governor
> And anyone with dirhams and dinars.

She then tells the caliph that she 'Will not forsake him by reason of the shifts of fortune or the perfidies of fate, because there is between us an unforgettable old companionship and unbreakable love bonding. Indeed, I should have patience with him in his stressful time, as I shared good fortune with him in better days.' The caliph marvels at her wisdom, love, and fidelity, and gives her a reward of 10,000 dirhams. The couple take the money and leave. Indeed, this story is a test for both marital partners and both display a high level of loyalty and commitment despite pressures and temptations. Surprisingly, the motif of forcing a husband to divorce his beautiful wife because a ruler becomes interested in her occurs even in the modern Middle East, as was the case, for instance, with the second wife of Saddam Hussein in Iraq.

Devotion and loyalty to an intimate partner despite misfortune and pressures appear in other stories too. In *Third Captain's Tale*, a wife prefers to stay loyal to her poor and ill husband and even uses her agency to rescue him from the wrath of the sultan who admires her beauty and wants to have her. In *Fatima and the Poet Muraqqish*, a woman insists on being loyal to her sexual partner and threatens to terminate the relationship if it proves otherwise. In *Sayf al-Muluk and Badi'at al-jamal*, the hero pays dearly and endures years of servitude for rejecting attempts of adultery and insisting on fidelity.

However, the story of Su'ad and her husband is contrasted with a different female agency in *Hind bint al-Nu'man and al-Hajjaj*. The very beautiful Hind is married to al-Hajjaj, the governor of Iraq, who spends a large amount of money to pay her bride-price. One day, however, he hears her reciting insulting verses and decides to divorce her. She gladly accepts the divorce and eventually accepts her marriage to the caliph. She demands that al-Hajjaj himself, on barefoot, should lead her camel to the town. When they arrive, she drops a dinar coin, which is made of gold, and asks him to pick up the 'dirham', which is made of silver. When he protests that it is not a dirham but a dinar, she says metaphorically, 'God be praised for compensating us with a dinar for the fallen dirham.'

Verifying the fidelity of a partner in a deliberate and calculated way is a motif appearing in many stories of the Arabian Nights. One day an old woman buys a necklace from a jeweller, in *Harun al-Rashid and the Youth Manjab*. The following day she takes him to a beautiful house owned by an attractive young woman. He eats with her and falls madly in love. The woman agrees to marry him, on condition that if he betrays her he will receive a thousand lashes on his right side and a thousand lashes on his left side, his tongue and hands will be cut off, and his eye will be plucked out. After a while, a Bedouin woman visits his shop and sells him a precious necklace. Instead of being paid with money, she just asks for a 'kiss on the cheek'. As her beauty confounds him, he lets her in and makes love to her. Immediately afterward, he is summoned to his wife, and his betrayal is revealed because the Bedouin woman was none other than one of the kitchen maids. He is tortured and thrown onto a garbage heap. It turns out that the woman is the sister of the vizier, and the couple are reconciled and the marriage is restored.

The vizier's sister is involved in another version of the story, in *Mock Caliph*. She marries a wealthy jeweller, and when one day she goes to the public bath, she asks him to wait for her return. However, the caliph's wife summons him to her room, and consequently, he is not there upon the return of his wife. She orders his execution but because of the intervention of the slave-girls, he is only whipped and thrown out of the palace. Since then he has sold all his possessions and plays a mock caliph every night. The caliph reunites the couple. A similar narrative appears in *First Lunatic's*

Story. A wealthy woman marries a merchant. One day a woman sells him a precious cock, and instead of payment, the woman only asks permission to kiss him on his cheek. When he agrees, she bites into his cheek and leaves a distinct mark. He presents the cock to his wife, but she is angry since the woman had been sent by her to test his faithfulness. Since he has not passed the test, he is chased away. The young man does not overcome his sorrow, ending up in the lunatic asylum. It turns out that the woman is the sultan's daughter, and the couple is reunited. It is notable that a woman taking initiative and showing sexual interest is narrated as an ordinary thing to happen in the different versions of the story.

The *Jewish Doctor's Tale* is also a story of testing love and fidelity with a tragic end. A young man from Mosul visits Damascus and rents a house. He meets a beautiful young woman and they develop an amorous and sexual relationship. One day she asks his permission to bring with her a younger and more beautiful girl, who accompanies her on her next visit. After a while, she urges him to sleep with the girl, with which he is happy to comply! The next morning, he finds the new girl is decapitated and the first girl is missing, realizing that the girl had been killed out of jealousy. It turns out that the two girls are sisters.

Infidelity and Femicide

The strong involvement of women in sexual infidelity would ineluctably result in subjecting them to vengeful violence that would include, but not necessarily be restricted to, femicide. Sexuality and violence are strongly interrelated, particularly when women are involved. The frame story of *Shahryar and His Brother* is about adultery and treachery of the wife and femicide as a punishment. King Shahzaman embarks on a journey to visit his brother, King Shahryar, but quickly returns to his palace to fetch something he had forgotten, to find his wife with a black slave making love in his own bed. When he sees them in that position, the world turns dark before his eyes, pondering to himself, 'If this is what happens while I have not departed the city yet, what would be the condition of this accursed woman during my absence at my brother's court?' Enraged, he kills both of them and resumes his journey. Full of grief, he fails to enjoy the warm reception his brother prepared for him, refusing to eat or participate in any activity.

One day, when his brother goes hunting and he stays behind, he stands in his apartment by a window overlooking a garden. A gate suddenly opens, and out in the garden come his brother's beautiful wife accompanied by ten female and ten male slaves. They go to a fountain, undress, and sit down together. Then the queen calls out, 'O Mas'ud!' and a black slave climbs down from a tree and comes to her, embracing her and she is reciprocating. He starts to make love to her, and likewise all the slaves to the accompanying women. They continue kissing, fondling, embracing, and fucking until the day begins to wane. Perceiving that the plight of his brother is even graver than that of his own because his brother is an even mightier king, Shahzaman feels happy again and contends that he is not alone in this quandary.

On his return, Shahryar notices the changes in his brother's state of mind and insists on an explanation. His brother tells him everything about their wives. They announce that they are going on a hunting trip but secretly return to the palace. The following day, they both watch the sexual orgy of the queen and the slaves. Deeply insulted by the situation, Shahryar suggests that they leave the palace and travel in search of knowledge about the nature of women that caused their miserable predicaments. After his return, he kills his wife and all the implicated slaves. In revenge, he starts the habit of deflowering a virginal bride every night, only to kill her the following morning. This bloody ritual lasts for three years until the arrival of Shahrazad.

The pattern of punishing the adulterous women by death, exemplified by the conduct of Shahryar and Shahzaman, is present in many tales of sexual perfidy in the Arabian Nights. In *Concubine and the Caliph*, a caliph spends each night with one of the forty concubines he has. In waiting for their turn, the concubines used to secretly receive their lovers in the palace, with the exception of one concubine. However, this concubine eventually decides to have a lover and invites a man to come to her in the palace. On his way to meet her the following day, he meets a friend and inexorably spends the night at the friend's house. In the morning, he rushes to the palace to meet his lover but instead he is shocked to see thirty-eight crucified men accompanied by thirty-eight dead concubines. He is told that the caliph has discovered their treachery the night before and had all of them executed. Thus, the man narrowly escapes death by sheer chance. In this story, a woman, in a circumstance of infidelity and deceit, causes a possible frightening death. Apparently, association with women tends to increase the risk of disaster, suffering, and death.

While adultery leads to the killing of the adulterous couple, fate could dictate otherwise, as in the story of *Unending Treasure*. A man meets a beautiful woman in Cairo and falls in love with her. She invites him to join her at night and reveals to him that she is the favourite concubine, Labiba. Some eunuchs catch them in bed and throw them in the river Nile to be drowned as a punishment. He survives and travels to Baghdad to inherit a vast treasure. One day, when he partakes in one of the Caliph Harun al-Rashid audiences in the palace, he recognizes one of the singers as Labiba and the lovers are consequently reunited. The above stories present infidelity within a context of the harem, where many slave-girls, *jawari*, compete for the attention of one man. Adultery in this context appears to be a subversive act; hence, adultery becomes politics.

An eagle tells Prophet Solomon a story, in *Solomon and the Queen of Sheba*. On one of their migratory flights, the birds see a wedding ceremony, where the groom promises his beautiful bride that he would love her even after her death. On the way back, the birds see the bride sitting on the grave of her husband. However, a handsome man persuades her with little effort to marry him. As he has to guard a certain thief's body on the gallows, she offers to hang her husband's body instead if the thief's body were stolen. When she offers to mutilate her dead husband's body to resemble the criminal, the young man suddenly turns out to be the personification of her marriage oath. Because she was readily willing to break her oath, the man kills her for her faithlessness.

When a couple moves to town, in *Qalandar with the Scarred Forehead*, the wife soon starts to behave differently. As the husband is warned one day that she is expecting her lover, he kills the lover and lets her know. In her anger, she wounds him with a knife, and he finally kills her too. Later, he decides to retire from the world and becomes a mendicant. Thus, this woman not only engages in adultery but also defends her perceived right to have multiple sexual partners, and in fact pays heavily for insisting on a way of life of duplicity. Perceiving him as a threat to her illicit affair with a lover, a sultan's wife decides to kill her stepson, in *Eleventh Captain's Tale*. When the horse warns him not to eat the poisoned food, the woman decides to kill the horse too, and so they escape and disappear. When the prince eventually returns, he finds out that his father is dead and the second wife and her lover rule the kingdom. He kills them both and restores the rule. In this story, infidelity is linked to violence and planning to kill for the sake of an extramarital sexual liaison. Indeed, violence breeds violence as the fate of this sexual experience is met with femicide. A horse warning a boy not to eat poisoned food prepared by his stepmother also appears in other Middle Eastern folklore traditions (Bushnaq 1986: 115).

A young boy travels from Cairo to Basra after hearing a story about a beautiful woman and falling in love with her, in *Qamar al-Zaman and the Jeweller's Wife*. An old woman helps him to become acquainted with the husband of the woman, a jeweller, and he is invited to their house. After the meal, the wife drugs them with a sleeping potion, and while they are asleep, she comes to Qamar and admires his beauty. She mounts on his chest and covers his face with kisses until it is red and swollen. Then she sucks his lips until the blood runs out into her mouth. Still, neither her heat is quenched nor her thirst assuaged. She does not cease kissing him, embracing him, and coiling leg with leg until dawn. The same thing happens the following night, but on the third night, he does not drink the potion and stays awake. She comes to him and they spend the whole night making love while her husband is fast asleep from the drug. She tells him that one night is not enough for her and that she would like to spend the rest of her life with him. She schemes to make her husband evict the lodger from their adjoining house and rents it out to the boy. She asks an architect to build a tunnel between the two houses so that they could meet in secret. The woman transports all the money and valuables to the lover's house and uses all kinds of tricks to deceive her husband. Finally, they depart for Cairo, but his father convinces him not to marry the treacherous and untrustworthy woman and marries him off to a noble girl instead.

One day the husband, dressed in rags and begging for food, enters the wedding festivities, which last for forty days. The father asks him whether this infidelity is the fault of the wife or his son, and he replies that the son is innocent, and the fault comes entirely from his wife. Thereupon, the father tells his son that he wants to test the jeweller to see if he is a cuckolded husband, *diyuth*, or a man who has no sexual honour, *'irdh*. If he forgives her, the father will kill him and then kill her because there is no good coming from the life of a cuckolded husband and adulterous woman, *zaniya*. The jeweller, however, kills the wife and her slave-girl. In rewarding him, the father offers him his daughter in marriage and gives him money, more than the treacherous wife had stolen from him. Later on, the jeweller wants to visit Basra and he hesitates to ask his wife to go with him. However, her father says, 'Here we do not have women who disagree with their husbands or women who are angry with their husbands.' After living together in Basra for five years, her husband dies and she turns down a proposal of marriage from the king of the city, by saying, 'In our tradition, there is no woman who marries twice, and I will not marry you even if you kill me.' She returns to her paternal home and stays unmarried until she dies. This tale illustrates many aspects of social life. Apart from exposing the intricate relationships that a married woman has with her husband and lover simultaneously, it also contrasts two women, one perfidious and the other faithful, and as such contrasts adultery and fidelity, as well as cunning and obedience.

Cunning and violence are intersected in other stories as well. In *Peasant's Wicked Wife*, a peasant in Egypt suspects his wife of adultery, and the wife plots to poison him together with his assistant. However, they catch her in bed with her lover and her husband kills them both. In *Confectioner, His Wife, and the Parrot*, the wife is slaughtered following the discovery of her infidelity. In contrast to all the stories where the adulterous woman is killed for her infidelity, in *Masrur and Zayn al-Mawsif*, the adulterous woman sees no solution but to kill her husband to enjoy her life with her lover. Adultery could also cause death in a different way. In the *Miller and His Wife*, a miller is married to a woman, but she is in an unrequited love with her married neighbour. When her husband discloses the secret of the treasure to his wife, she schemes with her lover to divide the treasure between them, to divorce their spouses, and to get married and join their newly acquired wealth. However, the man kills her and takes the treasure. Apparently, sharing knowledge with women is disastrous. Adultery is harshly punished in nonhuman creatures as well. In *Second Qalandar's Tale*, a jinni kidnaps a young woman and keeps her captive for twenty-five years. When a man reaches her place of captivity, they fall in love and spend happy times together. However, the jinni discovers the affair and brutally kills the woman because death is the traditional punishment for treacherous women in the world of the jinn.

Infidelity and Punishment

Femicide is not the only punishment for adultery. Rather, modalities of punishing infidelity are varied and extensive. Punishing adultery, particularly cases committed by women, is universal in all cultures, taking many forms. Medieval European literature narrates that infidelity was considered a grave crime and punished accordingly. Since adultery was a far more serious matter than fornication, it was usually punished severely. Although theologians maintained that extramarital sex was as sinful for a man as for a woman, canon law treated adultery primarily as a female offence (Brundage 1996: 42). Under both canon and Byzantine secular law, a wife's adultery was a more serious offence than a husband's. An erring wife could suffer mutilation, divorce, confinement in a convent, or a long period of exclusion from communion (Levin 1996: 339). Punishing sexual unfaithfulness is also narrated in medieval Islamic literature. Strikingly, there are three stories about adultery while the husband is away, where the dog witnesses the sexual act and intervenes to kill the adulterous couple (Irwin 1999: 203–5).

Punishment of female sexual infidelity is narrated in the Thousand and One Nights. The two wives who committed the act of sexual infidelity on the kings, in *Shahryar and His Brother*, remain unnamed in the tale and their only identification in this narrative is being the adulterous wives, which is a narrative punishment. While the women in the following two stories are punished for adultery, the type of punishment is unspecified. In *Vengeance of King Hujr*, a hostile tribe abducts the wife of a king. Spies overhear a conversation between the kidnapped wife and the leader of the tribe that is insulting to the king. Moreover, the wife makes love to the enemy chief. The king then attacks the camp and takes revenge. The wife of King Cypress, in *Diamond*, commits adultery with seven black men who are consequently killed and the wife is punished.

In *Abdallah the Fisherman and Abdallah the Merman*, the merman takes the fisherman into a tour of the world of the sea. Asked what will happen if someone commits adultery, the merman answers that if the convicted is a woman, she is expelled to the city of women. If she is pregnant, they leave her until she delivers the baby. If the child is a girl, then she is also banished with her mother and is called adulteress, daughter of an adulteress, and she remains a virgin until she dies. If the child is a boy, they take him to the king of the sea who puts him to death. Remarkably, nothing is said about the male adulterer, while killing or banishing the offspring of adulterous affairs is extraordinarily cruel. In *Third Shaykh's Story*, one day an old man, *shaykh*, surprises his wife in bed with an ugly black slave who frightens anyone looking at him. They are talking, laughing, kissing, and dallying. When the woman sees the old man, she casts a spell on him, transforming him into a dog. In his new form, he becomes friends with a butcher, whose daughter notices that he is a transformed human. She succeeds in releasing him and, furthermore, instructs him on how to turn his wife into a she-mule by means of a magic spell. Enchanting the adulterous party is also presented in *Jullanar the Sea-Born*. The trope of transforming humans into animal shapes as a punishment for perfidy is present in other Middle Eastern folktale traditions, as this is the case of a story where an adulterous woman is transformed into a dog and is relentlessly ill-treated (Bushnaq 1986: 94). Enchantment, *es-sehr*, is almost universally acknowledged to be a branch of satanic magic (Lane 1987: 83).

Castration as a punishment for infidelity appears in some stories. In *Three Eunuchs*, a slave became a eunuch because he had sex with the wife and son of his master. However, castration is not confined only to slaves and eunuchs. In *Aziz and Aziza*, when a woman lures Aziz, who is in a sexual liaison with Dalila, into sex and marriage and keeps him captive in her house for a year, Dalila promptly castrates him for his unfaithfulness upon his return. In *Coelebs the Droll Court's Jester*, a court jester marries a woman who has four lovers. When her husband is away, she hides her lovers in a closet, one after the other. The jester returns home, and the lovers devise a ruse to save themselves but the trick is revealed. The culprits are castrated and die, and the jester divorces his wife. While this punishment is harsh for the implicated men, the wife's share of the punishment is the divorce. Naturally, divorce could signify punishment but could also be a relief when marital harmony is lacking and matrimonial discord becomes unbearable.

Divorce unaccompanied by violence is also a viable option for cases of adultery in the narrative of the Arabian Nights. An astronomer's beautiful wife, in *Wife Who Vaunted Her Virtue*, boasts about her own virtue and nobility, and her husband is proud of it. Another man challenges the husband's trust by urging him to pretend that he is going on a journey. Instead, he returns home secretly to witness his wife deceiving him with three lovers. He divorces her. Ahmad is a married man in Cairo who has a bachelor friend, Mahmud, in *Man Who Understood Women*. Ahmad volunteers to teach his friend everything he needs to know about women, and Mahmud asks to be instructed how to find a lover. In following instructions, he inadvertently approaches his friend's wife, who wants to teach her husband a lesson and takes Mahmud as her lover. When Ahmad suspects what has happened, he tries to catch the couple on several occasions but fails every time. One day he has Mahmud tell his adventures in public, hoping that he will disclose his secret. Mahmud, however, is warned and reveals nothing. Ahmad sees no other way but to divorce his wife and Mahmud then marries her.

Remarkably, in some stories, not only is there no punishment for adultery but there is also an understanding and tolerance that one might call them stories of consented adultery. In *Admonished Adulteress*, the husband expects and rather understands that his absence will make the adultery of his wife inevitable and, consequently, recommends a friend of his to his wife in case she fails to control her sexual desires during his absence. In *Contest in Generosity*, two cousins in Baghdad grow up together and are in love. Yet, she is about to be married to another man, and when she cries on her wedding night, her husband allows her to take her cousin as her lover, and the lovers are subsequently reunited. A cycle of generosity is presented in another version of the story, *Thief Discovered by Storytelling*. A young woman who is deeply in love with her cousin is about to be married to someone else. On the wedding night, she confesses her love to her husband who generously allows her to visit her beloved. On the way, a thief who follows the example of her husband's generosity spares her. The lover, in turn, is also impressed and sends her back to her husband.

Infidelity and Fortune

While adultery is severely punished, it could also be ultimately rewarding in some narratives. Three sharpers are accustomed to looking for money in other people's belongings, in *Three Sharpers*, but for three days, they find nothing. As they are hungry, they present themselves before the sultan telling him that they used to be former masters of their profession. They discern that the queen's mother was a gypsy dancing girl, by observing her black eyes and her bushy brows. The sultan himself is then found to be the son of his father's cook because his mother has seen no other way of engendering a male child to ensure their continued rule. Stunned by the accurate judgments of the sharpers, the sultan becomes a dervish and concedes the realm to them. A similar motif is narrated in *King Who Kenned the Quintessence of Things*. A king, who becomes ascetic and worships God, justly concludes that the sultan of another city is the son of a baker, as his mother had seen no other way to engender a child and thus the continuity of the throne. He is richly rewarded. These two tales place the failure to conceive a child with the husband, contrary to the stereotype of blaming women in these cases. Because the husband is a king and succession to the rule is vital, the wife sees no choice but to use adultery to save the throne. Undoubtedly, these tales are still a manifestation of adultery as politics. Yet, it seems to be an act of infidelity for a 'good reason' and, therefore, unavoidable.

The politics of adultery is clearly illustrated in the funny tale of the *Sweep and the Noble Lady*. One day in the season of pilgrimage at Mecca, people hear a man saying, 'I beseech Allah that she may once again be in a rage with her husband so that I have a sexual intercourse with her!' The crowd beat him and take him to the governor, *emir*, of pilgrims, who orders him to be hanged. He implores the emir to hear his story out and then decide what to do with him. He is a scavenger who works in a sheep slaughterhouse, and one day, while his ass is loaded with rubbish, he sees people running away. He enters a small alley and waits, but a woman who is perfect in beauty, elegance, and amorous grace surrounded by thirty women and many eunuchs soon enter the same alley. They take the man to a luxurious house with magnificent furniture. He is then taken to an elegant bathroom and is soon joined by three damsels who seat themselves round him and undress him. One rubs his feet, another washes his head and the third scrubs his body, and after they finish, they dress him in new clothes, and sprinkle him with rose water. Thereupon, he is taken to a splendid saloon, where he finds the woman seated on a couch, surrounded by many damsels. The woman makes him sit by her side, orders food, and the damsels bring all kinds of luxurious food that he has never seen in all his life, followed by fruits, and serve wine, to the melodies of strings. While the man is drinking wine and enjoying himself, he is wondering if it is all not just an illusion of sleep. Later on, she takes him by the hand, leads him to the bed where they make love, and he sleeps with the woman until morning, while still wondering if he is in paradise or just dreaming.

In the morning, she gives him a handkerchief embroidered with gold and silver with 50 golden dinars in it. In the afternoon, a slave-girl comes to him to say that her mistress has called for him. He follows her to the house, again to experience another night of food, drink, and sexual intercourse with the woman, and in the morning, gets a similar amount of money. This situation lasts for eight nights, but on the last night, while he is sleeping with the woman, a slave-girl comes running and takes him into a closet to hide. He can see a handsome young man attended by a number of servants and soldiers. The man comes to the woman and kisses her hands, but she does not speak to him. However, he manages in the end to make peace with her. They spend the night together, and he departs in the morning, whereupon the woman comes to the hiding man to tell him that the other man is her husband, and she tells him her story.

It chanced one day that they were sitting in the garden within the house when her husband rose from her side and was absent a long while until she became tired of waiting, so she went into the house to search for him. She found him having sexual intercourse with one of the kitchen maids. When she saw this, she swore a great oath that she would commit adultery with the foulest and filthiest man in town. When she saw the poor man, she had been going round for days in quest of one who should answer this description and found none neither fouler nor filthier than this poor man. Now she quits her oath but also tells him that if her husband ever sleeps with the maid again, she will return the man to her favours. She gives him another 50 golden dinars and orders him to leave. With all the money he has received from her, he lives well and makes a pilgrimage to Mecca praying to God to make her husband repeat his adultery so that he can enjoy the same extravagant experience once again. When the emir of the pilgrims hears the man's story, he sets him free and tells the crowd to pray for him, for he is indeed excusable!

9

TALES OF CUCKOLDRY

CUCKOLDRY, A UNIVERSAL EXPERIENCE EXISTING IN ALL CULTURES, is heavily represented in the tales of Thousand and One Nights. Cuckoldry is strongly linked to, yet distinct from, adultery by involving a more sophisticated level of cunning. Acts of cuckoldry in these tales are performed with the help of old women whose agencies represent the highest level of cunning. A life of duplicity between husband and lover necessitates shrewdness, scheming, and deceitfulness, which are well represented in the narrative. In fact, the cunning of women in these tales is in harmony with the medieval Islamic canonical literature that devotes many sections to the cuckoldry and adultery of women performed through using their wiles. For example, the famous work of Nafzawi, *The Perfumed Garden*, contains a whole chapter 'On the Deceits and Treacheries of Women' (Irwin 1994: 166).

It is interesting to explore how the husband and the lover are brought together within a context of cuckoldry and infidelity. Cuckoldry is the intersection of infidelity and cunning bringing together two opposite poles that are otherwise widely apart. When the husband and the lover cannot be the same person, two men intersecting in the life of a woman becomes inevitable. A lover encroaching on marital life, causing drama, adventures, and consequences is a constant trope in the narrative of cuckoldry. Thus, the contest between lovers and husbands in the Arabian Nights often works to the disadvantage of the husbands who are easily deceived by their wives. What distinguishes cuckoldry from ordinary adultery is that it dares to bring husbands and lovers together, sometimes while the illicit sexual intercourse is performed. Cuckoldry by its very nature is the agency of women at the expense of their husbands. It is an adulterous act but with more amusements where the wife together with her lover derive great pleasure in deceiving and cuckolding her husband. Both men and women amuse themselves at the expense of the cuckolded husband, who is presented in the narrative as a fool, stupid, and deserving of the cuckoldry act.

The cuckolded husband is often presented as an old man, or much older than his wife. This age difference between husbands and wives furnishes a background to, and a contributing factor in, the recourse to cuckoldry. It is suggested that this age difference might contribute to sexually deprived or unsatisfied young wives married to old men. Cuckoldry then provides not only compensatory, or at least complementary, sexual pleasure for the wife, but also a tool for subverting the marital order predicated on age and unequal power between spouses. Cuckoldry thus functions as a punishment, of the husband, for the many vices of marriage and unfulfilled expectations in marital life. Furthermore, tales of cuckoldry show that sexuality during the medieval time is so alluring and inexorable that an age difference does not stand in the way of seeking and obtaining sexual pleasure.

Cuckoldry functions as a rationale for the narrative of the Arabian Nights. The frame story of the two brothers, *Shahryar and His Brother*, contains an explicit motif of cuckoldry. During their journey, the kidnapped bride forces them to make love to her next to her jinni abductor. Even though they were deprived of their subjectivity, they nevertheless did cuckold the mighty demon, as the slaves in their palaces cuckolded them by having sexual access to their wives. Admittedly, the bride was not cuckolding her husband but her abductor in revenge for kidnapping her on her wedding night. Yet, one still wonders of the possibility that the two wives performed their act of cuckoldry with conscious awareness of it being a deliberate revenge against the way they were situated in their particular gender reality, for instance, the harem situation. By establishing a nexus between cuckoldry and retribution, cuckoldry becomes a deliberate gender politics. The cuckoldry acts by the bride become her politics of dealing with her situation of incarceration and, consequently, a routinized aspect of her life. This normalized life of cuckoldry is symbolized by the collection of seal rings, demanded from every male she forces to participate with her in the politics, or game, of cuckoldry.

Moreover, this narrative shows that cuckoldry could lead to further cuckoldry and the cuckolded can become a cuckolder, as was the case with the two brother kings. After being cuckolded by the black slaves, they eventually had the opportunity to cuckold other males. By doing this, the cycle of cuckoldry comes to a close where a man is situated as both active and passive in relation to cuckoldry, which becomes an inevitable and integral part of sexual life. Yet, cuckoldry in this situation is also related to hierarchy. The black slave is inferior to the king, in the double sense of being black and slave, which makes his cuckoldry an even worse transgression. On the other hand, the king cuckolded a jinni who is inferior to the human despite his mightiness. This hierarchy of cuckoldry could perhaps explain why Shahryar would not resign to his fate even after cuckolding the demon. This cycle of cuckoldry and the space created for cuckoldry in return does not seem to have helped Shahryar to overcome his predicament or soothe his anger and sense of victimization at the hands of his wife. Rather, turning into a killing machine appears to be the only possible revenge for cuckoldry for the emotional and severely wounded king.

Deceitfulness and Cunning

Sexual perfidy is strongly associated with the use of cunning, particularly by women. The son of a wealthy merchant, in *House with the Belvedere*, travels to Baghdad and rents a house. One day an old woman passes by and asks him if he has already seen the upper storey and the balcony. He climbs the stairs and reaches a roof terrace, from where he sees a beautiful woman in the adjoining house. He asks the old woman to arrange a meeting with her. She agrees and instructs him to buy a face veil from a certain merchant's shop. The merchant turns out to be the young woman's husband. The old woman takes the veil, burns one of the corners, and goes to the house of the merchant, pretending to look for a place to perform her prayers. Before leaving, she slips the veil under a cushion. The merchant finds it and, suspecting his wife of adultery, sends her to her mother. The old woman visits her there and promises to reconcile her with her husband. Under the pretext of going to a wedding, she then takes her to the young man's house, where the couple spend seven delightful nights. Then the young man is instructed to go to the shop and, when the old woman walks by, ask her about the veil, to allay the suspicion of the merchant. In this way, the woman is reunited with her husband, and the adultery has been performed cunningly.

Another version of the tale appears in *Crone and the Draper's Wife*. A draper is married to a beautiful woman. A young man desires her and asks an old woman to help him arrange a meeting and she advises him to buy some turban cloth and burn it in two places. Dressed as a devotee, she enters the house of the woman under some pretext and leaves the cloth behind. When her husband finds the cloth he becomes suspicious, and his wife asks the old woman to help her. She sends the young man to her house to mend the cloth, and he has sexual intercourse with the woman. Then they think up a ruse to dispel the husband's suspicion by letting him know that the old woman left the turban there. Conspicuously, the wife in both tales is ready for adultery, engaging in it unreflectively and without hesitation. Interestingly, there is a suspicion when no adultery is committed and trusting when it did happen. Does the suspicion of adultery inadvertently contribute to an adulterous act?

A man gives his wife a dirham with which to buy some rice, in *Woman Who Made Her Husband Sift Dust*. The rice merchant seduces her and lets his servant secretly fill her sacks with sand and stones. When the woman returns home, her husband is surprised to find the sack is filled with dust. The woman immediately thinks up a plausible story, pretending that she lost the dirham and therefore took the soil from the spot. This story represents a casual adulterous affair, but the responsiveness of the woman is unmistakeable. She cheats on her husband, yet insists on inventing a story even when she becomes aware that the merchant cheated her with her purchases. A man brings his wife a fish, in *Woman's Trick Against Her Husband*, and asks her to prepare it. She puts the fish in a jar of water and goes to a wedding party together with a lover. She stays away for a whole week, during which time her husband looks for her everywhere. When she returns home to receive the scolding from her husband, she takes the fish out of the jar alive and pretends that she has been away for only a short while. The neighbours cannot believe that the fish has stayed alive for a whole week, and they believe her.

Oblivious of the adulterous affairs of his wife, a man in Cairo, in *Woman Who Humoured Her Lover at Her Husband's Expense*, boasts about his wife's virtue, obedience, and piety. One day the woman promises her lover a baked goose, and asks her husband to invite his friends for a meal and has him slaughter two geese. She lets her lover have the prepared geese, and when her husband returns with a friend, she sends him away to fetch more guests. Meanwhile, she frightens his friend by telling him that her husband intends to cut off his testicles, and the man runs away in horror. When the husband returns with more guests, his wife pretends that his friend took the geese and ran away. He follows the man, shouting that he should at least let him have one, thinking of the geese while the friend is thinking of his testicles. A similar trope appears in Middle Eastern folkloric tradition. One day a traveller asks for a shelter, and the host asks his wife to cook a couple of chickens for the guest. Smelling the rich steam, the woman could not resist tasting the food and soon nothing is left. The woman informs the guest that whenever a guest arrives, her husband has the habit of cutting off their ears and roasting them over the fire for her son to eat. The guest escapes and when her husband asks why the guest was running away, she replied that he has snatched the chickens out of the pot and run away. The husband gives a chase, shouting, 'Let me have one, at least; you may keep the other!' (Bushnaq 1986: 33).

A young man falls in love with a married woman of unsurpassed beauty, in *Wife's Device to Cheat Her Husband*. As she is chaste, she refuses to comply with his advances. When her husband is on a journey, he approaches an old woman for help. The old woman feeds a dog with peppered meat so that its eyes shed tears. She then visits the woman and tells her that the dog is actually an enchanted girl who once rejected a man who loved her. Fearing that she will be enchanted too, the woman now concedes. At this point, the old woman cannot find the young man and takes another man from the street to her house. When the woman notices that the man the old woman has brought to be united with her is none other than her own husband, she starts screaming. In this manner, she avoids being suspected herself, and her husband is forced to swear that he has never been unfaithful to her. This story also appears in the medieval literature about the cunning of women (*Jins-al ʿinda al-arab* 1997 I: 94–5).

In *Confectioner, His Wife, and the Parrot*, a merchant who travels frequently buys a parrot for his beautiful wife, who he loves and guards jealously. The woman is in a secret relationship with a young man who comes to her house whenever the husband is absent. The parrot reveals their secret to the husband, but she denies the accusation by blaming him for believing a bird that has no brain. Later on, she contrives a ruse to discredit the parrot's talk. The next time her husband is away, the lovers, while covering the cage, produce a counterfeit thunderstorm by pouring out water, making noise, and producing flashes of light. The parrot informs its master about the storm, which makes him angry because the weather was fine. His wife insists on killing the parrot for deceiving him, which he does. The husband eventually discovers her adultery and slaughters her. He swears that he will never marry a woman again in his life.

The king of Isfahan's favourite concubine, in *Adulteress Who Tested Her Husband's Trust*, falls in love with a young silk merchant and has him smuggled into the harem in a trunk. Suddenly the king enters and wants to inspect the trunk. She tells him that her lover is inside, and when he becomes furious, she pretends that it was only a test of his trust. She permits him to open the trunk, but now the king wants to demonstrate that he also trusts her and leaves without inspecting. In *Shoemaker's Wife*, the shoemaker does not want his wife to leave the house, for he suspects her of visiting her lover and, therefore, he binds her to a pillar. When he goes to sleep, his wife convinces her neighbour to take her place for a while. When the man wakes up and calls for his wife, the other woman does not dare to respond in order not to betray herself. He wants to teach her a lesson and cuts off the tip of her nose, still thinking her to be his wife. When his wife returns from her lover, she again changes places with her neighbour and then asks God to perform a miracle in restoring her nose. As her husband has witnessed the 'miracle', he confesses to having been wrong about her.

In *Captain of Police*, a man in Egypt is appointed a captain of police. He asks an old woman to search for a bride for him, and she brings him a fat woman with whom he is satisfied. The woman soon takes their neighbour as a lover, and one night they are caught in the act. She hides her lover and tells her husband the story of her own adultery, blindfolding him with her veil so that her lover can escape. The king's executioner, in *Lady and Her Two Lovers*, sends his servant to a married woman he loves. The servant seduces the woman when suddenly his master arrives at the house. The woman hides the young man in an underground chamber. The executioner makes love to her, but suddenly her husband knocks on the door. She tells her lover to take his sword and curse and threaten her when her husband enters, then leave the house in a rush. She informs her husband that the fellow was chasing a young man who had fled to the house and hidden in the underground chamber. In this way, she saves all her lovers and even earns the praise of her husband.

Curiously, women have used cunning even to rescue their adulterous husbands from trouble. A married man is in love with the judge's daughter, in *Muhammad the Shalabi and His Mistress and His Wife*. While the lovers are having a romantic meeting, a police officer surprises them and puts them in jail. His wife disguises herself as a male slave, visits them in prison, and exchanges clothes with the lover, who escapes in men's clothes. When the chief of police reports the case to the sultan, the judge's daughter is found peacefully in her home, and the supposed culprits turn out to be husband and wife, 'mistakenly' detained by the police.

Cunning is not an exclusive domain for women, however, as the following stories implicate men too. A man called Khalbas, in *Khalbas and His Wife and the Learned Man*, is married to a beautiful woman who has a lover. In their neighbourhood lives a learned man who also has a beautiful wife. The lover tells Khalbas that he is in love with the learned man's wife and asks him to attend the assemblies in the scholar's house and speak up loudly toward the end of each session in order to warn him, to which he agrees, and during the assemblies, the lover stays with Khalbas's wife unnoticed. After some time, however, the scholar becomes suspicious and prevents him from speaking up, in order to check on his own wife. It turns out that the scholar's wife is innocent, while Khalbas has been fooled all the time.

A merchant is married to a beautiful woman, in *King's Son and the Merchant's Wife*. To protect her from the covetous eyes of other men, he builds a pavilion for her outside the town. One day, a prince passes by and sees the woman. He writes a letter to her and shoots it into the pavilion with an arrow. She responds to his letter, and he asks her to pull up a thread with a key fastened to it. He then hides inside a trunk that is deposited in the merchant's pavilion. The woman opens the trunk with the key she has previously been given, and the two enjoy blissful sexual intimacy for some time. When the king requests his son's presence, arrangements are made to have the trunk taken from the merchant's house. As it happens, the trunk falls open during transport and the secret is discovered. Interestingly, this story conveys the message that secluding women for fear of adultery is a botched strategy and that suspicion of women often leads to contrary outcomes, which is also a valid lesson for modern Middle Eastern societies.

Youth Who Would Futter His Father's Wives is a story where erotica is intersected with adultery, ethical incest, cunning, violence, and killing. A certain good-for-nothing son has the habit of seducing his father's wives. Whenever his father marries, the son would seduce his wife, and when his father discovers the fact, he would divorce her and take another wife. One day his father marries a particularly beautiful woman and when he is away on a journey, the son conceives a ruse. He kneels with his backside up in the air and pretends that this posture is healthy, as it allows the air to enter the body. When the wife is impressed by his expertise and imitates him, he points out that her second opening should be blocked, and he volunteers to take care of that himself. When his father finds out about the trick, he again divorces his wife. To prevent his son from behaving so boldly, the father now marries two women at the same time. As he is about to go to town one day, he realizes that he has forgotten his shoes. Meeting his son at that very moment, he sends him home to fetch the shoes. The son pretends to the women that his father ordered him to make love to both of them. When they do not believe his words, he calls to his father, asking if he meant both or only one. The father replies, 'Both!' and the two women give in. The women enjoy his youthful vigour, and from then on, the son regularly has sexual intercourse with both of them. When one day they are having fun together, the father returns home early and catches them in the perfidious act. He has them all arrested, and while the young man is executed on the spot, the two women are later strangled.

A certain notable, in *Page Who Feigned to Know the Speech of Birds*, buys a male servant at the slave market. One day the servant overhears his master telling his wife that she should go and divert herself in the garden. The servant hides food and drink in the garden and accompanies her the next day. He pretends to understand the language of birds, who tell him where he can find food and drink. As the woman trusts him, he then makes her believe that the birds urge him to have sexual intercourse with her, and she lets herself be persuaded. When the woman's husband surprises them having sexual intercourse, they pretend that she is lying on the ground because she has fallen from a tree. Not only is cunning used in committing adultery, but also in discovering adultery. In *Lover Exposed by Way of a Special Perfume*, a merchant approaches a king with a complaint that he had deposited some money with his wife, who later pretended that the money was stolen. The king gives the man a flask of a very special perfume and tells him to present it to his wife, expecting that she will give it to her lover. The king orders that his men should watch the city gates and detect the smell of the perfume. In this way, the lover is finally caught.

Drugging the Husband

Drugging the husband to commit adultery is also part of the cunning used in this collection of tales. In *Ensorcelled Prince*, a prince is happily married to his cousin for five years, but one day he overhears a conversation between two of his slave-girls pitying him for having a deceitful wife. They tell each other how poor their master is, who is wasting his youth with his accursed *qahba*, harlot wife, who gives him a sleeping potion each night and then leaves him to visit her lover until dawn while their master is unaware and fast asleep. They say, 'May God curse all unfaithful and adulteresses!' When the prince hears this conversation, the light in his eyes becomes darkness, and the following night, he pretends to drink the potion and falls asleep. He hears his wife saying, 'Sleep out your night and never rise again, by Allah, I hate you and I hate your image, I am tired of your company and I do not know when God will take away your life!' Then she puts on her best dress, perfumes herself, and leaves the house, secretly followed by the prince.

He sees his wife with a fat-lip black slave, lying upon a bed of sugarcane refuse and wrapped in an old cloak and a few rags, who starts to reproach her for being late. She replies, 'Oh my lord and my love and solace of my eyes, do not you know that I am married to my cousin whom I hate his look and abhor his company?' The lover swears that if she is ever late again, he will terminate their company and never stick his body on her, cursing her as a stinking bitch, the most despicable of whites. She stands weeping and humbling herself to him, saying, 'O my love and fruit of my heart, if you are angry with me, who is left for me, and if you reject me, who shelters me, oh my beloved and light of my eyes?' She is overjoyed when he forgives her and asks if there is anything to eat, to which he says there are cooked rats' bones and a little millet beer left. After eating and drinking, she undresses and joins him in his bed naked. Her husband, who is watching what is happening, first intends to kill them both. He strikes the slave with his sword, but he only wounds him, returning to his palace without harming his wife, who did not have a chance to recognize who the interloper was.

Dressed in mourning clothes, his wife returns to the palace and tells him that she received news that her parents and brothers have died, and therefore she needs to weep and lament. After a year of mourning, she requests that he should build for her a tomb within the palace to be called the house of lamentations, and she transports the slave to this place when it is ready. She visits him morning and evening and weeps and moans over him, and this continues for another couple of years. One day, when his patience has finally run out, the prince enters the tomb to find her weeping and reciting verses, and in his turn, he recites verses of wrath. Hearing this, she rises to say, 'Oh you dog, it was you who did this to me, wounding the beloved of my heart, and wasted his youth, and he is for three years neither dead nor alive!' He replies, 'O the foulest of whores and filthiest of the fucked women who are enamoured with slaves; it was indeed I who did this!' The prince draws his sword to kill her, but she is faster and being a powerful sorceress she petrifies his lower half into stone and then enchants his kingdom into a lake inhabited by coloured fish. Every day, she strips him, gives him a hundred lashes with a whip, so that the blood runs down and his shoulders are torn, while he is too paralysed to defend himself, and then dresses him with a shirt of haircloth to increase his affliction. In the end, the two lovers are killed, the prince and his kingdom are back to their normal state, and the prince marries another woman. The story highlights a dynamic drama of the intersecting relationships with a lover and a husband in the life of a woman. The wife of the king of China, in *Merchant's Daughter Who Married the King of China*, used to drug her husband at night and have an adulterous affair with a lover in a royal garden outside the city. The king kills the queen and her lover and marries the girl who had witnessed the adulterous acts. Drugging the husband is also employed in *Qamar al-Zaman and the Jeweller's Wife*.

Husbands, Lovers, and Treachery

A foolish man, in *Numskull Who Does Not Count the Ass He Is Sitting on*, rents ten donkeys to sell wheat. He rides on one of the donkeys and drives the others before him. As he counts only nine donkeys, he steps down from the one he is riding, and now he counts ten and is satisfied, but when he climbs on the donkey's back, he counts nine again. In a similar way, he counts the side rooms of his house as being three instead of four. His wife then makes him believe that one of the side rooms left to visit his beloved. He sets out in pursuit of the missing room. When he arrives at the mill, the miller, who is one of his wife's lovers, tells him to rest, as the side room will surely pass by. When the fool is fast asleep, the miller shaves off his beard. As the fool wakes up, they make him believe that someone stole his beard. He is told to stay with the miller for thirty days until the person who took his beard returns. After thirty days, his beard has grown again and he is satisfied. Now his wife announces that she will go to visit her sister. Instead, she goes to visit her lover and returns only after a week. When her husband complains about her long absence, she argues that she was away for only an hour, since she left on Friday and returned on Friday.

In *Fuller and His Wife and the Trooper*, a fuller is married to a beautiful woman whose lover is a soldier. The soldier rents the adjoining house and digs a tunnel to his lover's house. She tells her husband that her sister, who looks exactly like herself, has come to live next door. They manage to deceive the fuller, and when he is asleep, they dress him in a military uniform. The woman pretends not to know who he is, and the other fullers do not recognize him. Finally, the fuller travels to Isfahan to join his regiment, as instructed in a letter he finds in his pocket. In *Qadi-Mule*, a tax collector in Egypt is often obliged to leave his house, and so his wife has taken a lover. One day, when the husband is away at the market to buy some provisions, the lover takes the husband's mule to sell it. When the husband returns, his wife makes him believe that the mule was actually an enchanted *qadi*, judge. She instructs him to go to the court and lure the *qadi*-mule back to the house. When the husband does as he is told, the *qadi* thinks he is mad and gives him some money with which to buy a new mule. However, the husband goes to the market and sees his own mule, but he refuses to buy it again.

A poor man and his wife have a beautiful daughter, in *Qadi and the Ass's Foal*. A judge asks for the girl's hand in marriage, and although he is extremely ugly, the proposal is accepted. He has a young and handsome clerk who becomes the young woman's lover. One day, the judge falls ill and returns home early. His wife puts him in bed and goes to the bathhouse. In the meantime, her lover enters the house and slips into bed, thinking that his beloved is lying there. The judge is deeply shocked, grabs him, and locks him up in a chest. He then goes to the bathhouse and tells the women to send his wife out. On hearing this, she disguises herself and leaves the bathhouse without being seen. At home, she manages to release her lover from the chest and puts an ass's foal inside instead. She returns to the bathhouse and comes out to meet her husband, who is furious. The husband takes along four witnesses and opens the chest. When the foal appears, everyone thinks that he has gone mad. The husband is so outraged that he drops dead on the floor. While this tale displays a remarkable talent of cunning on the part of the wife, it is also explicit that this marriage is a mismatch between her beauty and the ugliness of her husband. The poverty of the parents leaves them little choice but to accept marrying off their daughter to an established high-ranking judge, despite his extreme ugliness. The outcome of adultery and cuckoldry is hardly surprising in the context of this marital bonding.

When her husband is away, in *Cairene Youth, the Barber and the Captain*, a captain's wife sends an invitation to her lover, who is having a shave at the barber's shop. The lover goes to her house while the barber follows him, insisting that he return to his shop to finish his shave. The captain returns home sooner than expected and notices the barber in front of his house. The barber asks him to send the young man out of the house and the captain is enraged. Inside, the lover hides in the shaft of the cistern and cannot be found. As the captain rummages about the house several times in a rage, the barber finally offers to help him. Just as the barber suggests that he should inspect the cistern, the captain's wife reproaches him for believing such a stupid fellow. Now the barber is kicked out of the house, and afterward, the captain and his wife enjoy themselves with sexual intercourse. When the captain has fallen asleep, the young man escapes from the house, and the barber is given a beating.

A young man in Hamadan, in *Singer and the Druggist*, is highly skilled in singing to the lute. Travelling to another town, he meets a druggist who gives him advice about ways to become famous. While he tours around the city, a beautiful woman invites him into her house: 'What do you say about meat and drink and the enjoyment of a lovely face, and getting some money?' They eat, drink, and make love. Thereupon, she sits in his lap and they play, laugh, and exchange kisses until the day is half gone. When her husband comes home, she hides the singer in a mat in which she rolls him up. When the husband sees the disorder in the room and the smell of liquor, he questions his wife about it, but she replies that she had a drink with her female friend who has just left. When her husband leaves the house for his shop, the lovers return to their pleasant time until evening when she gives him money for pleasing her sexually and asks him to come back the next day. The first thing the singer does on the following day is to visit the druggist in his shop to tell him about his adventure with the woman and her horned cuckolded husband, and the druggist suspects the woman to be his own wife. That day he comes home early to check on his wife, but she has hidden her lover in a chest. This goes on with different hiding places for some days, and the singer always escapes safely and tells the druggist about his adventures, who is convinced that his house is the scene of the adulterous adventures but always fails to catch them together. Finally, when forced one day to escape over the roof, a neighbouring Persian catches him but he escapes a severe beating for being a suspected thief, only by proving he is a talented singer.

Using cunning to commit adultery while the husband is watching is a motif pertinent to the Arabian Nights collection of tales. In *Wife and Her Two Lovers*, a man is married to a beautiful woman who has two lovers, a melon farmer, and an oil merchant. The oil merchant requests the woman to arrange for him to have dinner together with both her and her husband. The woman organizes a meal in the dark in which he participates in secret. When he is discovered, the woman pretends that he must have been hiding inside the dish her husband has just bought. On her husband's advice, she agrees to guard him until they can return him the next morning. While her husband is sleeping, she visits her lover in his room and spends the night with him. The melon farmer wishes to make love to her while her husband is watching. The wife proposes to her husband that they visit some of her relatives, and on the way, she wants to rest in a melon field and asks him to pick a melon. When he does so without asking permission, the melon farmer gets angry and demands that he restore the melon to its stalk. As the husband is unable to comply, he suggests acquitting him by having sexual intercourse with him. When the man rejects the suggestion, the farmer agrees to have intercourse with the wife as compensation. While he does so, he orders the man to hold up his balls, explaining that should they touch the ground, his field would go dry. The man does exactly the opposite, believing that he has ruined the melon farmer. The *Arabian Nights Encyclopedia* (Marzolph and Leeuwen 2004 I: 447) refers to another jocular medieval Middle Eastern tale where the cowardly husband aims to insult his wife's lover by having sex with his own wife.

During an outing in a garden, in *Simpleton Husband*, a woman climbs a tree and pretends to witness her husband making love to a woman before her own eyes. When he denies this, she urges him to climb the tree and see for himself. Then the lover appears and starts making love to the woman before the eyes of the watching husband. When he climbs down from the tree, the lover quickly hides. This trick is repeated several times until the husband believes that the place must be enchanted by a jinni. In another version of the tale, a woman digs a hole in a tent in a garden where she hides the lover and has her husband climb a tree. While he is watching, she makes love to her lover. When the husband protests, she makes believe that the place is enchanted, climbs a tree and mockingly pretends to see her husband making love to a woman.

Using a trick of sight to commit adultery while the husband is watching appears also in medieval European literature. A bawdy, humorous medieval French fabliau narrates that a priest arrives at his lover's house; he yells out that he can see her and her husband having sex through the open window. The husband replies that they are only eating, but the priest swears he sees them having sex. The husband changes places with the priest and to his shock, sees the priest making love to his wife. When he cries out, the priest assures him he is only eating. The husband is befuddled by the magic window that seems able to transpose the acts of eating and sex to the watcher (Harper 2008: 86).

The story of *Masrur and Zayn al-Mawsif* is an interesting narrative of a married woman who goes to great lengths in cunningly using her beauty, sexuality, and interfaith tensions to get rid of her merchant husband and to live happily with her merchant lover. One night the Christian merchant Masrur has a dream in which a bird of prey snatches from his hands a dove that he likes very much. The next day, he walks on the street and hears a woman recite a poem. He looks into her garden and is overwhelmed by the scent, the sounds, and the woman's beauty. To introduce himself, he asks for some water and starts a conversation. The woman, Zayn al-Mawsif, tells him that she is married to a Jewish merchant who is away on a journey, that she had a dream the night before in which she was being abducted by a bird. The overlap in their dreams confirms their bond, and Masrur accepts her invitation to share her meal. Then the woman challenges him to play chess with her for money. Enchanted by the delicacy of her wrist, he loses each game and eventually owes her all his possessions. When he becomes desperate, the woman finally gives in to his amorous and lustful wishes. She restores to him everything he has lost and thinks up a plan to mislead her husband. He is to pretend that he wants to do business with her husband and win his confidence. When the husband returns and Masrur approaches him, he soon becomes suspicious, particularly since the mockingbird he keeps in his house appears to be familiar with Masrur. Moreover, his wife in her sleep talks about her lover. When the husband is certain about the relationship of the two, he sells his possessions and departs together with his wife.

When he learns what has happened, Masrur is stricken with grief. He visits the house where his beloved used to live and reads the poems she has written on the doors. Knowing her whereabouts, he sends her passionate letters. When her husband finds out that the couple is corresponding with each other, he has his wife locked up and put in fetters. Now the blacksmith who has made the fetters falls in love with her and sings her praise just as the *qadi* is passing by his workshop. The *qadi* summons her to court and falls in love with her, and the judges of the other law schools follow his example. Using her charm and beauty, she manipulates the judges to her advantage. The judges accuse the husband of having married her illegally and jail him accordingly. Meanwhile, she manages to sneak out of town to return to her beloved. On the way, she visits a monastery where all the monks become infatuated with her, and she has to find a way to escape their advances. When she is finally reunited with her beloved, she learns that her husband has been released and thus schemes a ruse to get rid of him for good. Pretending that she has died, her slave-girl takes the husband to the cemetery. She then pushes him down into an empty grave and buries him alive. The lovers enjoy a happy life together, far away from the incongruous husband.

IO

LESBIAN ENCOUNTER

Lesbian desire in the narrative of the thousand and one Nights is more ambiguous and less explicit than, for instance, pederasty. While this narrative is essentially reverberating medieval erotic literature, yet there is a scant inclusion of female same-sex yearning in the intertextuality. Medieval treatises contain many anecdotes about lesbian love and same-sex intimacy. These anecdotes associate lesbian love principally, if not exclusively, with tribadism, *musahaqa*, and with cultural refinement, *zarf*. These narrations imply a rather more enduring lesbian affection, expressing a distinct subculture identity. The first known lesbian couple emerged in the seventh century in Iraq. Females cross-dressing as men was a widespread phenomenon during the Abbasid period, known as *ghulamiyyat*. Medieval Arabo-Islamic literature is full of anecdotes about female same-sex attachments and cross-gender dressing (Amer 2009: 218–19; 2012: 388–9; Boswell 1989: 15–16; Bullough 1996: 224–5; Burton 2010; Clot 1986: 157–8; Cuffel 2007; Guthrie 2001: 198; Habib 2007: 65; Irwin 1994: 122; 1999: 159–77; P. Kennedy 2007: 18; Kugle 2010: 242; Malti-Douglas 2001: 134; Naaman 2013: 356; Nasr al-Katib 1977: 88; Reynolds 2006b: 250–1; Roth 1996: 322; Rowson 1991: 68). In fact, the richness of medieval erotic anecdotes might disprove the contention of Foucault (1990), and others, that homosexual identity, and the very conceptualization of sexuality, is a modern construct. Comparative sexuality, i.e. comparing different sexual partners or different modes of sexuality, which was part of the medieval canonical literature and the Arabian Nights regarding pederasty, has no space in the narratives related to lesbianism in the Arabian Nights.

However, the Arabian Nights presents lesbian encounters as accidental, temporary, distracting, and disruptive sexuality. It portrays female same-sex desire as antagonistic to the culturally legitimate heterosexual love. Lesbian love is not seen as having an independent existence from heterosexuality, or a parallel liaison to it as is the case with tales of pederasty. It is always depicted in relatedness to heterosexuality, in a correlation of tension and disharmony. Tales of lesbian love are presented either in a context of the conflict with heterosexual love, and thus an obstacle, negative, and deflective, or in a context of otherness where opponents are lesbianized, a pejorative and insulting connotation. Lesbian fantasies and experiences are condemned and presented as casual, accidental, innocent, and trivial. Real lesbian partners and mutual commitment to a serious female homosexual relationship have no space in the narrative. However, the Arabian Nights is not unique in this regard. No evidence of lovemaking between women or of women kissing and embracing each other has surfaced in the medieval Nordic literature (Jochens 1996: 390). Murray (1996b: 191) comments that studying lesbianism in historical perspective is not an easy task for many reasons: 'Of all groups within medieval society lesbians are the most marginalized and least visible. All the difficulties attendant upon the study of female sexuality and male homosexuality are exacerbated in the case of medieval lesbians. These difficulties are theoretical, methodological, and evidential.'

Lesbian Experiences

Some stories of the Thousand and One Nights narrate a tolerant presentation of female same-sex desire, albeit with some reservation and negativity. In *Khalifa the Fisherman of Baghdad*, Caliph Harun al-Rashid has bought Qut al-Qulub, a beautiful and well-educated slave-girl. The caliph becomes so infatuated with her that he deserts his wife, Zubayda, and his entire collection of concubines, and locks himself with the new girl for a whole month, except for the Friday prayers. Zubayda becomes jealous and plans to get rid of the new rival. While the caliph goes on a hunting trip, she invites her for dinner. She is so stunned by her beauty, intelligence, recital of verses, and music playing that she almost becomes enamoured with her, saying that there is no blame on her husband to be in love with such a woman. Female beauty is a temptation not only for men but also for women. Royal women admiring female beauty also appears in *Hasan of Basra*. Women admiring female beauty, which may or may not imply lesbian fancies, is narrated when the jinniyah enters the public bath and the royal palace where all the attending women, including the caliph's wife, admire her extraordinary beauty.

A beautiful woman gives money to a constable, asking for help, in *First Constable's History*. She tells him that she is in love with the judge's daughter and needs his help getting into the house. She will wait in the street at night while he makes his nightly tour of inspection. As she does not have a place to stay, he should ask the judge to lodge her for the night. The next morning, however, the judge claims that the woman had stolen 6,000 dinars from his house. While this story contains no direct lesbian experience and presents a case of roguery, yet it is striking that pretence of lesbian love and desire is accepted and taken as a serious, or at least not out of the ordinary, thing.

In *Mahmud and His Three Sons*, Sulayman reaches the City of the Lovers, where everyone owns a garden and enjoys the pleasures of love. The vizier's son invites him to a social gathering where ten female singers are to talk about their sexual adventures. The first woman is used to being a lesbian, initiated into sex by rape. This story suggests a correlation between sexual violence, rape, and homosexuality. This connection implies that homosexuality is not a natural choice, but mainly induced by external factors, most importantly, sexual violence. Still, it is noteworthy that this narrative portrays lesbian experiences as part of the sexual configuration and landscape of sexuality. Revealing and talking about homosexuality seems to be socially accepted and tolerated. It is presented as a choice, among many choices of sexual desires. A female jinni who hates men abducts a woman shortly before her marriage, in *Damir and al-Anqa'*. Friendly jinn kill the abductor and rescue the woman. What would motivate the jinniyah in this kidnapping when women do not constitute the object of hate for her? Is it possible that there is a lesbian inclination in this narrative? While hating the opposite sex does not necessarily mean same-sex desire, yet it could possibly be the case in this story.

The following couple of tales present lesbian desire and experience in a context of the direct conflict with heterosexuality. A woman with a broken heart in Basra tells a boon companion a story about her unhappy love for a young man, in *Jubayr ibn 'Umayr and the Lady Budur*. One day while her slave-girl is combing her hair, the girl who admires her beauty bends her head and kisses the woman on the cheek. At that very moment, her lover suddenly enters the room. Angry to see someone else is sharing with him his beloved, he immediately departs reciting the verses,

> If in love, I must share with another one
> Then I leave my beloved and live alone.

Since that day, he has left her and refuses to communicate with her. This discord continues for a whole year until their love is finally resuscitated. However, this tale has a note of reconciliation in the end. While this rapprochement is desirable from the perspective of the two lovers, yet it obviously signifies the end of the lesbian fancy that has caused the commotion in the relationship. Thus, the triumph of heterosexuality is evidently communicated in the story. By contrast, the following story has no note of reconciliation, signalling a total demise of heterosexual love.

A beautiful but sad woman in Basra, in *Lovers of Basra*, reveals to a poet that she is in love with a young man who does not want her anymore. The woman has a slave-girl who was very fond of her. One day, the slave-girl, who was enamoured with her, threw herself on her with non-stop bites and pinches. The two women were playing about with each other, one time the slave-girl was on her, and another time she was on her slave-girl. With the effect of drink, the slave-girl untied the woman's underwear, and the underwear went down due to their interplay. While they were in that position, her male lover suddenly entered the house to see them in that situation. In consequence, he broke off all contacts with her. It has been for three years and the lover still refuses to talk to her, causing her to be in this wretched situation.

This is the only story in the collection of the Arabian Nights that depicts more details about female same-sex intimacy. Naturally, this intimacy could be a normal and a common case of female homosociality. Yet, the narrative in this story tends to induce the reader, and the listener, to speculate lesbian interaction in this case. However, even though the story is presenting just one occasion of lesbian intimacy, the fact that these two women share life together and live in the same house with daily contact might suggest a more durable physical intimacy than merely the single incident mentioned in the story. The high point of this juncture is that it comes into conflict with heterosexual attachment. Short of this confrontation, lesbian fantasies are not only going smoothly and unsuspected, but they also tend to provide pleasure for the partners. Obviously, pleasure is present in the sexual contact to warrant its durability. The fact that this intimacy is associated with drinking gives the experience some kind of normalcy and acceptance. While the slave-girl is making the advances, the young woman seems not only to be enjoying the outcome but reciprocating as well.

Nonetheless, there is a heavy price to be paid for lesbian transgression, illustrated in losing the only socially legitimate norm of sexual contact, heterosexual relationship. Consequently, the choice becomes either/or, with no space for bisexuality. Enjoying both sexual experiences is not tolerated, and sexuality has to be regimented through dominant heterosexuality. Accordingly, the young woman suffers because of the constrained sexual arrangement. The fact that she is forced to lose the prospect of the other form of sexuality, heterosexuality, makes the woman very depressed indeed. Likewise, losing the lesbian option would also make the woman depressed when and if she resumes the heterosexual liaison. The absence of one form

of sexuality tends to disturb the woman while she was living happily by
having both worlds of sexuality.

The story, however, is silent about what has subsequently happened to the
lesbian relationship. Most probably, it did not continue considering the state
of melancholy that the woman finds herself in because of losing her male
lover. While the woman is surely depressed for losing her male lover, it could
also be the case that she is miserable because she is denied the choice of
having and enjoying both, the heterosexual and the lesbian. She is unhappy
because she is forced to relinquish one form of sexuality for the benefit of
the other, which is against her wish to revel in both. This is particularly so
because the story clearly portrays the young woman to be enjoying the lesbian exploration and deriving real pleasure and happiness out of it. Yet, the
narrative not only denies the lesbian relationship the possibility of developing, but it also condemns lesbian homosexuality as a cause for misery and
suffering.

Thus, the previous two stories are more daring in presenting same-sex
fantasies. It is remarkable, however, that both stories of lesbian experiences
occur in Basra, a port town in the south of Iraq that is known for cultural
refinement and, accordingly, a natural place for open and expanded sexual
imagination. The poet tells the young woman, 'How does love not touch
you when you live in Basra?' It is true that he was referring to heterosexual
love, but the poet was not shocked by the details of the same-sex intimacy,
neither when he was listening to the woman nor when he himself was narrating the story to the caliph. Nevertheless, heterosexuality and homosexuality are brought together in these stories but only in disharmony and conflict.
These sexual inclinations are presented in a contest and mutually exclusive
arrangements. The one is negating the other, and never in coexistence since
there is room for only one form of sexuality. In this respect, the narrative is
unambiguous regarding which form of sexuality is socially expected to have
pre-eminence and permanency.

However, one wonders about the perspective of the male lover in the
stories. The lover is not deserting his beloved necessarily or solely because
she is engaging in lesbian relationships, a socially condemned sexual attachment. It is equally plausible that he is deserting her because someone else is
sharing the woman with him, as this is stressed in the recited verses. In that
case, it makes little difference whether the rival is a female or a male. Love
and sexuality are strongly related to monogamy and a kind of mutual own-
ership by the couple. Thus, promiscuity, regardless of gender, is the credible
cause of deserting the lover rather than the condemned lesbianism. Hence,
the conjunction of homosexuality with promiscuity is what causes distress

and confusion in romance and gender relationships. The lover was estranged from his lover not because he saw her accepting a kiss from her slave-girl, but he was hurt and scandalized by his sense of the exclusiveness proper to love (Gerhardt 1963: 132).

Thus, lesbian tendencies come in direct conflict with socially legitimized heterosexuality, with little vagueness as to the expected outcome of this tension. This tension, however, is well illustrated in the tale of *Three Unfortunate Lovers*. A man has a daughter who was in love with a young man, who in turn was in love with a singing girl, who in turn was in love with the man's daughter. One day the singing girl sang sad verses about unrequited love. The young man who was attending the performance and who was impressed by the beauty of the verses asked the singer whether she permits him to die. She said she would permit him to die if he is a true lover, and the man put his head on a pillow and died. When the man's daughter heard the news, she also put her head on a pillow and died. When the singing girl heard of this, she also died.

All the three lovers die in one day because of the misery brought out by unreciprocated love. The triangle of three lovers through a parallel and convergence of heterosexuality and homosexuality not only fails to ensure happiness but also causes agony and death. Thus, heterosexuality and homosexuality should not mix but instead should rather be separate. Bringing these two sexual experiences together is dysfunctional and one-sided. The three people that were involved in these relationships are not in harmony, but in a relationship of tension, negation, and mutual exclusivity. The only intersection in this regard is misery and death. While the main trope of this story is tragedy associated with unrequited love, it is also evident that same-sex love and desire is disastrous, risky, and dangerous, if not lethal.

Stigmatizing Lesbian Tendencies

Some stories in the Thousand and One Nights tend to associate lesbianism with derogatory language and social stigmatization. The narrative is demonizing lesbians and lesbianism, or put differently, 'lesbianizing' opponents, understood in a negative sense. Hasan marries a beautiful jinni-princess and takes her back home with him, in *Hasan of Basra*. She manages to return home with her children and her sister scolds her for marrying without their consent, marrying a human being, and for subsequently abandoning her husband and separating the children from their father. With the help of an old woman, Hasan eventually succeeds in taking them back home. The old woman requests that they should take her with them and not leave her with the callous, *fajira*, whore, and *musa-hiqa*, tribade lesbian sister. Moreover, encouragement of heterosexuality is strongly pronounced in this story. Hasan's foster-sister tries to convince the princess to marry Hasan by saying that women are created for men, and women cannot live without men. She adds, 'If we knew that women can live without men and if men are expendable in the lives of women, we would have discouraged him from his wish to marry you.' The old woman reiterates the same message.

In *Umar ibn al-Nu'man*, Dhat al-Dawahi swears to avenge the death of her granddaughter Princess Abriza, who had been raped by King al-Nu'man and was killed by one of his slaves, after failing to rape her. She disguises herself as a pious woman, manages to enter the palace, and wins the trust of al-Nu'man, enough to poison him. When his son returns to the kingdom, people at the palace tell him about the wicked woman who killed his father. They tell him that she is an accursed old woman, a witch of all witches, mistress in sorcery and deception. She is a crafty, debauched, and perfidious prostitute with bad breath, red eyelids, yellow cheeks, pale face, bleared eyes, leprous body, greyish hair, lumped back, faded complexion, and running nostrils. She is a plague of plagues and calamity of calamities, a corrupt unbeliever who has no religion. They continue to say that she mostly stays with her son King Hardub for having access to the virgin damsels of the palace, because she loves tribadism, *musahaqa*, and is unable to live without it. She teaches any damsel she fancies the skill of tribadism and rubs saffron on her until she faints away for excess of pleasure. She bribes damsels with jewels to tribade with her. She provides many favours on the damsel who complies with her and influences her son the king to desire the damsel as well. However, she schemes to destroy those damsels who repel her. Her granddaughter disdains her and hates to lie with her because of the ill smell from her armpits, the smell of her fart is worse than that of a carcass, and her body is coarser than palm fibre.

Thus, the Christian warrior Abriza used to have lesbian relationships with other women, including her grandmother. However, because of her love affair with a Muslim prince, her religious conversion to Islam secured the triumph of her heterosexual over lesbian orientation. This narrative resonates with medieval Arabic epics. Cuffel (2007: 138) argues that these women's 'incorrect' or incomplete sexuality in the form of lesbian behaviour mirrors their 'incorrect' or incomplete understanding of God. Just as Christianity was an intermediate step to Islam, so too was same-sex love between women a stage on the way to heterosexual love directed toward the Muslim male hero.

Transsexuality and Homosexual Intimacy

There are few stories in the Arabian Nights that directly portray the issue of transsexuality. A princess in India changed sex with a jinni, in *Sea Rose of the Girl of China*. However, when she later wanted to change it back the jinni refused, for discovering that sex for a female is more intense than for a male. The sultan of Egypt wants to kill a scholar, in *Shihab al-Din*, but he escapes by changing appearance with a slave-girl, who regains her true appearance only after she is beheaded.

Three stories in the collection tend to associate transsexuality with magic power and water. A magician arrives at the royal palace in Baghdad, in *Warlock and the Young Cook of Baghdad*. He changes a cauldron with water into a sea and transforms the vizier into a mermaid swimming in the sea. A fisherman catches the vizier, who eventually marries a young man and gives birth to seven children. As he jumps into the water again, he surfaces in the cauldron and finds the magician and the king waiting for him. The king of Egypt visits the house of a magician, in *Hasan the King of Egypt*. While refreshing himself in a basin of water, he suddenly finds himself transformed into a woman on an island. A Frankish boat picks him up, and he eventually marries the Frankish king and bears him a child. After giving birth, the woman goes to wash, and the king suddenly finds himself back in the magician's house. The accompanying vizier and imam go through the same experience. In *Enchanted Spring*, a jealous vizier takes a prince to a spring with magic power, knowing that any man who drinks from this spring will immediately change into a woman. A jinn-prince takes him to another spring and he changes back into a man after drinking water.

The *Arabian Nights Encyclopedia* (Marzolph and Leeuwen 2004 I: 175) states that the motif of the change of sex by means of contact with water is common to many cultures. In the popular belief of numerous cultures, water, in general, is supposed to possess magic qualities. Excitingly, these tales of transsexuality, magic, and water are the only narrative in the collection depicting male homosexuality, albeit indirectly, apart from the dominant theme of pederasty. While these experiences are performed via sex change and with the aid of magic, they still convey homosexual couples uniting in marriage and having children together. This is the only reference to a homosexual coupling in the tale collection.

The narrative of the Thousand and One Nights contains more stories about cross-gender dressing than about transsexuality per se. However, cross-dressing in this narrative is always done for tangible purposes, never for transsexual experiences as such. Cross-dressing is a literary device and not a statement of sexual preference (Irwin 1994: 171–2). The cross-gender dressing is related to gender spatial configuration and often leads to gender complications and consequences. Most of these tales narrate about women cross-dressing to men, indicating a lower social status of women relative to men. In this narrative, cross-dressing is a literary device enabling women to have wider access to public space with its power, status, wealth, ruling, and heroism.

Intriguingly, in all the stories of the Arabian Nights where a woman becomes a king because of cross-dressing, she ends up relinquishing the throne to her husband, lover, or brother. Thus, the gained power via cross-gender dressing proves to be transitory and the more legitimate male power is eventually restored. Hence, the challenge to social hierarchies that gender cross-dressing entails seems to be uncertain and ephemeral. By contrast, stories about men cross-dressing to women are much fewer and are mostly done to get access to women and the harem, a rather restricted, private, and inferior social and gender domain. The *Arabian Nights Encyclopedia* (Marzolph and Leeuwen 2004 II: 584–5) states that the main narrative asset of the harem is its sacrosanctity and inaccessibility. It is the quintessential enclosure, locking women in and excluding any interference from outside.

Cross-dressing and transvestic exploits prove to be instrumental in allowing the trespassing of the heavily controlled border between men and women (Epps 2008: 126). Smuggling lovers to the harem requires dressing them in women's clothing. In *Taj al-Muluk and the Princess Dunya*, an old woman dresses the prince in women's clothes, telling him to follow her, to sway from side to side, and to neither hasten in his walk nor take heed of any one speaking to him. For a whole month in the harem, the lovers are alone together passing the night in kissing, embracing, and coiling leg with leg, while their love is growing. A princess smuggles a prince into her apartment, disguised as a slave-girl, in *Ardashir and Hayat al-Nufus*, but a eunuch eventually discovers them and denounces them to the king. Smuggling into the harem appears in *Ni'ma and Nu'm*, *Lovers of Syria*, and *Three Sisters and Their Mother*. Marzawan disguises as a woman to have access to his foster-sister, in *Qamar al-Zaman and Budur*.

Other stories narrate other purposes for men dressing as a woman. In *Merchant's Daughter Who Married the King of China*, a king disguises himself as a woman and visits a merchant's daughter to find out the truth about his wife's infidelity. He eventually marries her. In *First Larrikin's History*, some tricksters deceive a man by paying him much less than what his calf is worth. To teach their leader a lesson, he dresses as a woman and joins the gang. As the leader prepares to spend the night with the presumed woman, he tricks him into binding himself and then gives him a heavy beating. The leader then goes to the bathhouse to recover from his wounds, and the larrikin enters disguised as a sick man and flogs the leader once again. Finally, he lures the tricksters away from their camp. When the camp is empty, he flogs the leader, who stays behind, for the third time. Then he leaves the country.

Women dressing up as men have more representation in the Arabian Nights. Suspecting their mother of committing perfidy, in *Salim and His Sister Salama*, Salama and her brother abandon home, dressed in men's clothes. During their journey, they are separated, and she becomes a king in a town and when she eventually reunites with her brother, she relinquishes the throne to him. Dressed as a man, a woman becomes a king and surrenders the throne to a husband or lover appears in *Qamar al-Zaman and Budur*, *Ali Shar and Zumurrud*, and *Devotee Accused of Lewdness*. In *Woman Who Regained Her Loss*, a woman decides to travel as a merchant and, dressed in men's clothes, sets out for Alexandria and Cairo. Soon she becomes rich. In *King's Son of Sind and the Lady Fatima*, Princess Fatima disguised as a man shows her command of the martial arts as a heroic fighter and she even captures the enemy king. The princess of Baghdad, in *Zunnar and the King of Iraq's Daughter*, dresses as a slave and travels to convince a proud king of their marriage. In *Two Viziers and Their Children*, two Bedouin women dress as men and travel to search for their husbands. *Sitt al-Banat and the King of Iraq's Son* is about a princess who dresses as a blacksmith to search for her lover.

Cross-dressing intersected with bestiality is narrated in *King's Daughter and the Ape. Muhammad of Damascus and Sa'd of Baghdad* is a story where cross-gender dressing is performed with the intention of exploiting pederastic tendencies to take revenge. The narrative about women dressed as men deciding to play a pederastic homoerotic game on their unsuspecting male lovers, yet ending in heterosexual intercourse, is found in three tales, *Qamar al-Zaman and Budur*, *Ali Shar and Zumurrud*, and *Fifth Captain's Tale*. In *Muhammad the Shalabi and His Mistress and His Wife*, the wife dresses up as a male slave and visits the prison where her husband and his lover are detained on charges of adultery. She gives the male clothes to the lover to escape from prison. The cunning associated with the double cross-gender dressing saves the lovers from the adultery charges, paradoxically, with the help of the wife.

Some stories narrate that cross-gender dressing could lead to indirect lesbian infatuation. A woman disguised as a man becomes friends with a princess, yet people accuse them of illicit sexual relation, in *Devotee Accused of Lewdness*. A daughter dresses up as a man and the princess falls in love with her, in *Three Sisters and Their Mother*. While being smuggled into the harem, she is caught and sentenced to death. However, it is discovered just in time that she is a woman. She is spared and the king marries her. Cross-gender dressing leading to suicide and death is presented in *Ameny*. Fleeing to Baghdad dressed as a man, Princess Ameny enters a cave, where she finds a young woman being harassed by a black slave for not yielding to his desires. She kills the slave, and the young woman says that she is a princess kidnapped by the slave who had previously killed her beloved cousin. They go to her town, and the woman asks Ameny, who is still dressed as a man, to marry her. When the marriage takes place, Ameny at first tells her that she has pledged chastity and finally reveals her identity. The princess kills herself and Ameny is sent away to be captured by robbers and sold as a slave. Two cousins are in love and elope together, in *Lovers of Syria*. After they are accidentally separated, the young woman reaches a town disguised as a man and becomes a king. She consents to a marriage with the vizier's daughter to avoid revealing her identity. She does not initially touch her but eventually opts to tell her secret. She finally marries her lover.

Dressed as a man, Princess Budur marries Princess Hayat al-Nufus, in *Qamar al-Zaman and Budur*. After avoiding her for a while, Budur reveals her identity and the bride keeps the secret, and they feign virginal blood to show her parents. When Budur and her husband are reunited, Hayat al-Nufus becomes the second wife. In the relationship between Budur and Hayat, Matarasso (1982: 38) connotes that Budur giving herself over to accomplishing erotic desires with her partner corresponds to her ambivalence and bisexuality. This sexual polymorphism expresses a variable combination of homosexuality and heterosexuality and a libidinal plasticity with a multitude of erotic possibilities. Amer (2007, 2008) overenthusiastically and with unwarranted certainty argues that the two princesses establish a lesbian relationship and that the ultimate outcome of heterosexual marriage has integrated, rather than negated, the lesbian liaison. She upholds that the lesbian relation is embedded in the polygamous household of the harem (2008: 157) and 'is maintained at the end of the tale under the cover of the harem, "protected" by the socially and politically legitimizing polygamous marriage' (108). Thus, Amer subscribes to Matarasso's reading of the narrative and goes even further. It seems that this is an inaccurate reading of the text, where some predetermined convictions are enforced to reach an implausible and hasty conclusion. On the other hand, Amer (:157) also states that Budur not only abdicates in his favour but she offers him a second wife; the cross-dressed woman remains ultimately subordinated to traditional gender hierarchy and the upholding of heteronormativity. Binary heterosexual relations are upheld and validated in the end (2007: 111).

Rather than forming a lesbian couple, Budur and Hayat are trapped as husband and wife in a matrimonial heterosexual sense. They end up becoming co-wives sharing one common husband where intimacy is centred on a man rather around them as a couple. The polygamous marriage is the initiative of Budur, telling Hayat, 'You too will be his wife.' For these women, the polygamous marriage seems to be an optimal solution to the bizarre situation they find themselves trapped in, which is contrary to the claim of a normal, happy lesbian couple. Abdicating the throne to her husband and playing an instrumental role in establishing a polygamous marriage tends to dispel, rather than assert, the claimed lesbian agency of Budur. The fake virginity blood is a show performed for the benefit of the parents in a context of the patriarchal conception of female honour. By preserving the virginity of Hayat to her real, heterosexual husband, both women demonstrate their adherence to the established code of honour, rather than challenging it. Moreover, both women heavily invest in seeking incestuous liaisons with their stepsons, which is a fact that furnishes further demonstration of having heterosexual rather than lesbian interest and inclination. Surprisingly, this episode of incest is completely missed in Amer's analysis despite its relevance to the discussion. In fact, revealing their incestuous adventures has led to their disgrace, rejection, and insignificance, which is contrary to the claim of a proud and happy lesbian life.

Thus, there is little justification for the claim of a lesbian couple in this story. A more acceptable reading would establish the relationship to be no different from those in any other stories narrating complexities resulting from the cross-gender dressing. In fact, the narrative is clear about a relationship of homosociality between the women. Hayat says that she would have been happier if Budur was her brother. Budur asks, 'And if I were your sister, would you have loved me as much?' to which she replies, 'Even more. I would have always been with you, slept with you, in the same bed with you.' This clearly indicates a case of sisterly bonding, a kind of homosociality between siblings, cousins, and friends, which is still considered normal social behaviour in Middle Eastern cultures even today. Likewise, co-wives and the harem often form homosocial bonding. To be sure, the boundaries between homosociality and homosexuality are perhaps more fluid than rigid in a situation of harem due to sexual and emotional depravity. Burton (2010) states that the harems are hotbeds of sapphism and tribadism. Nonetheless, a distinction between these two grounds is still in order. Homosocial must be distinguished from homosexual and by no means implies a sexual relationship, but rather a social relationship between two individuals of the same gender (Malti-Douglas 1991: 15; 2004 I: 34).

Contrary to the claim that Budur did not enhance her social standing because of the cross-dressing (Amer 2007: 122), her situation has changed dramatically. Cross-dressing enabled her to travel freely and to reach the highest level of power by becoming a king. She was able to exercise the patriarchal, privileged position of a husband when she married Hayat. Cross-dressing enabled her to play a homoerotic game against her husband where the power structure between the two has been radically inverted. This game was fully initiated by her and it was performed against the will of the rejecting and reluctant husband. Budur, who initially showed female weakness, tries to assume the role of a man, or rather the role of a master, while Qamar is reduced to virtually a slave-like existence (Beaumont 2002: 84). Budur takes full advantage of the power of royalty by becoming, through marriage with Hayat, a sovereign (Matarasso 1982: 25). Budur and Zumurrud disguised themselves as men to travel in security and to advance their fortune (Irwin 1994: 172).

Women attempted to redress the inequalities of their gender role by cross-dressing or taking on the guise and role of a man because it gave them a new status in society and allowed them to do things not normally allowed to women (Bullough 1996: 232). Thus, by cross-dressing, Budur gains greater wealth and power, a wife, and a reversed relationship with her husband, albeit provisionally. The narrative of the Arabian Nights unequivocally confirms the instrumentality of cross-gender dressing. Yet, it also confirms that this functionality is transitory because ultimately dominant, culturally legitimate social values, and models of power and social hierarchy re-establish themselves.

II

TEMPTING PEDERASTY

M ALE HOMOSEXUALITY IS WELL REPRESENTED IN THE THOUSAND and One Nights but exclusively in its pederastic form. During the medieval period, pederastic relationships thrived in the Middle East, as in ancient Greece and Rome (Johansson and Percy 1996: 158–9). Boswell (1989: 14) discusses that there is an even more overwhelming emphasis on homosexual eroticism in medieval Islam than in classical Greek or Roman writing. It is probably fair to say that most pre-modern Arabic poetry is ostensibly homosexual, and it is clear that this is more than a literary convention. Falling in love with a teenage youth and expressing this love in verse were not punishable offences, and a significant number of Islamic scholars asserted that such behaviour was not objectionable (Rouayheb 2005: 153). Lagrange (2000: 172–3) contends that medieval writers did not deal with man-to-man attraction any differently than with heterosexual relations, depicting similar consequences. Homosexual desire and activities were prominent among the political, intellectual, and commercial elites of the Abbasid culture. Homoerotic desire became integrated into the social order and erotic discourse became a crucial aspect of articulating cultural elite identity in medieval Arabic culture (Sharlet 2010: 37). In his 'Terminal Essay', Burton (2010 X: 178–219) holds pederasty to be geographical and climatic rather than racial, by suggesting that the Middle East forms part of a vast Sotadic Zone where there is a blending of the masculine and feminine temperaments, making pederasty popular and endemic.

The medieval proliferation and sophistication of the pederastic inclination is well reflected in the Arabian Nights. Pederasty is not only tolerated but also celebrated in this literature. This narrative addresses pederasty in a less ambiguous and a less conflictual presentation vis-à-vis heterosexuality. Pederasty is considered to have an independent sexual existence, parallel to heterosexual relationships. The relative merit of each of these forms of sexuality is widely thought, compared, and debated. The ascendancy of pederasty in medieval society in combination with a flourishing heterosexuality tends to indicate the dominant position of men in society. The influx of eunuchs and slave-girls provides men with an expanding access to pederasty as well as heterosexuality. This increasing outlet for sexuality corresponds to the higher gender status of men supported by religion and culture. In fact, pederastic activities not only do not tarnish the reputation of men but also support the hegemonic masculinity ideal in society.

Nonetheless, this masculine ideal is exclusively assigned to the active role of pederasty, to the exclusion of the passive role of the beardless, *amrad*, young male. By involving intergenerational partners, pederasty by its very nature is a patriarchal construction encompassing a dominant macho adult and a weak, insignificant minor. The age asymmetry pertinent to pederasty tends to make the active and passive roles highly polarized and mutually exclusive. This construction of sexual roles sheds some doubts about considering pederasty as a homosexual activity or at least making it a very distinct form of male homosexuality. A man and a teenager rather than equal partners perform this homo practice. The penchant for *amrads* can be recognized as same-sex desire only in the measure that *amrads* are constructed as male gendered (Lagrange 2008: 188).

Thus, pederasty is a patriarchal and intergenerational homosexuality performed by unequal men with differential status and age asymmetry and predicated on penetration and inequality. The unbalanced power structure and relation pertinent to this sexual activity is palpable and unambiguous. In many parts of the world where gender order and sexual morality have been challenged and where heterosexuality and homosexuality connote equal partnership between adult individuals, this kind of sexual practice is considered paedophilia and as such outlawed and criminalized. By contrast, prevalent social construction of masculinity, gender, and sexuality has not yet been seriously challenged in the Middle East. Consequently, it is no wonder that pederasty is still the dominant form of male homosexuality in these societies. Murray and Roscoe (1997a: 302) reason that pederasty has long been the idealized form in Middle Eastern cultures.

The often-claimed Middle Eastern tradition of social tolerance of homosexuality is not supported by either mainstream literature or by the stories of the Arabian Nights. Apparently, confusing pederasty and homosexuality would create ambiguity and the ensuing falsely, or at least highly exaggerated, claimed tradition of flourishing and condoning of homosexuality in the region. While the narrative of the Thousand and One Nights presents and tolerates pederasty, yet it is utterly silent on male homosexuality. This is by no means a unique finding. A survey of medieval Scandinavian literature found no evidence of an exchanged homosexual role (Jochens 1996: 387). To be sure, there is an indirect reference to the male homosexual union in the Arabian Nights. With the help of magic power and contact with water, a man transformed into a woman leading to a homo marriage union via gender change is presented in *Warlock and the Young Cook of Baghdad* and *Hasan the King of Egypt*. Yet, these experiences belong to the realm of magic rather than real life occurrences. Moreover, in contrast to pederasty, this literature provides a much less tolerating, if not condemnatory and conflictual, presentation of another form of homosexuality, lesbianism.

However, rejoicing pederasty does not mean that it is a straightforward or noncontroversial issue even in the narrative of the Arabian Nights. This is clearly illustrated in the story of the relative excellence of sex with young boys versus sex with women. Pederasts were suspects and vilified in the stories of *Ala' al-Din Abu l-Shamat* and *Mercury Ali of Cairo*. In the game of pederasty in *Qamar al-Zaman and Budur*, homosexual tendencies are presented as a corrupted nature. While there is a wish for a different, natural sexual inclination, the narrative admits that corrupted tastes do not heed to good counsel and, therefore, these tastes are not only inevitable but should also be tolerated. This tolerance is concomitant with a hope for forgiveness of sins by the divine power. Thus, while the narrative presents the enforced compliance of Qamar al-Zaman with the order of the king as a triumph of pederasty, this success, however, immediately becomes transitory and ineffective to the advantage of heterosexuality when Budur reveals her identity.

The homoerotic game in this story and other similar stories end up with sexual intercourse between a wife and a husband, signalling the final triumph of heterosexuality and its naturalization in gender and sexual relations. It is important to note that the matter-of-fact tolerance of homosexuality that pervades the written text nonetheless occurs within a heterosexual norm (Boone 1993: 27). The pre-eminence and perpetuity of heterosexuality over any other sexual 'deviation' and 'corruption' are also evident in the tale of *Qamar al-Zaman and the Jeweller's Wife*. The story presents homosexual pederasty merely as a temptation, a desire that is either fulfilled or not, yet the real and legitimate sexuality is heterosexuality that will necessarily triumph in the end. Moreover, rejecting, overcoming, and resisting homo tendencies would eventually be rewarded with women, heterosexuality, and happiness.

Admiring Male Beauty

Beauty is a central concept in romantic and sexual relationships in the medieval Middle East and its literature. The *Arabian Nights Encyclopedia*

(Marzolph and Leeuwen 2004 II: 493) states that one of the principles of the experience of beauty in Arab culture is the association of beauty with pleasure and well-being and, therefore, it is considered healthy and thera-peutic. It also adds, 'Besides women, stereotypical descriptions of beauty also apply to young men, whose handsome appearance is typically asso-ciated with wealth, noble descent, and moral qualities' (494). Thus, in the androgynous approach to beauty, physical beauty that is strongly related to pleasure applies to both women and young men. The beauty of the boy is admired and compared to the beauty of women. In a culture where male beauty is a source of appreciation, expressions of admiration and even attraction to male beauty would be so familiar that they would not provoke surprise (Boswell 1989: 21).

Lagrange (2008: 170) asserts that the canons of adolescent beauty in the classical imaginary were not clearly gendered. The terms used to describe young heroes in the Thousand and One Nights and the standards of beauty that are applied to them are identical for boys and girls. Rowson (1991: 58) concurs by saying that the canons for the beauty of boys are virtually the same as those for women, a fact underlined by the extraordin-ary prominence of the question of the beard in homoerotic poetry and anecdote since the wearing of beards was the single most potent symbol of manhood. Boswell (1989: 20) argues that archetypes of beauty in the Muslim world, like in the Greek world, are more often seen in masculine than in feminine terms, beauty is thought to be a great asset to a man, and the uni-versal archetype of beauty, to which even beautiful women are compared, is Joseph.

Not only is the beautiful Joseph mentioned in the Qur'an but also the beardless young males of paradise attending to the needs of the believ-ers. Mystical Islam has developed this orthodox religious injection to a sophisticated level. Among the various meditative practices developed by circles of the Sufis was that of *nazar*, the contemplation of a beauti-ful pubescent boy, who was considered a 'witness' (*shahid*) to the beauty of God and the glory of His creation (Rowson 1991: 62). In mystical Islam, God is beautiful and loves beauty: 'all beauty is the beauty of God' (Rouayheb 2005: 37). Beauty is divine, and 'to behold it was to behold one of the attributes of God' (95). Sufism and the practice of hypnotic boy gazing, wherein the practitioner stares at a lovely youth until achiev-ing transcendence, were gaining ground as popular spiritual compet-itors to official religion (Kassim 2008: 309). Burton (2010 X: 178–219) emphasizes that there is a noble sentimental side to the pure love of boys since it unites in the soul the creature with the creator. This platonic affection regards youths as the most pure and beautiful objects in this phenomenal world, which is different from the always sexual love of the other sex.

While the jinn are impressed with the beauty of both the prince and the princess, in *Qamar al-Zaman and Budur*, the jinniyah is forced to admit that 'the two upon the couch might be twins save in the matter of their middle parts'; 'If there is equality between a male and a female, the male bears off the prize.' The male jinni pronounces, 'I have never seen so many perfections in a boy.' Thus, a male jinni is fascinated with the male human beauty while the female jinni does not show the same fascination with the female human beauty.

The vizier of Yemen, in *Vizier of Yemen and His Young Brother*, has a younger brother who he guards jealously. He hires an old man as his teacher, but the teacher falls in love with the boy. He agrees with the boy to climb over the wall when his brother is asleep to spend a night of pleasure. The vizier surprises the two together, but after the sheikh has recited a poem, he is pardoned.

The sultan's vizier receives a handsome Christian youth, in *Al-Malik al-Nasir and His Vizier*. When the sultan asks him how the young man came into his possession, the vizier answers that he received him as a gift. He then presents the boy to the sultan. The other viziers spread a rumour that he still loves the young man, implying he would like to have him back. To try him, the sultan sends him a love letter allegedly written by the young man. The vizier sees through the ruse, however, and sends an adequate answer, declaring that his 'Reason is not entangled in the toils of passion'. Even though the singer, in *Singer and the Druggist*, is engaged in an adulterous affair with a married woman, he sees in a neighbouring house a young male slave, as if he were the full moon, and he professes lustful love to him. The slave agrees and invites him to come to his sleeping place at night. In the dark, however, he takes out his penis, spits on it, and slips it into, mistakenly, the sleeping master of the house, who beats him and ties him to a tree as a punishment. The slave displays an active role in the story by quickly consenting to this affair of pederasty. *Three Eunuchs* is a story narrating about a slave demonstrating an active agency of being himself a pederast by having sexual intercourse with the son, in addition to the wife, of his master. However, this transgression proved to be costly for the slave as he was consequently castrated, thereby becoming a eunuch.

A beautiful young boy secluded by his parents is a motif in *Qamar al-Zaman and the Jeweller's Wife*. A son is kept secluded at home until he is fourteen years of age. When his father finally takes him to the market his beauty stuns everybody. Oblivious to the nature of their relationship, people

think that there is a pederastic relationship between the two. One merchant
recites the verses,

> You have created beauty as a temptation to us
> And said, O my servants fear me and abstain
> Behold, you are beautiful and love beauty
> How, then, your creatures from loving refrain

One of the people who gather to admire the boy is a dervish who intensely
gazes at the boy, telling verses in admiration of the boy's beauty and bursts
out crying. Enraged by what is happening and regretting listening to his
wife, the merchant decides to close his shop and go home with his son,
but the dervish follows them and asks to be their guest for the night. Even
though the father suspects that the dervish has pederastic intentions towards
his son, he nonetheless consents to the dervish's request because the dervish
says that the guest is God's guest, to which the father says welcome to the
guest of God. However, a homoerotic game is played on the dervish to know
if he has any pederastic wishes with the intention of punishing him accordingly. Later on, when asked why he was staring at the young boy if he had
no sexual desire for him, the dervish says that the boy has a striking similarity
with a very beautiful woman he fell in love with in Basra.

When Prince Taj al-Muluk enters the market, in *Taj al-Muluk and Princess
Dunya*, and the merchants look at his beauty and grace, they are confounded.
One merchant says, 'Surely, the gate-keeper of paradise left the doors open
and so this lovely youth came out.' Another merchant says that he is one of
the angels. When the supervisor of the merchants looks at the prince and his
companion Aziz, he rejoices and has a great affection for them. He prefers the
love of young men to that of women. He says, 'This is a fine catch, glory to
Him who created them and fashioned them out of the vile water!' The next
day, after taking a bath that results in increasing their charm, the two young
men go to the market and when the supervisor meets them, he sees two
gazelles, with red cheeks, black eyes, and shining faces, as if they were two
lustrous moons or fruit-laden saplings. Seeing their hips quivering, he feels
strong emotion and desire. He cannot contain himself but puffs, snorts, and
devours them with his eyes. When he recites verses praising their beauty after
having a bath, they insist that he should join them for a second bath. He can
hardly believe his ears and hastens to join them. Taj al-Muluk takes him by
one hand and Aziz by the other, carries him into a cabinet, and he submits to
them while his emotions are sharpened. Taj al-Muluk proceeds to wash him,
while Aziz pours water over him and he thinks himself in paradise. Admiring
the beauty of young males in the market is also presented in the story of the
Dervish and the Barber's Boy and the Greedy Sultan.

The Pederast Abu Nuwas

The Thousand and One Nights contains a number of stories involving the celebrated poet Abu Nuwas (d. 814 or 815), who is considered one of the greatest of classical Arabic literature and is well known for his poems of revelry, obscene verses, *mujun*, and homosexual pederasty. Born in Ahwaz of a Persian mother and an Arab father, he spent his childhood and adolescent life in Basra, a cultural heartland. His mentor poet Waliba al-Asadi, whose poetry is homoerotic and licentious, took him to Kufa as a young apprentice. The mentor was attracted sexually to the young poet and may have had erotic relations with him. P. Kennedy (2007: 4) states, 'Whether or not this predisposed Abu Nuwas to visit this behaviour upon others when he was older can only be mooted, but certainly Abu Nuwas's relationships with adolescent boys when he had matured as a man seem to mirror his own experience with Waliba.' In Basra, he became enamoured with Janan, a born slave-girl, but their relationship was complicated, oscillating between attraction and antipathy expressed in animated poetic exchanges (8). It is also reported that it was he who was largely responsible for the demise of their relationship having refused to accede to her condition that he give up sleeping with boys. He moved to Baghdad soon after the relationship ended with a heavy heart (9).

Literary expression of the admiration of male beauty and infatuation with beardless young boys brings poetry and pederasty together in an unequivocal nexus. This connection is also found in earlier Greek Mediterranean culture (Rowson 1991: 77). Yet it was unknown in the Islamic world until the early Abbasid period. The link between poetry and pederasty represents the development of love poetry, *ghazal*, into a new literary genre of verses and prose, *mujun*, libertinism. This literary shift reflects the urban society that was expanding and flourishing at that time and a departure from the platonic poetry, *hub 'udhri*, of the bedouins and the desert life. It celebrates sensual pleasure and tends to embrace homosexual tendencies by including the praise of the beloved beauty and the love poetry about boys, *mudhakkarat*.

The most famous initiator and representative of this new literary genre is Abu Nuwas, together with few other *mujun* poets. Abu Nuwas had a crucial influence in establishing the enduring fashion for homoerotic poetry and anecdote in Arabic (Rowson 1991: 77). He is the most flagrant example of those who were to transgress and subvert societal codes and also to take pleasure in their transgression or to ridicule the codes (Lagrange 2008: 168). Abu Nuwas was the greatest of the poets who celebrated both the joys of wine and the beauty of the boys who served that wine (Irwin 1994: 154). Wine drinking and pederasty tended to go hand in hand, in literature at least (155). He was famous above all for his *kham-riyyat* verses in praise of wine.

Abu Nuwas was not only encouraging wine drinking and wantonness with the hope, or rather the philosophy, of divine forgiveness but also dared to say that stopping debauchery is, in fact, a sin. He recites, 'To keep souls away from what they love is a great sin' (Wright 1997: 12). Hence, the stigma of committing a sin is subverted and inverted. In the story of *Ma'ruf the Cobbler and His Wife*, Abu Nuwas recites these verses on the habit of wine drinking,

> Halt blaming me, for blaming is a seduction
> And treat me with the medicine that has caused my malady
> From a cup-owner, take it
> She [wine] has two lovers, fornicator and sodomite

In the narrative of Alf Layla wa Layla, Abu Nuwas is associated with the legendary Caliph Harun al-Rashid. However, the *Arabian Nights Encyclopedia* (Marzolph and Leeuwen 2004 II: 468) states that Abu Nuwas was never such a close companion to Harun al-Rashid as the anecdotes in the Arabian Nights suggest. He gained access to the court only after Harun's death when he became a boon companion of Caliph al-Amin. When Harun al-Rashid asks for Abu Nuwas, in *Harun al-Rashid and the Damsel and Abu Nuwas*, he is found in a tavern where he has been held for a debt of 1,000 dinars he had squandered in feasting with a young boy.

In *Abu Nuwas with the Three Boys*, the poet buys everything he needs for a festive evening and goes out to look for company. He sees three handsome, beardless young men, equal in the perfection of beauty 'as if they were youths of the gardens of paradise, *wildan al-jinan*', and all hearts yearned with a desire to the graceful bending of their shapes. Abu Nuwas loves to spend happy time with youth; as the poet says, 'A greybeard is amorous and likes nice faces and music.' He approaches the boys with poetic verses inviting them to accompany him for a merry time of food, drink, and fucking: 'Fuck each other and put my penis between you.' They consent to spend the evening with him, saying, 'We hear and obey.' After eating and drinking, they appeal to him to judge who is the handsomest and shapeliest of them. He signals to one and recites verses after kissing him twice. Then he points to another and continues his verses after kissing him on the lips. Then he nods to the third and continues his verses after kissing him ten times. When the wine creeps to his head, he recites more verses: 'A delight is incomplete, but with someone who drinks and nice faces are his cup boons.' Whenever he needs a kiss, he takes it from the lips of one of his companions. The poet says, 'God bless them! Right sweet has my day with them been. We drink the wine cup, both mixed and pure, and we agreed to fuck the one who falls asleep.'

When everyone is getting drunk, suddenly Caliph Harun al-Rashid enters. To reprimand him, the caliph says, 'I have appointed you judge, *qadi*, of the pimps,' whereupon Abu Nuwas responds, 'Do you have a case to present before me?' Full of rage, the caliph leaves the house while Abu Nuwas continues his night of merriment and delights. When Abu Nuwas comes to the palace the next day, he is punished and ordered to take off his clothes. They bind an ass's saddle on his back and force him to make a tour around the lodgings of the slave-girls. Seeing Abu Nuwas in this state, the vizier asks him what offence he has committed, to which he answers, 'I made the caliph a present of the best of my verses and he made me a present in return with the best of his clothes.' When the caliph hears this, he laughs and not only pardons him but also rewards him with some money.

Notably, the youths are happy with the sexual role they play in this tale, not only in allowing the poet to do what he wants with them, but they also find joy and a merry time, even playing a game of contest about their beauty and charms. The term used to describe the beardless youths in this story is taken from the Qur'an. Qur'anic verse 56: 17–18 states, 'There shall wait on them immortal youths with bowls and ewers and a cup of purest wine' (Koran 1974: 110). Verse 52: 24 states, 'There shall wait on them young boys of their own as fair as virgin pearls' (117); while verse 76: 19 states, 'They shall be attended by boys graced with eternal youth, who to the beholder's eyes will seem like sprinkled pearls. When you gaze upon that scene you will behold a kingdom blissful and glorious' (18). 'And there pass among them immortal youths; if you were to see them, you would reckon them pearls scattered about in profusion' (Pinault, 1992: 141). The youths of paradise have been a source of inspiration for homosexuality among Muslims since the beginning of Islam (H. Kennedy 2008: 184). Al-Jahiz states, 'God described them in more than one place in His book and created a desire for them in His saints' (182). This terminology of describing the beauty of male youths shows the influence of religion on literature, including the Arabian Nights.

Burton (2010) classifies pederastic activities of the Arabian Nights in three categories. He considers the debauchery of the three youths by Abu Nuwas, who lures them with wine and falls to kissing and fondling them, is the worst, the grimmest, and the most earnest phase of perversion. He contrasts this type of pederasty with the funny and practical joke of Budur and Zumurrud, and with wise and learned debate of the reverent woman.

A similar story about Abu Nuwas and three boys also appears in canonical literature. *The Three Egyptian Lads* is a documented anecdote presenting Abu Nuwas as a predator in disguise who rapes and sodomizes three young boys in Fustat, in Egypt, by pretending to be a porter. In the morning the poet proudly recites verses that tell the whole story (Lagrange 2014: 237–8).

Trade and Pederasty

Reflecting the most important economic activity of the time, commerce, a significant part of the tales of the Thousand and One Nights is about merchants and their lives. Essentially, by its very nature of manly activity, the profession of trade that often entails many and long travels is conducive to the spread of pederasty. Being away from their wives and concubines and the absence of women from the trade caravan concomitant with the availability of many young boys who extend their assistance, whether for making their living or for travel, or both, make male homosexuality in the form of pederasty a rather compelling necessity and temptation.

Afraid of his son attracting admirers, the chief of merchants in Egypt, in *Ala' al-Din Abu l-Shamat*, ordered that his beautiful son Ala' al-Din Abu l-Shamat would live in a basement where no stranger will see him. Irwin (1994: 171) states, 'A leitmotif in the *Nights* is the seclusion of a beautiful boy by his parents in order to protect him from lascivious men.' However, when the son becomes a young boy, his father takes him to the market. Oblivious to the fact that the chief merchant has a son, the merchants think that the young boy is his lover, saying that this man is 'Like a leek, with a grey hair but a green heart'. The merchants decide to discharge their chief, but he succeeds in convincing them that the boy is, in fact, his son, inviting them to celebrate the coming of the child.

One of the guests is a merchant by the name of Mahmud al-Balkhi who likes young boys. When he sees the boy, he becomes enamoured with him, asking the other young boys to convince him to travel with him, and promises them a good quality dress each. They succeed in convincing him by arguing that sons of merchants have no pride other than travelling to make business and profit. Finally, Ala' al-Din persuades his parents and joins the caravan of al-Balkhi heading towards Baghdad. On the route, al-Balkhi invites him to eat with him, and after they have finished their meal, he wants to kiss the young boy and to rape him. Ala' al-Din withdraws his sword and reprimands the merchant. However, later on during the journey, some Bedouins attack the caravan and take all their possessions, and when they reach Baghdad, al-Balkhi invites Ala' al-Din to his house. Once again, he tries to kiss him yet is reproached by the young man. The merchant tells him that he is enamoured

with him and that if he complies with his desire, he will give him twice the
wealth he has lost, reciting the verses,

> A lover does not heal from what is afflicting him
> By embraces and kisses but by fucking

Ali al-Zaybaq, a sharper in Cairo, is invited by a friend to come to
Baghdad, in *Mercury Ali of Cairo*. He joins a trade caravan consisting of forty
merchants and offers his help to a Syrian merchant. The merchant, who
loves boys, accepts and fancies the young and beardless, *amrad*, Ali. When the
caravan stops for the night sleep, the merchant sleeps next to Ali, but when
the merchant wants to embrace Ali, he cannot find him. He thinks to himself
that perhaps one of the other merchants has already arranged to sleep with
Ali for the night. He sleeps with the intention of reserving Ali for himself the
following night. However, Ali manages to reach Baghdad without experiencing any pederastic advances. A young and beardless young boy is often
thought of as an object for homo-pederastic desire. When the merchant does
not find Ali beside him during the night, he immediately thinks that Ali is
having homosexual activities with another merchant who is faster than he is
in arranging an affair with the young boy.

Pederasty versus Heterosexuality

One of the facets of the complexity and dynamism of sexual life in the medieval Middle East is the tendency to compare different aspects of sexuality. This
comparative sexuality includes comparing the merits of pederasty and heterosexuality, of women and beardless boys as sexual partners, of vaginal and
anal intercourse, and of anus and vagina in relation to sexual pleasure. This
comparative literary exercise results in a hierarchization of sexual pleasure
derived from penetrating different body parts. This literature reflects a dominant male sexuality treating women and beardless boys as sexual objects. It is
about the pleasure that a man can derive from a penis penetrating a vagina or
an anus. This sexual contrasting extends to the gender aspects by comparing
the merits of men versus women. The vice versa direction, from the gender
to the sexual, is also valid. The gender and sexual comparative evaluation is
part of a more extensive literary trend that compares any opposite things, not
unlike the Greek literary traditions.

During the Abbasid period, preference for sexual intercourse with slave-
boys became fashionable. In the ninth century, al-Jahiz wrote a famous literary
debate on whether sexual intercourse is more pleasurable with a male slave,
ghulam, or with a female slave, *jariya*. This treatise about greater excellence,

tafdhil, was entitled, *mufkharat al-jawari wa 'l-ghilman* (*Boasting Match Between Slave-Girls and Page-Boys*). This work had a great influence on medieval mainstream literature because sexual contrasting became a repeated theme in these texts and the narrative device of a boasting match a well-established genre in the Arabic literature (Boswell 1989: 15; H. Kennedy 2008: 175–6; Kugle 2010: 87; Nasr al-Katib 1977; Rosenthal 1997: 25; Rowson 1991: 58).

The Arabian Nights was not absent from this mainstream literary debate. An explicit debate over the excellence of pederasty versus heterosexuality forms the main theme of the tale of *Man's Dispute with the Learned Woman*. Sitt al-Mashayikh, literally meaning Lady of the Elders, is a pious, intelligent, and well-read female preacher from Baghdad who visits Hamah one day. She became famous for engaging in debate and dispute over issues of theology with scholars who used to visit her at her house. One day a scholar takes his friend with him to attend one of these discussion meetings. However, the friend is mainly preoccupied with gazing at her handsome young brother's face and admiring his beauty without paying any heed to what she is saying. The preacher turns to the friend and says to him, 'It seems to me you are one of those men who prefer men to women,' to which he replies, 'Without a doubt.' The narrative contains a long debate between them on the merit or demerit of sexual pleasure with boys or girls, extending to their merit and demerit as gender.

Women and Pederasty

Obviously, pederasty is an all-male activity. Still, it is an interesting question to explore whether women are involved in the pederastic activity, particularly in the narrative of the Arabian Nights. Pederasty is a sexual activity predicated on the penetration of the anus and age and status unevenness. However, what is the most important determinant of pederasty is the beauty of the young male rather than the anus. To be sure, the anus is very important for pederasty but this form of sexuality is not performed with any or all men. Rather it is performed on the young male and what is penetrated is the anus of a beardless boy. The anus makes sense in pederasty only in conjunction with young and beardless male beauty. Additionally, not all pederastic desires are acted upon. Most of these desires are imaginary, chaste, platonic, and reduced to admiring male beauty without necessarily involving action, actualized by a penetration of the anus. For example, admiring male beauty is one of the pillars of Sufi practices and literature.

However, as far as women are concerned, the desire to penetrate the male anus is presented in the tales of Alf Layla wa Layla. In this narrative, women play homoerotic games for fun and pleasure in the stories of *Ali Shar and Zumurrud, Qamar al-Zaman and Budur*, and *Fifth Captain's Tale*. A woman using pederasty for other purposes appears in *Muhammad of Damascus and Sa'd of Baghdad*. Yet, one can speculate that the female desire to penetrate the young boy could even go beyond the imaginative mind with the use of dildo. The medieval erotic literature mentions that women are used to employing the dildo in their same-sex desires and activities. There is also an anecdote describing a woman's use of a dildo to sodomize an effeminate man (Rowson 1991: 67–8).

Leaving the anus aside, the age asymmetry of pederasty could be appealing to women as well. After all, they are accustomed to age differences with their husbands, and so pederastic activities are a way of reversing the age differences to their advantages this time. Are mature women attracted to the beauty of young beardless males as men are? Beauty has an androgynous nature and is associated with youth, making it appealing to both men and women. Women infatuated with the beauty of the beardless males appear in several stories.

In *Qamar al-Zaman and Budur*, a female jinni admires the astonishing beauty of the young boy Qamar al-Zaman while he is asleep. In addition, Budur demonstrates that female resistance to the charm of male beauty is very weak and lacking self-control of her sexual lust for the young boy. A woman prospers as a merchant and wants to marry a young man, in *Woman Who Regained Her Loss*. Impressed by the beauty of the young boy, in *Vizier's Son and the Bath-Keeper's Wife*, the wife of the bath-keeper engages in adulterous sex with the boy while the husband is waiting outside the room. In *Ali with the Large Member*, two wives commit adultery with two young men hired as cattle-herders by their husbands. In *Lady and Her Two Lovers*, a married woman has a lover but does not mind having an extra affair with his young messenger.

Queens desiring young men and copulating with, or making advances on them, appear in the stories of *Diamond, Ali and Zahir from Damascus* and *Jullanar the Sea-Born*. When Badr al-Din enters the bridal salon, in *Nur al-Din and His Son Badr al-Din Hasan*, all the attending women gaze at his beauty, wishing to be united with him, and envy the one who is going to marry him. In the story of *Woman Who Had a Boy and the Other Who Had a Man as Lover*, two women debate the merit of having a young boy or a man as the most appropriate and satisfying sexual partner for women. This dispute results in the triumph of the adult man as a sexual partner.

Yet we have the reverse outcome in the story of *Qamar al-Zaman and the Jeweller's Wife*. The woman drugs her husband and the fourteen-year-old boy guest with a sleeping potion, and while they are asleep, the wife comes to the boy and admires his beauty. She climbs on his chest and covers his face with kisses until it is red and bloated. Then she sucks his lips until the blood runs out into her mouth. Still, neither her heat is subdued nor her thirst alleviated. She does not stop kissing him, cuddling him, and encircling leg with leg until daybreak. The next morning when Qamar al-Zaman washes his face, his cheeks and lips burn him and the host says that surely this comes from the mosquito bites. Qamar al-Zaman asks him if it happened to him as well, but the man says no, and adds, 'Whenever I have a guest like you, he complains in the morning of the mosquito bites, and this only happens when the guest is beardless, like you. If the guest is bearded, the mosquitoes do not trouble him. What is hindering them from me is my beard. It seems that mosquitoes do not love bearded men.' This funny but brilliantly and smartly narrated dialogue leaves no doubt that the beauty of young males appeals to women as well. Adult women engaging in a sexual liaison with boys existed in some part of Europe during the Middle Ages, with condemnation though. For instance, a law issued in 731 in Italy declared that union between mature adult women and small boys who were under the legal age was illegal (Balzaretti 2008: 19).

HEDONISTIC NARRATIVE

Homoerotic Game of Pederasty

Several stories of the Thousand and One Nights depict women playing a mischievous homoerotic trick on their lovers. The slave-girl Zumurrud is abducted and forced to separate from her lover Ali Shar, in *Ali Shar and Zumurrud*. However, she manages to escape in disguise as a man and becomes a king in another town. When one day, the wandering Ali Shar comes to her town, she decides to play a homoerotic game with him. The king sends him to the bath and then provides him with sumptuous food and drink. He then asks him to rub his feet. He starts rubbing his feet and legs and finds them softer than silk. The king tells him to go higher with the rubbing, but he says that he will not go higher than the knee. The king rebukes him that disobeying his orders will earn him an ill-omened night and that if he obeys the order, the king will make him his lover and one of his princes. Ali Shar asks him in what he should obey him, and the king commands him to put off his trousers and lie down on his face. He protests that he has never done this before, weeping and lamenting but the king threatens to cut off his head if he refuses his bidding.

The king mounts on his back, Ali Shar feels something softer than silk and butter, and he thinks to himself that this king is better than all the women are! The king then turns over on the ground, and Ali Shar says to himself, thank God that his penis has not erected. The king, however, tells him that his penis does not usually erect unless it is rubbed with hands, 'So come, and rub it until it stiffens, or else I kill you.' The king lies down on his back, takes Ali Shar's hand, and sets it on her vagina, and Ali Shar finds a pussy softer than silk, white, and great, resembling in heat a hot bath or the heart of a lover whose passion is troubling him. He thinks to himself that it is a wonder that the king has a pussy, and lust, *shahwa*, gets hold on him and his penis hardens to the utmost. When she sees this, she bursts out laughing and reveals her identity of being Zumurrud, his slave-girl. He throws himself upon her, as a lion upon the sheep, kissing, embracing, and making love to her, and she reciprocates in great ecstasy.

A similar homoerotic development occurs in *Qamar al-Zaman and Budur*. Budur is separated from her husband Qamar al-Zaman and, disguised as a man, becomes the king of the Ebony Islands. When she finds out that her husband exists in another town, she decides to bring him to her palace. Without revealing the identity of her husband, she orders the captain of the ship to bring back her former cook who has destroyed his kitchen boy by embraces that were too severe. On the boat bringing the husband, the captain tells him, 'So you are the one who loves little boys and who destroyed the King's kitchen boy.' At the royal palace, Budur plays a homoerotic game with the unsuspecting husband before revealing her identity. She bestows many favours on him and advances him in official ranks, making him the treasurer. Yet, Qamar al-Zaman is oblivious to the reasons of the entire honour and favours that he is receiving from the king. He starts to suspect unpleasant motives behind the king's kindness, and thinks about leaving the kingdom.

The king tells him the reason for his favours is because, 'I love you for your exceeding grace and surpassing beauty. If you grant me my desire of you, I will increase your honours and favours and make you a vizier, despite your tender age.' On hearing this, he is confounded and his cheeks flush with redness, and he replies that he would rather forsake these favours if they involve committing a sin. He continues to be unyielding, saying that he has never done these things before. The king tries to convince him by saying that at his age he should not be afraid of committing sins or doing forbidden things. He orders him to comply with his decree, foreordained by God, of *wisal*, sexual contact with him, reciting homo verses,

> Do not you see the various kinds of fruits on the market
> Some people are for the fig and others for the sycamore tree
> With her charms, she wants me to forget you
> Do I turn infidel after being a believer
> O' unique beauty, your love is my faith
> And my choice of all doctrines
> I have forsworn women for your sake until
> People believing that today I am a monk
> Do not compare a boy with a wench and do not listen
> To denunciator who says, it is bawdiness
> I ransom you and I chose you with intent

For you neither lay eggs nor menstruate
If all are inclined to communion with harlots
The wide land will be too narrow for our offspring
She offered me an exquisite pussy
And I said I am not fucking
She turned away saying
Fucking front wise in our days has been abandoned
She turned and showed me a buttock
As it was a lump of silver
And I said, well done my lady

The penis smooth and round was made
With anus best to match it
Had it been made for cunts' sake
It had been formed like a hatchet

My penis is big, and the little one says to me
Stab with it at my inwards and be bold
I replied that this is unlawful, but he tells me
It is lawful to me, and I fucked him the traditional way

When Qamar al-Zaman hears these verses, the light in his eyes becomes darkness and he says that the king has many women and slave-girls of unsurpassed beauty that could satisfy his desires without him. The king says that he is right, but 'They cannot heal him from his passion for him, for when tastes and inclinations are corrupted they do not heed to good counsel.' The king recites even more homo verses and Qamar al-Zaman becomes certain that there is no escape from complying. He says to the king that if this is necessary then 'Swear to me that this is done only once, even though this will not help in rectifying a corrupted nature.' The king promises him that and says, 'Hoping that God in his favour to us will erase our great sins, for the range of divine forgiveness is not too narrow to embrace us and absolve us of the excess of our transgressions and bring us to the light of righteousness out of the darkness of error.' The king recites these verses,

People hallucinate about us something and resolve
On it with their souls and hearts
Come, let us justify their suspicions, and relieve them
From guilting us once and then repent

The assurances of the king make Qamar al-Zaman consent and so he goes with the king to his bed, taking off his trousers with feelings of shame and tears in his eyes. The king smiles and turns to him, kissing, clasping, and coiling leg with leg, and tells him, 'Put your hand between my thighs so that my penis might stand up from prostration.' He weeps and says that he is not good at these things but the king insists that he should comply with his order. He puts out his hand with a heart of fire for confusion, to find his thigh suppler than butter and softer than silk. Touching the thighs pleases him and he moves his hand in all directions until it reaches a dome abounding in benedictions and movements, saying to himself, 'Perhaps the king is a hermaphrodite, neither male nor female.' He tells the king, 'O king, I cannot find any manly gear, like other men, why do you do these things.' When the king hears this, he laughs until he falls backward and says, 'O my beloved, how quickly you have forgotten the nights we have spent together.' Budur reveals her identity, they embrace and kiss each other, and they lie down on the bed of delight. Matarasso (1982: 21) names this game as simulated homosexuality where Budur simulates a homosexual scene. Thus, by disguises and ruse, Budur inverts the uninvertible difference of sexuality (37), making surreptitious use of disguises and jokes for transgression (35).

A dervish admires the beauty of a fourteen-year-old boy and forces himself as a guest in the house of the boy, in *Qamar al-Zaman and the Jeweller's Wife*. The father thinks to himself that if the dervish is in love with his son and makes homosexual advances on him, he will kill him. He instructs his son to try to seduce the dervish to know his real intention and punish him accordingly, while he is watching from a hiding place. The boy starts to offer himself to the dervish, and sits in his lap, but the dervish refuses. The boy insists on asking why the dervish denies himself the pleasure of sexual intercourse when the boy is enamoured with him. When the dervish becomes angry with the boy and threatens to tell his father, the boy replies that his father knows about his homosexual propensity and does not prevent him from acting on these desires. The dervish replies that being devoted to the love of God, he is interested neither in boys nor in girls. This, however, does not discourage the boy from inviting the dervish to admire the beauty of his face, the redness of his cheeks, and the sweetness of his lips. He reveals his beautiful legs and says that his breast is even more beautiful than the breast of girls. The dervish, on the other hand, insists that this is a forbidden act and starts to pray to ward off the seduction of the boy. He keeps praying when he sees that the boy is waiting for him to finish his prayer to resume his advances. Finally, the boy throws himself on the dervish, starting to kiss his face, telling him that if he does not make love to him, he will tell his father that the dervish has homosexual intentions against him and surely his father will kill him for these evil intentions.

The father, who is watching everything, finally enters the place and is convinced that the dervish has no sexual desires toward his son. The father asks the dervish why, since he has no sexual intention, he then was crying and staring at his son all the time. The dervish starts to tell them the story of how he was in Basra one day when he saw a very beautiful woman and fell in love with her. When he saw the boy he could not help noticing the striking similarity of beauty with the woman, and that is why he cried in grief over the woman. Hearing the story, the son becomes infatuated with the woman, deciding to travel from Egypt to Basra to search for her. Now, the tale takes quite a different turn by shifting from temptations of peder-asty to heterosexuality. However, the extent and the persistence that the boy shows in seducing the dervish are remarkable indeed. It is difficult to imagine an innocent, virginal fourteen-year-old boy using all these seduc-tive techniques and tricks to convince the dervish to indulge in a homosex-ual liaison. One wonders whether this signifies a narrative exaggeration or a real homosexual tendency developed by many years of seclusion from the outside world. Homoerotic games are also narrated, briefly, in *Fifth Captain's Tale*, *Muhammad of Damascus and Sa'd of Baghdad*, and *Wife and Her Two Lovers*.

Narrative of Sex and Fun

One day, the paralytic brother of the barber, in *Barber's Tale of His Second Brother*, meets an old woman who invites him to a wealthy house where he will enjoy food, drink, and embracing a beautiful face until dawn, on the condition that he would obey the woman of the house in whatever she wishes. She takes him to a nicely decorated room and soon a troop of young women enter, with a woman in their midst whose beauty shone as if she was the full moon. After eating and drinking, the women start to laugh at him, ridicule him, and slap him on the neck repeatedly. The old woman makes him believe that the young woman is passionately in love with him and if he tolerates all this, he will have sexual intercourse with her at the end of the day. Tempted by the expectation of sexual pleasure, he shows no protests when the woman orders his beard and moustache to be shaven and his eyebrows dyed or when the women throw cushions, oranges, and limes at him when ordering him to dance. The old woman tells him that there is one last thing for him to do in order to have the woman. When the woman gets drunk, she does not allow any man to have her until she puts off her clothes, remains completely naked, and orders the man to do the same. Then she runs before the man from place to place, as if she flees from him until the man has an erection, at which she stops and gives herself to him. They undress and the young woman tells him that if he wants to have her, he has to follow her. He runs after her until he suddenly falls through a trapdoor and descends in the middle of a crowded market, to endure another beating from passers-by for being beardless and naked with an erect penis. Dalila and her young daughter play a trick on a handsome young merchant in *Dalila the Crafty and Her Daughter*. She tells him that she would like to offer her rich daughter in marriage to him, and give him the capital to open two shops instead of one. The young merchant tells himself that he has asked God for a bride, and he has answered him with three things: money, clothes, and a pussy.

Porter and the Three Ladies of Baghdad is a story depicting a sexually charged atmosphere. A beautiful woman in Baghdad asks a porter to follow her and carry her purchases. Arriving at her house, the porter encounters two other beautiful young women and refuses to leave. Since the porter is a witty fellow, the women consent to his participating in the party. A hilariously funny and luxurious evening of eating, drinking, dancing, singing, reciting verses, laughing, and making sexual jokes soon follows. The porter falls to toying, kissing, biting, groping, cuddling, and fondling with all the three women, as if he sits in paradise among the paradisiac female slaves, *huri*. When drunkenness ensues, one of the women undresses completely naked and throws herself in the basin. She plays with the water, takes water in her mouth and spurts it at the porter, and washes her limbs and between her thighs. Then she comes out of the water and throws herself into the porter's lap, telling him while pointing to her private part, 'O my lord, o my love, what is the name of this?' The porter answers that it is her womb, but she scolds him for being shameless and clasps his neck. 'Your vagina, *fargiki*' answers the porter, to get a slap on the nape of his neck. 'Your pussy, *kusuk*,' he offers another guess, and she gives him another slap and says what an ugly word, he should be ashamed. 'Your cunt, *zanburik*,' he said, which makes the other women join in slapping him and reproaching him. Whatever he says, they laugh at him, reprimanding him, and beating him more and more until his neck aches. Finally, he asks, 'What is its name for you?' to which they reply that it is the 'sweet basil of the dykes, *habaq al-jasur*'.

They resume drinking and after a while the second woman undresses and sits in the porter's lap, to ask the same question while pointing to her genitalia: 'O light of my eyes, what is the name of this?' He replies with all the names he knows: vagina, vulva, pussy, including also the sweet basil of the dykes, but they keep laughing, slapping, and rebuking him. She finally says that it is 'the peeled sesame, *al-sumsum al-maqshur*'. Another round of drinking passes and then the third woman strips and throws herself in the basin, and the porter watches her naked beauty as if she is a piece of the moon. He looks at her naked body and breasts and at her heavy quivering buttocks. She leaves the basin and sits on his knees, asking the same question while pointing to her pudenda. No names he mentions, including the sweet basil of the dykes and the peeled sesame, can save him from further admonishments, being laughing at, and slapped, until she finally says, it is 'Abu Mansur Inn, *khan*'.

Afterward, another round of drinking passes and now the porter puts off his clothes and jump in the basin and then throws himself into one of the women's lap and while pointing to his genitalia he asks them what is the name of this. They say it is 'your penis, *zubak*', but he says no, and takes of each a kiss. They say, it is 'your phallus, *ayrak*', but he says no, and gives each of them a hug. They say, it is 'your impalement, *khazukak*', but he rejects their guess. They name cock, yard, prick, dick, but he keeps saying no, while incessantly kissing, hugging, and fondling the women to his heart's content. They laugh and say, 'O brother what is its name?' and he replies, 'Do not you know? This is the mule break-all, browses on the basil of the dykes, gobbles up the peeled sesame, and lays by night in the khan of Abu Mansur.' They laugh until they fall backward, and then they all resume drinking. Naaman (2013: 363–4) states that this narrative is a flirtatious verbal game in which the parties involved delight in expressions pertaining to the strictly tabooed realm of human sexuality and sex organs. The euphemisms the women choose to use for their own genitals appear to be figurative and based on their organs' shape: an unshaved or bushy vulva for the first woman, a shaved vulva for the second woman, and the canal forming the vagina for the third woman.

Narrative of Sexual Intercourse and Pleasure

A poor cobbler marries a princess, in *Ma'ruf the Cobbler and His Wife*. When the couple is finally alone on their wedding night, they put off their clothes, sitting down on the bed and toying with each other. He places his hand on her knee and she sits down in his lap and pushes her lips into his mouth. He takes her in his arms, strains her fast to his breast, and sucks her lip until the honey runs out from her mouth. He lays his hand under her left armpit, upon which his guts and hers crave for coition. He pats her between the breasts and his hand slides down between her thighs. She girdles him with her legs, and he inserts his penis into her and she cries of joy when he deflowers her. They spend such a wonderful night not to be reckoned among lives, for it is full of fondling each other, embracing, sucking, and fucking until morning. A merchant travels from Baghdad to Egypt and meets a beautiful woman in the market, in *Christian Broker's Story*. They express love and the woman asks him whether she should come to him or he should come to her. The next evening he goes to her house. His host is crowned with pearls and jewels, has her eyebrows pencilled, and her hands stained with henna. She embraces him and presses him to her breast, and set her mouth on his and sucks his tongue, and he hers. They spend a wonderful night full of playing, kissing, and fucking and this continues night after night.

A king buys a beautiful slave-girl, in *Jullanar the Sea-Born*. He marvels at her beauty and symmetry. He presses her to his breast, seats her on his knees, and sucks the dew of her lips, which he finds sweeter than honey. A vizier buys a slave-girl of stunning beauty and intelligence for the king, in *Nur al-Din and the Damsel Anis al-Jalis*, but keeps her in his house for a few days so that she recovers from a long journey. When his son sees her, just after she has had a bath, he immediately falls in love with her. Despite the warnings of the vizier about the notoriety of his son with young women, she reciprocates his love because she is impressed by his beauty, resembling the moon at its fullest. He asks her if she is the slave-girl that his father has bought for him, and she says yes. He embraces her, lifts her legs, and makes them surround his waist, while she knots her hands around his neck and meets him with kisses, sighs, and amorous gestures, *ghanaj*. He sucks her tongue and she his, and he deflowers her maidenhead.

In *Mus'ab ibn al-Zubayr and A'isha bint Talha*, Mus'ab intends to marry A'isha and asks another woman to describe her for him. She reports that her face is more beautiful than health, with large eyes, an aquiline nose, smooth cheeks, a mouth like the mouth of pomegranates, and a neck like a ewer of silver. She has two breasts like twin pomegranates, a slender belly with a navel like a casket of ivory, a buttock like a hummock of sand, plump thighs, and legs like columns of alabaster. He marries the woman and, impressed by her beauty, has sexual intercourse with her seven times on their wedding night. In a female gathering, a woman tells an anecdote that one day she was in the house of A'isha when her husband came in to her, she yearned to him, and he fell upon her. She puffed, snorted, and made use of all rare and strange movements, while the visiting woman heard everything. When her husband went out, the woman asked her, how does she do all this while the woman is still in her house? To which A'isha replied that there is nothing wrong with a woman who brings her husband all the excitations and rare movements. The woman said, 'You do all this during the night.' Ai'sha replied that what she did is during the day, but by night, 'I do even more than that, for when he sees me, desire stirs in him and falls on the heat. He extends it to me and I obey him and that is what you see.'

Impressed by their beauty, the jinn unite a young boy and young girl one night, in *Nur al-Din Ali and His Son Badr al-Din Hasan*. She tells him to take her and press her to his bosom. She lifts her dress to her neck to reveal her pussy and buttocks, at which sight desire stirs in him who also unclothes. She draws him to her, saying, 'O my love, you are keeping me waiting. Quench my desire with your love and let me enjoy your loveliness!' She then recites these verses,

> For God's sake, rest your legs between my thighs
> For that is all I presently want in the world.

He draws her to him, embracing her, and putting her legs around his waist. He then sets up the cannon, aims it at the fortress, fires, blasts it, and penetrates her to find her unpierced pearl and a filly that none but he had ridden. They enjoy their sexual intercourse so much that they repeat it fifteen times during that night. Euphemistic description of sexual intercourse as a figurative military attack on a fortress is not unique to the Nights, as it is also referred to in the canonical literature (Naaman 2013: 346). One day Abu Suwayd and his friends enter a garden to buy some fruits, in *Abu Suwayd and the Pretty Old Woman*. They see in a corner an old woman with a pretty face but white hair. He says to her, 'O old woman if you dye your hair in black, you will be prettier than a girl will.' The woman, however, replies with these verses,

> I dyed what life has dyed
> My dye did not endure and only the dye of time remains
> In old days, I was clad in a garment of my youth
> And I used to be fucked from behind and front

To which Abu Suwayd cried, 'How sincere are you, o old woman, in your yearning for forbidden things, *haram*, and in your false repentance from sins.' Two women engage in a debate, in *Woman Who Had a Boy and the Other Who Had a Man as Lover*. One of them has a man for a lover, while the other one loves a beardless boy, *amrad*. They start disputing the respective merits of their lovers. She says, 'O sister, how could you tolerate the harshness of your lover's beard as it falls on your breast when he kisses you, and his moustaches rub your cheek and lips?' To which the other woman replies that the beard is a manly attribute and that the young man ejaculates quite soon, whereas the older man takes his time. She continues to say, 'O silly woman! how shall I lie under a boy, who will be hasty with me in emission, and leave a man, who, when he takes breath, clips close and when he enters, goes leisurely, and when he has done, repeats, and when he pushes, pushes hard, and as often as he withdraws, returns?' Now the other woman says, 'I forsake my lover, by God!' The motif of abandoning young lovers to the advantage of older and more experienced lovers also appears in *Mahmud and His Three Sons*. However, anecdotes about women preferring beardless men exist in the medieval erotic literature (Nasr al-Katib 1977: 79).

One night the lovers Aziz and Dalila finally meet in a garden, in *Aziz and Aziza*. She comes to him and strains him to her bosom, and kisses him and sucks his upper lip, while Aziz sucks her lower lip. He puts his hand on her waist and presses it and they both come to the ground. She undoes her trousers and they fall to embracing, toying, biting, coiling of legs, soft speech, and coquetry until her sense fails her and she swoons away. That was indeed a heart-gladdening and eye-opening night. Since then they frequently meet in the garden to spend delightful nights together.

However, while he is walking by himself in a deserted alley one evening, an old woman lures him into a certain house and locks the door. A young woman emerges, embraces him to her bosom, throws him to the floor, kneels upon his breast, and kneads his belly with her hands until he has lost senses. She then takes him by the hand while he is unable to escape because of her intense clasp. She tells him that if he wants to live then he should marry her, 'You are a handsome youth, and I desire you according to the ordinance of God. Whatever you want of money and clothes will come to you, and I will not impose any toil on you. All I ask of you is to do with me as the cock does.' When Aziz asks what the cock does, she laughs, claps her hands, and falls over on her back for the excess of laughter. Then she asks him if he really does not know what the cock's business is, and he says no. She says, 'The cock's business is to eat, drink, and fuck. All I ask of you now is to gird your loins, strengthen your resolution, and fuck the best you can.' She marries him, accordingly. She undresses and comes in a fine shirt to Aziz to take him to bed, saying that there is no shame in what is lawful. She lies down on her back and draws him to her breast. She heaves a sigh, followed by amorous gestures, and then pulls her shirt above her breast. Seeing her in that position, Aziz finds himself penetrating her after sucking her lips, while she is moaning and making a show of bashfulness. This reminds him of the poet's verses,

> When I lifted her dresses to uncover the roof of her pussy
> I found in it tightness as my humour and subsistence
> I pushed halfway into her and she heaved a sigh
> I said what is the sigh for, and she said surely for the rest of it

The woman tells him, 'O my beloved, to it and do your best, for I am your slave-girl, so take her. My life on you, give it to me, all of it, let me take it in my hand and thrust it inside me.' She does not stop making coquetry, sobs, sighs, and amorous gestures while they are kissing and fondling until their screams can be heard from the road. The woman locks Aziz inside the house for a whole year doing nothing except the cock's business of eating, drinking, and fucking.

Narrative of Vaginas and Penises

One very hot day, Queen Zubayda, in *Harun al-Rashid and Queen Zubayda in the Bath*, was bathing naked in a pool surrounded by trees in the royal garden. The caliph furtively watched her through the screen of the leaves. He saw her completely naked with all her secret charms displayed for the water was not deep enough to cover her. When she noticed him, she felt ashamed for being exposed to the caliph naked, so she placed her hands on her vagina, but it escaped from between them, due to its immensity and plumpness. The caliph turned and went away. While Hasan is enjoying the scenery in a garden, in *Hasan of Basra*, suddenly ten birds descend on the terrace, take off their garment of feathers, and change into ten beautiful girls, who start swimming and playing in the basin. When they come out of the pool, he marvels at their beauty and loveliness. He casts a glance at the naked chief damsel to see what is between her thighs, a goodly rounded dome, like a bowl of silver or crystal. Hasan eventually marries her. Later on in the story, Hasan goes to search for his wife, and an old woman takes him to a place to see if his wife is among them. Hasan unobtrusively watches while the women undress, wash, and play in the river. His penis rises when he watches what is between their thighs, of various kinds, soft and domed, plump and cushioned, large-lipped, perfect, and ample.

However, most of the tales in this category are about the penis. This is hardly surprising considering that it was men who narrated and wrote these tales. A judge arbitrates a marital conflict in *Second Captain's Tale*. Before consenting to the suggested reconciliation, the wife asks him a riddle: first, it is a bone, then a nerve, then a piece of flesh. The *qadi* himself does not know the solution, but his fourteen-year-old daughter tells him that the answer is a man's penis. She explains that between the ages of fifteen and thirty-five, the penis is hard as a bone, then on to the age of sixty, it is as sensitive as a nerve, then after the age of sixty, it becomes just a useless piece of flesh.

One day, in *Hashish Eater*, a man goes to a public bath, *hammam*, where he finds himself to be the only customer. After he has cleaned himself, he swallows a piece of hashish. Falling asleep, he has a fantastic dream of having a beautiful girl in his arms, kissing her, and setting her between his thighs.

Just as he is about to penetrate her, he is awakened by some other visitors, 'Awake, you who is good for nothing; it is noon time and you are still asleep.' He scolds them for having awakened him too soon, 'Would not you have waited until I had put it in!' They reprimand him in turn for being naked with an erect penis. While a man is sleeping at the house of his host, in *Foolish Schoolmaster*, he hears a loud screaming coming from inside the house and he goes to investigate the matter, to find his host in his last gasp with his blood streaming down. The host explains that he sits meditating on the work of God. Everything he creates for man has certain uses. He creates the hands to seize, the feet to walk, the eyes to see, the ears to hear, and the penis to fuck, except these two testicles. There is no use in them, so he took a razor and cut them off. The guest leaves him, questioning the schoolmaster's intelligence.

Bukhayt tells the story of how he became a eunuch, in *Three Eunuchs*. He became a slave when he was five years old, and grew up with the daughter of his master. One day when he was twelve years old and the girl was ten, he found her sitting in an inner room, perfumed with essences and scented woods, and her face shone like the round of the moon on its fourteenth night as if she had just come out of the bath. When they began to play, his penis rose and became a big key. She threw him down and mounted his breast, straddling him until his penis became uncovered. She took it in her hands and started to rub it against the lips of her pussy, outside her trousers. At this, heat stirred in him and he put his arms around her, while she tied her hands around his neck and strained him to her with all her might, until, before he knew it, his penis pierced her trousers, penetrating her vagina, and did away her maidenhead. He was castrated because of this adventure and the girl married a young man eventually. However, their adventure did not end there, as he became her eunuch, and they continued to enjoy kissing, embracing, and sleeping together.

In *Singer and the Druggist*, the master of a house ties the intruder to a tree as a punishment. While he is still in that position, a beautiful slave-girl who sympathizes with him and desires him starts to rub his penis until it rises upright. She asks him to make love to her in return for releasing him. He tells her to loosen him first and he will then do it. She expresses her fear that if she frees him, he will not do it, and suggests having her standing while he is still bound. She opens her clothes, inserts his penis into her, and falls to toing and froing.

The jinn wager a beauty contest between a very beautiful prince and princess while they are asleep, in *Qamar al-Zaman and Budur*. When Qamar al-Zaman wakes up, he finds a young woman lying beside him, whose breath is more fragrant than musk, and whose body is softer than cream and her beauty impresses him. When looking at her, clad in a hazel shirt without trousers, his instinct heat begins to stir in him, and the desire of fornication is awoken. He puts out his hand, loosening the collar of her shirt to reveal her bosom, with its breasts like globes of ivory, whereupon he feels an exceeding desire for her. When Budur wakes up, she finds a young man lying beside her, the loveliest of God's creatures, with eyes that put to shame the fair maids of paradise, a mouth like Solomon's seal with sweet saliva, lips the colour of coral, and cheeks like blood-red anemones. When seeing his beauty and grace, she is seized with passion and longing, telling him to awaken from sleep to enjoy her beauty: 'Awake and look on the narcissus and the tender green and enjoy my body and my secret charms and dally with me and tousle me from now until the break of day.' She becomes enamoured with him, looking at him with a thousand sighs, and her heart flutters and her guts yearn, telling him, 'Speak to me my beloved, tell me your name for you have captivated my mind.' She opens the bosom of his shirt and kisses him. She puts her hand on his breast, and for the smoothness of his body, it slips down to his navel and then to his penis. Whereupon her heart is throbbing and her desires stir in her, for the lust of women is fiercer than that of men, and she blushes. She kisses him on the mouth and all over his body. Then she takes him to her breast, laying one of her hands under his neck and the other under his armpit, and falls asleep by his side.

In *Harun al-Rashid and the Two Slave-Girls*, two slave-girls, *jawari*, one from Kufa and one from Medina, massage the hands and feet of the Caliph Harun al-Rashid. When the caliph has an erection, the girl from Medina takes his penis in her hand and rubs it. The other girl tells her, 'I see that you would keep the whole of the capital to yourself; give me my share of it.' To which the girl from Medina claims it as hers by quoting a hadith of Muhammad, 'Who has quickened the dead, the dead belongs to him.' Now the other girl pushes her away, and takes the caliph's penis all in her own hand and responds with another hadith, 'Game belongs to him who takes it, not to him who raises it.' In another version of the tale, *Harun al-Rashid and the Three Slave-Girls*, the caliph has sexual intercourse with three slave-girls, originating from Mecca, Medina, and Iraq. As the caliph has an erection, the girl from Medina takes his penis in her hand and rubs it, but the girl from Mecca quickly draws it to herself. The girl from Medina says that this is unjust aggression, quoting the hadith of the prophet, 'Who revives a dead land, it is his,' to which the other girl replies by quoting another hadith of the prophet, 'Game belongs to him who catches it, not to him who raises it.' Now, the Iraqi girl pushes them both away and takes it to herself, saying, 'This is mine until you settle your contention.'

A rich Omani merchant, in *Harun al-Rashid and Abu Hasan the Merchant of Oman*, settles in Baghdad. One day he visits a brothel but decides to stay there for months, squandering all his wealth on the beautiful girls. He is very impressed with the beauty of the daughter of the brothel's owner. The following erotic verses are referring to her,

> She said and verily desire ran riot on her side
> While the dusky night let down the darkness like a tide
> Night, in your blackness, is there no one to keep my company
> Is there no fucker for this pussy
> She smote it with her palm and sighed
> The sighing of the sorrowful, the sad, the weeping-eyed
> The beauty of the teeth appears with the tooth-stick
> And the penis is for pussies like the tooth-stick.
> O Muslims, do not your penises erect
> Is there no one among you to answer the complainer
> My penis thrust out erect from underneath my clothes
> And said to her I come to you, I come to you
> I untied the laces of her knickers; she made a show of fear and said
> Who are you? And I said, a youth answering your call
> I was routing her with what was like her wrist
> A lusty routing, that full sore the buttocks mortified.
> Until when I rose after three intercourses
> She said is there more, I said there is

In a gathering of pleasure in a garden, in *Ali Nur al-Din and Maryam the Girdle-Girl*, friends of Nur al-Din insist that he should taste the wine. They liken the wine to the medicine that is useful to the body despite its bitterness, and they start telling him about the many health benefits of wine. It digests the food, dispels care and anxiety, dissipates smells, clarifies the blood, adds colour, enlivens the body, encourages the coward, and fortifies the strength of a man for sexual intercourse, *jima'*. During this gathering, a female singer joins them, whose beauty, the sweetness of her voice, and the eloquence of her speech impress Nur al-Din. He falls in love with her, bends to her, and strains her to his breast. She does the same and lets herself to his caresses and kisses. Then, he kisses her on the mouth and they start to kiss each other after the manner of the billing of doves, *zaq al hamam*.

Afterward, he travels to Alexandria and one day he sees a beautiful girl for sale in the slave market. The broker wants to sell her to an old man, and she reprimands him as if he is mad or afflicted in wit to do so. She asks him whether it is permitted by God to sell the like of her to a decrepit old man, who said of his wife these verses,

> She says to me with a wounded pride
> When she has invited me to that which might not be
> If you do not fuck me the fuck of a man to his wife
> Do not rebuke me for becoming a cuckold

As if, your penis is made of wax for its flaccidness
Whenever I rub it with my hands, it softens even more
I have a penis that sleeps because of meanness and evil omen
Whenever one I love with my desire complies
Yet, when I am at home by myself
It requests stabbing and fighting
I have an ill penis with much brusqueness
It treats those who honour it, with reproach
If I sleep, it stands up; if I rise, it lies down,
God has no mercy on those who have pity on it.

Then, the slave-girl chooses Nur al-Din as her buyer and gives him money to pay for her price. Their first night is special and immensely sensual. She puts off her clothes and lies down beside him. She kneads him until he awakes, finding by his side a girl like pure silver, softer than silk, with swelling breasts, brows like bended bows, eyes like gazelles' eyes, cheeks like blood-red anemones, slender belly, thighs like two pillows stuffed with ostrich feathers, and between them what the tongue fails to describe. He turns to her and presses her to his breast, sucks first her under lip and then her upper lip and slides his tongue between her lips. He finds her an unpierced pearl that no one has mounted before him, and so he does away with her maidenhead. They are united together by a love that knows no breach or separation. He rains down kisses upon her cheeks, like the falling pebbles into the water, and besets her with stroke upon stroke, like the thrusting of spears in a raid. He finds all the desirable attributes of the paradisiac *huri* in this slave-girl. Later on in the story when the couple flee and the army of her father reaches them, she realizes that fighting is impending and so she asks him if he has a stomach for fighting, to which he replies in verses,

O Maryam, spare me the pain of reproaches
Do not kill me or prolong my suffering
How should I be a warrior
When I am afraid of raven's croaking
If I set eyes on a mouse, I tremble in horror
And I piss in my pants out of fear
I do not love thrusting but in bed
The pussy knows the ascendancy of penises
This is a wise judgment,
And any contrary judgment is not right.

CONCLUSION

S EXUAL LIFE IN THE NARRATIVE OF THE THOUSAND AND ONE NIGHTS, or the Arabian Nights, is impressive, rich, and complex where the erotic account is explicit. This narrative shows that there is a high regard for sexuality in social life. Urbanization and economic prosperity have resulted in an intellectual refinement and a flourishing of various kinds of literature, including erotic treatises. Canonical literature of erotica reverberated in the Arabian Nights through a process of intertextuality and literary interaction. A flourishing economy, expanding trade, and increasing wealth and incomes led to the influx of slave-girls and eunuchs, providing significant sources of various sexual desires and fantasies. A still relaxed gender mixing coupled with a positive outlook on sexuality strengthened this development. The participation of women in this social arrangement is instrumental and well represented in the narrative. Sexuality is so alluring that people overcome various barriers to fulfil their sexual desires. Distance, faith and religious differences, gender tension and segregation, or virginity prove to be no barrier to a fluid and inevitable sexuality that seems to be an unstoppable destiny.

However, while active female sexuality has enriched medieval sexual life, the narrative is mostly, if not exclusively, written and narrated by men, for mostly male audiences. Concerns about the sexuality of men are highly reflected in these stories. While this narrative focuses on female sexuality, yet subconscious male sexual interests and worries are evident. Because sexuality is important for men in the construction of their male ego and masculine ideal, female sexuality becomes exaggerated and is perceived as ravenous and insatiable. This unappeasable sexuality drives women to search for large penises and to engage in promiscuity and bestiality. In bestiality and demonic sexuality, the narrative portrays men competing with animals and jinn over the access to female sexuality and the sexual favour of women. Women are heavily represented in the sexual interaction between jinn and humans. Men too are part of this interaction and the very existence of the world of jinn is accepted and rationalized by religious beliefs. The narrative also depicts violent and taboo aspects of sexuality, such as rape, particularly as politics and a retributive instrument, and incestuous attachments.

The narrative of the Arabian Nights presents a rather prevalent promiscuous life in forms of both polygamy and polyandry. People take multiple sexual partners, including the harem, and women take advantage of the religiously sanctioned stipulation of having an interim husband to get back at their husbands after a divorce. In this promiscuous life, sexual infidelity is widespread but severely punished, including femicide. Interestingly, the whole narrative about sexual perfidy is utterly related to women, as treacherous creatures by nature, presenting an essentialized perception of women and their sexuality, while men's treachery is taken for granted and overlooked. This essentialization and the hidden concerns of men are well portrayed in the narrative of cuckoldry, displaying highly sophisticated levels of deceitfulness and cunning by women who lead a life of duplicity, to the disadvantage of the husbands who often find themselves trapped in a distressed and confusing gender reality. These stories subscribe to a culture of suspicion of women. Consequently, suspicion of women and female cunning become interwoven and mutually reinforcing. Sexual unfaithfulness is a central theme in the narrative of the Thousand and One Nights. This motif provides the framework and rationalization for the entire collection of tales.

Material prosperity and refined culture contribute to a plurality of sexual expressions and sexual desires. Subsequently, homosexuality becomes an important part of the sexual configuration of medieval life. Homosexuality is one of the most interesting manifestations of the rich sexual world of the Arabian Nights. Male homosexuality is totally centred on pederastic attractions, which is related to, but quite distinct from, homosexuality. In contrast to homosexuality constructed through equality and mutual roles, pederasty is a patriarchal activity related to the admiration of the beauty of beardless young boys. In this sense, women too are involved in pederastic desires. The male-dominated economic activity of trade, away from women, is highly conducive to a flourishing pederasty. Sufi mysticism with its doctrine that beauty belongs to God is vital in feeding pederastic tendencies, and so are the wine-drinking parties. Male beauty and pederastic desirability go hand in hand with an increasingly flourishing obscene poetry, particularly the dominant role of the legendary poet Abu Nuwas. Resonant to medieval erotology, the Arabian Nights contains a heated debate on the relative excellence of pederasty versus heterosexuality.

However, the confusion about pederasty and male homosexuality gives the false impression that the Middle East and its literature are forbearing toward homosexuality. The narrative of the Arabian Nights does not support the often-claimed tradition of social tolerance of homosexuality in the region. Yet, this narrative, like canonical medieval erotica, presents open-mindedness toward pederastic infatuations. Nevertheless, this broad-mindedness is not extended to lesbian attractions and desires, which are mostly depicted in direct conflict with prevalent and socially legitimate heterosexuality. Lesbian tendencies are stigmatized, particularly in a context of otherness. Little is narrated about transsexuality in the Thousand and One Nights, but there are many stories of cross-gender dressing, which seem to reflect gender hierarchies in society. Women who consequently gain more power, status, and wealth perform most of this cross-dressing. Men cross-dressing to women are mainly performed to have access to the harem, which is an inferior social domain compared to their privileged positions in society.

The stories of the Thousand and One Nights are an unequivocal erotic narrative coupled with explicitly libidinous poetry, whether in pederasty or heterosexuality. The unambiguous sexual accounts embroil homoerotic games, sexual verbal games of openly naming sexual organs, and stories of sexual intercourse, fun, and pleasure. The epicurean narrative is one of the reasons for the popularity of this collection of tales, but also one of its perceived notoriety. Yet this hedonistic narrative was resonant with an equally sexual pleasure-seeking medieval erotic literature. All this erotic literature, including Alf Layla wa Layla, represents an epoch in the history of the Middle East where sexual outlooks were liberal, open-minded, and relaxed. The historicity of this reality is important, particularly when contrasted with the more sexually rigid present-day cultures dominating the region.

Many aspects of sexual and human relationships in these tales tend to transcend time and appeal to modern time as well. Issues addressed in this collection of tales are highly relevant to present life in the Middle East and beyond. Astonishingly, medieval liberal attitude to sexuality is sharply contrasted with a very conservative and condemnatory outlook to sexuality in present-day Middle Eastern cultures. Positive sexuality reflected in these tales is part of the tradition of this region and should, therefore, be regarded as an incentive to discard the many cultural and religious taboos engulfing sexual life in these societies. In this regard, highlighting and discussing the issues addressed in the Thousand and One Nights, including sexual and gender issues, is an important tool in rebuilding a more dynamic, open-minded, and tolerant Middle East.

Arguing against orientalist criticisms, the argument that the Middle East during the Middle Ages was a sexually liberal society and culture is often invoked, generating a misleading satisfaction at the expense of scrutinizing current realities. While this debate accuses the orientalists of adopting an ahistorical approach to the region, the Middle East itself tends to subscribe to the very same allegation of ahistoricity. Obviously, the once liberal medieval epoch falls into an unambiguous divergence with the present-day rigid and conservative region and, therefore, the spirit and outlook of that era need to be internalized and owned, rather than externalized as an argument that is mainly raised to score points with the West. This would entail the resuscitation of Alf Layla wa Layla.

Irwin, an influential authority on the subject, states that the Arabian Nights is a product of a medieval culture that was confident, tolerant, and pluralist. Astoundingly, the very opposite of these attributes characterize the current situation in the Middle East. Leaving aside the depressing domains of politics and economics, gender and sexual myths are still venerated and unchallenged, thereby creating one of the most sexually repressive and segregated gender realities across cultures. When the Middle East decides that it no longer makes sense or is no longer possible to remain an exception to a worldwide and cross-cultural tendency of liberalizing sexual and gender realities and moralities, the Thousand and One Nights will undoubtedly prove to be an instrumental and valuable tool in creating a new cultural, social, and gender reality. In the currently debilitating situation, the region needs remedies to political, social, and cultural paralysis and rigidity. The framework, the stories, and indeed the entire narrative spirit of the Arabian Nights are condensed to finding a way out of a difficult and violent impasse. In this endeavour, imagination, exercised as politics, proved to be instrumental. What the Middle East really needs today is an imaginative mind able at critically scrutinizing realities with a positively imagined future. The imaginative Shahrazad, the queen of the literary narrative of the Arabian Nights, is highly relevant to the present-day Middle East.

The literary product of the Thousand and One Nights represents one of the most important Middle Eastern contributions to world literature. This narrative still inspires and influences various literary expressions worldwide. The various translations of this work helped not only in reviving this literature but also in popularizing it and making it one of the most celebrated works of world literature. Not only has the European adoption of the Arabian Nights been successful in making this work an outstanding and popular literature, but also in instrumentally using it to overhaul the austerity of the sexual morality of the Victorian period, dominating British and Western societies until the nineteenth century. Sad to say, this sexually rigid morality is still prevalent in the Middle East. Yet, Alf Layla wa Layla is not a deceiving illusion of a desert mirage or a distant past, but rather animated, brilliant, powerful, valuable, culturally indigenized, and most importantly, highly accessible.

SELECT BIBLIOGRAPHY

Abbott, Nabia 1949. 'A ninth-century fragment of the "Thousand Nights": New light on the early history of the Arabian Nights'. *Journal of Near Eastern Studies*, 8 (3): 129–64.

Adang, Camilla 2003. 'Ibn Hazm on homosexuality: A case-study of Zahiri legal methodology'. *al-Qantara*, 24 (1): 5–31.

Alf Layla wa Layla. 1835–6. 2 vols. Cairo: Bulaq Government Press.

Alf Layla wa Layla. 1880–3. 4 vols. n.a.: al-Haydari Printing.

Alf Layla wa Layla. 1889–90. 5 vols. Beirut: al-Matba'a al-Katholikia.

Alf Layla wa Layla. Wiki Organization, various volumes. https://ar.wikisource.org/wiki/

Alf Layla wa Layla. Wikipedia. https://ar.wikipedia.org/

Allen, Roger and Richards, D. S. (eds) 2006. *Arabic Literature in the Post-Classical Period*. Cambridge: Cambridge University Press.

Amer, Sahar 2001. 'Lesbian sex and the military: From the medieval Arabic tradition to French literature'. In Sautman, Francesca Canadé and Sheingorn, Pamela (eds), *Same-Sex Love and Desire Among Women in the Middle Ages*. New York: Palgrave, pp. 179–98.

2007. 'Cross-dressing and female same-sex marriage in medieval French and Arabic Literature'. In Cuffel, Alexandra and Britt, Brian (eds), *Religion, Gender, and Culture in the Pre-Modern World*. New York: Palgrave Macmillan, pp. 105–35.

2008. *Crossing Borders: Love Between Women in Medieval French and Arabic Literature*. Philadelphia, PA: University of Pennsylvania Press.

2009. 'Medieval Arab lesbians and lesbian-like women'. *Journal of the History of Sexuality*, 18 (2): 215–36.

2012. 'Naming to empower: Lesbianism in the Arab Islamicate World Today'. *Journal of Lesbian Studies*, 16 (4): 381–97.

Arabian Nights. Various e-books editions, Project Gutenberg. www.gutenberg.org/

Attar, Samar and Fischer, Gerhard 1991. 'Promiscuity, emancipation, submission: The civilizing process and the establishment of a female role model in the frame-story of 1001 Nights'. *Arab Studies Quarterly*, 13 (3–4): 1–18.

Babayan, Kathryn, and Najmabadi, Afsaneh (eds) 2008. *Islamicate Sexualities: Translations Across Temporal Geographies of Desire*. Cambridge, MA: Harvard University Press.

Balzaretti, Ross 2008. 'Sexuality in late Lombard Italy, *c.*700–*c.*800 AD'. In Harper, April and Proctor, Caroline (eds) 2008. *Medieval Sexuality: A Casebook*. New York: Routledge, pp. 7–31.

Beaumont, Daniel 2002. *Slave of Desire: Sex. Love, and Death in The 1001 Nights*. Madison, WI: Fairleigh Dickinson University Press.

Belcher, Stephen 2007. 'Hunters and boundaries in Mande cultures'. In Cuffel, Alexandra and Britt, Brian (eds), *Religion, Gender, and Culture in the Pre-Modern World*. New York: Palgrave Macmillan, pp. 167–82.

Bellamy, James A. 1979. 'Sex and society in Islamic popular literature'. In Sayyid-Marsot, Afaf Lutfi al. (ed.), *Society and the Sexes in Medieval Islam*. Malibu, CA: Undena Publications, pp. 23–42.

Bencheikh, Jamel Eddine 1997. 'Historical and mythical Baghdad in the tale of Ali b. Bakkar and Shams al-Nahar, or the resurgence of the imaginary'. In Hovannisian, Richard G. and Sabagh, Georges (eds), *The Thousand and One Nights in Arabic Literature and Society*. Cambridge: Cambridge University Press, pp. 14–28.

Bettelheim, Bruno 1976. *The Uses of Enchantment: The Meaning and Importance of Fairy Tales*. New York: Alfred A. Knopf.

Boone, Joseph 1993. 'Framing the phallus in the Arabian Nights: Pansexuality, pederasty, Pasolini'. In Wayne, Valerie and Moore, Cornelia (eds), *Translations/Transformations: Gender and Culture in Film and Literature East and West*. Honolulu, HI: University of Hawaii Press, pp. 23–33.

Borg, Gert 2000. 'Lust and carnal desire: Obscenities attributed to Arab women'. *Arabic and Middle Eastern Literature*, 3 (2): 149–64.

Boswell, John 1989. 'Revolutions, universals, and sexual categories'. In Duberman, Martin, Vicinus, Martha, and Chauncey, George Jr. (eds), *Hidden from History: Reclaiming the Gay and Lesbian Past*. New York: Meridian, pp. 1–33.

Brundage, James A. 1996. 'Sex and canon law'. In Bullough, Vern L. and Brundage, James A. (eds), *Handbook of Medieval Sexuality*. New York: Garland, pp. 33–50.

Bullough, Vern L. 1996. 'Cross dressing and gender role change in the Middle Ages'. In Bullough, Vern L. and Brundage, James A. (eds), *Handbook of Medieval Sexuality*. New York: Garland, pp. 223–42.

Bullough, Vern L. and James A. Brundage (eds) 1996. *Handbook of Medieval Sexuality*. New York: Garland.

Bürgel, J. C. 1979. 'Love, lust, and longing: Eroticism in early Islam as reflected in literary sources'. In Sayyid-Marsot, Afaf Lutfi al. (ed.), *Society and the Sexes in Medieval Islam*. Malibu, CA: Undena Publications, pp. 81–118.

Burton, Richard F. 2010 [1885–88]. *The Arabian Nights*. 10 vols. London: Halcyon Classic.

Bushnaq, Inea (trans. and ed.) 1986. *Arab Folktales*. Harmondsworth: Penguin.

Clinton, Jerome W. 1985. 'Madness and cure in the 1001 Nights'. *Studia Islamica*, 61: 107–25.

Clot, André 1986. *Harun al-Rashid and the World of the Thousand and One Nights*. London: Saqi.

Colligan, Colette 2006. *The Traffic in Obscenity from Byron to Beardsley: Sexuality and Exoticism in Nineteenth-Century Print Culture*. New York: Palgrave Macmillan.

Crispin, Philip 2008. 'Scandal, malice and the Kingdom of the Bazoche'. In Harper, April and Proctor, Caroline (eds), *Medieval Sexuality: A Casebook*. New York: Routledge, pp. 154–72.

Cuffel, Alexandra 2007. 'Reorienting Christian "Amazons": Women warriors in medieval Islamic literature in the context of the Crusades'. In Cuffel, Alexandra and Britt, Brian (eds), *Religion, Gender, and Culture in the Pre-Modern World*. New York: Palgrave Macmillan, pp. 137–66.

Cuffel, Alexandra and Britt, Brian (eds) 2007. *Religion, Gender, and Culture in the Pre-Modern World*. New York: Palgrave Macmillan.

Damrosch, David 2011. 'The Thousand and One Nights'. In Damrosch, David (ed.), *Gateways to World Literature*. New Jersey, NJ: Longman, pp. 606–47.

Dawood, N. J. 1973. *Tales from the Thousand and One Nights*. London: Penguin.

Duran, Khalid 1993. 'Homosexuality and Islam'. In Sweidler, A. (ed.), *Homosexuality and World Religions*. Valley Forge, PA: Trinity Press International, pp. 181–98.

Epps, Brad 2008. 'Comparison, competition, and cross-dressing: Cross-cultural analysis in a contested world'. In Babayan, Kathryn and Najmabadi, Afsaneh (eds), *Islamicate Sexualities: Translations Across Temporal Geographies of Desire*. Cambridge, MA: Harvard University Press, pp. 114–60.

Farag, Rofail F. 1976. 'The Arabian Nights: A mirror of Islamic culture in the Middle Ages'. *Arabica*, 23 (2): 197–211.

Farmer, Sharon and Pasternack, Carol Braun (eds) 2003. *Gender and Difference in the Middle Ages*. Minneapolis, MN: University of Minnesota Press.

Finke, Laurie A. 1996. 'Sexuality in medieval French literature'. In Bullough, Vern L. and Brundage, James A. (eds), *Handbook of Medieval Sexuality*. New York: Garland, pp. 345–66.

Foucault, Michel 1990. *The History of Sexuality*. Vol. 1. Harmondsworth: Penguin.

Gelder, Geert Jan van 2004. 'Poetry and the Arabian Nights'. In Marzolph, Ulrich and Leeuwen, Richard van (eds), *The Arabian Nights Encyclopedia*. Santa Barbara, CA: ABC-Clio, vol. 1, pp. 13–17.

Gerhardt, Mia 1963. *The Art of Storytelling*. Leiden: E. J. Brill.

Ghazoul, Ferial J. 1996. *Nocturnal Poetics: The Arabian Nights in Comparative Context*. Cairo: The American University in Cairo Press.

Goitein, S. D. 1979. 'The sexual mores of the common people'. In Sayyid-Marsot, Afaf Lutfi al. (ed.), *Society and the Sexes in Medieval Islam*. Malibu, CA: Undena Publications, pp. 43–62.

Grossman, Judith 1980. 'Infidelity and fiction: The discovery of women's subjectivity in Arabian Nights'. *The Georgian Review*, 34 (1): 113–25.

Guthrie, Shirley 2001. *Arab Women in the Middle Ages: Private Lives and Public Roles*. London: Saqi.

Habib, Samar 2007. *Female Homosexuality in the Middle East: Histories and Representations*. New York: Routledge.

Haddawy, Husain 1990. *The Arabian Nights*. New York: W. W. Norton.

Hämeen-Anttila, Jaakko 2014. 'What is obscene? Obscenity in classical Arabic literature'. In Talib, Adam, Hammond, Marlé, and Schippers, Arie (eds), *The Rude, the Bad and the Bawdy*. Cambridge: Gibb Memorial Trust, pp. 13–23.

Hammad, Hiyam Ali 1986. *al-mar'a fi alf layla wa layla* [*Women in Thousand and One Nights*]. Cairo: Nahdhat al-Sharq.

Hammond, Marlé 2014. 'The foul-mouthed fahla: Obscenity and amplification in early women's invective'. In Talib, Adam, Hammond, Marlé, and Schippers, Arie (eds), *The Rude, the Bad and the Bawdy*. Cambridge: Gibb Memorial Trust, pp. 254–65.

Hamori, Andras 1974. *On the Art of Medieval Arabic Literature*. Princeton, NJ: Princeton University Press.

1976. 'Notes on two love stories from the Thousand and One Nights'. *Studia Islamica*, 43: 65–80.

1983. 'A comic romance from the Thousand and One Nights: The tale of two viziers'. *Arabica*, 30 (1): 38–56.

Harper, April 2008. '"The Food of Love": Illicit feasting, food imagery and adultery in old French literature'. In Harper, April and Proctor, Caroline (eds), *Medieval Sexuality: A Casebook*. New York: Routledge, pp. 81–97.

Harper, April and Proctor, Caroline (eds) 2008. *Medieval Sexuality: A Casebook*. New York: Routledge.

Heath, Peter. 1987–88. 'Romance as genre in "The Thousand and One Nights"'. *Journal of Arabic Literature*, I (18): 1–21; II (19): 3–26.

Hoffmann, Thomas 2009. 'The intercourse of prayer: Notes on an erotic passage in the Arabian Nights and the Islamic ritual prayer'. In Holm, Bent, Nielsen, Bent Flemming, and Vedal, Karen (eds), *Religion, Ritual, Theatre*. Frankfurt: Peter Lang, pp. 63–76.

Hovannisian, Richard G. and Sabagh, Georges (eds) 1997. *The Thousand and One Nights in Arabic Literature and Society*. Cambridge: Cambridge University Press.

Irwin, Robert 1994. *The Arabian Nights: A Companion*. London: Penguin.

     1999. *Night and Horses and the Desert: The Penguin Anthology of Classical Arabic Literature*. London: Penguin.

     2015. 'The Dark Side of "The Arabian Nights"'. *Critical Muslim*, 13 (1), www.criticalmuslim. io/the-dark-side-of-the-arabian-nights/

     2016. 'Medieval Basra: City of the mind'. *Critical Muslim*, 18 (3), www.criticalmuslim. io/medieval-basra-city-mind/

Jayyusi, Salma Khadra 2006. 'Arabic Poetry in the post-classical age'. In Allen, Roger and Richards, D. S. (eds), *Arabic Literature in the Post-Classical Period*. Cambridge: Cambridge University Press, pp. 25–59.

Jins-al 'inda al-arab: nusus mukhtarah. [*Sexual Life of the Arabs: Selected Texts*], 1997. 3 vols. Köln: al-Jamel Publication.

Jochens, Jenny 1996. 'Old Norse sexuality: Men, women, and beasts'. In Bullough, Vern L. and Brundage, James A. (eds), *Handbook of Medieval Sexuality*. New York: Garland, pp. 369–400.

Johansson, Warren and Percy, William A. 1996. 'Homosexuality'. In Bullough, Vern L. and Brundage, James A. (eds), *Handbook of Medieval Sexuality*. New York: Garland, pp. 155–89.

Kassim, Dina al. 2008. 'Epilogue: Sexual epistemologies, East in West'. In Babayan, Kathryn and Najmabadi, Afsaneh (eds), *Islamicate Sexualities: Translations across Temporal Geographies of Desire*. Cambridge, MA: Harvard University Press, pp. 297–340.

Kennedy, Hugh 2008. 'Al-Jahiz and the construction of homosexuality at the Abbasid court'. In Harper, April and Proctor, Caroline (eds), *Medieval Sexuality: A Casebook*. New York: Routledge, pp. 175–88.

Kennedy, Philip 2007. *Abu Nuwas: A Genius of Poetry*. Oxford: Oneworld.

Kirby, W. F. 1887. 'The forbidden doors of the Thousand and One Nights'. *The Folk-Lore Journal*, 5 (2): 112–24.

Knoblauch, Ann-Marie 2007. 'Promiscuous or proper? Nymphs as female role models in ancient Greece'. In Cuffel, Alexandra and Britt, Brian (eds), *Religion, Gender, and Culture in the Pre-Modern World*. New York: Palgrave Macmillan, pp. 47–62.

Koran, The 1974. Translated with notes by N. J. Dawood, 4th revised edition. Harmondsworth: Penguin.

Kraemer, Joel L. 1993. *Humanism in the Renaissance of Islam: The Cultural Revival during the Buyid Age*. Leiden: Brill.

Kruk, Remke 2004. 'The Arabian Nights and the popular epics'. In Marzolph, Ulrich and Leeuwen, Richard van (eds), *The Arabian Nights Encyclopedia*. Santa Barbara, CA: ABC-Clio, vol. 1, pp. 34–8.

Kuefler, Mathew S. 1996. 'Castration and eunuchism in the middle ages'. In Bullough, Vern L. and Brundage, James A. (eds), *Handbook of Medieval Sexuality*. New York: Garland, pp. 279–306.

Kugle, Scott Siraj al-Haqq 2010. *Homosexuality in Islam: Critical Reflection on Gay, Lesbian, and Transgender Muslims*. Oxford: Oneworld.

Lagrange, Frédéric 2000. 'Male homosexuality in modern Arabic literature'. In Ghoussoub, A. and Sinclair-Webb, E. (eds), *Imagined Masculinities: Male Identity and Culture in the Modern Middle East*. London: Saqi, pp. 169–98.

2008. 'The obscenity of the vizier'. In Babayan, Kathryn and Najmabadi, Afsaneh (eds), *Islamicate Sexualities: Translations across Temporal Geographies of Desire*. Cambridge, MA: Harvard University Press, pp. 161–203.

2014. 'Modern Arabic literature and the disappearance of mujun: Same-sex rape as a case study'. In Talib, Adam, Hammond, Marlé, and Schippers, Arie (eds), *The Rude, the Bad and the Bawdy*. Cambridge: Gibb Memorial Trust, pp. 230–53.

Lane, Edward William 1987 [1883]. *Arabian Society in The Middle Ages: Studies from The Thousand and One Nights*. London: Curzon Press.

Lapidus, Ira M. 2002. *A History of Islamic Societies*. 2nd edition. Cambridge University Press.

Leeuwen, Richard van 2014. 'Love or lust: Sexual relationships between humans and jinn in The Thousand and One Nights and the djinn in The Nightingale's Eye'. In Talib, Adam, Hammond, Marlé, and Schippers, Arie (eds), *The Rude, the Bad and the Bawdy*. Cambridge: Gibb Memorial Trust, pp. 208–20.

Levin, Eve 1996. 'Eastern orthodox Christianity'. In Bullough, Vern L. and Brundage, James A. (eds), *Handbook of Medieval Sexuality*. New York: Garland, pp. 329–43.

Littmann, E. 2012. 'Alf Layla wa-Layla'. In Bearman, P., Bianquis, Th., Bosworth, E., van Donzel, E. and Heinrichs, W.P. (eds), *Encyclopedia of Islam*, 2nd edition. http://referenceworks.brillonline.com/browse/encyclopaedia-of-islam-2

Mack, Robert L. (ed.) 2009. *Arabian Nights' Entertainments*. Oxford: Oxford University Press.

Macnaghten, W. H. 1839–42. *Alf Layla wa Layla*. 4 vols. Calcutta: Baptist Mission Press.

Mahdi, Muhsin 1973. 'Remarks on the 1001 nights'. *Interpretation: A Journal of Political Philosophy*, 3 (2–3): 157–68.

1984. *Kitab alf layla wa layla min usulihi al-arabiya al-ula [The Thousand and One Nights from the Earliest Known Sources]*. 3 vols. Leiden: E. J. Brill.

1995. *The Thousand and One Nights*. Leiden: E. J. Brill.

1997. 'From history to fiction: The tale told by the king's steward in The Thousand and One Nights'. In Hovannisian, Richard G. and Sabagh, Georges (eds), *The Thousand and One Nights in Arabic Literature and Society*. Cambridge: Cambridge University Press, pp. 78–105.

Malti-Douglas Fedwa 1991. *Woman's Body, Woman's Word: Gender and Discourse in Arabo-Islamic Writing*. Princeton, NJ: Princeton University Press.

1997. 'Shahrazad feminist'. In Hovannisian, Richard G. and Sabagh, Georges (eds), *The Thousand and One Nights in Arabic Literature and Society*. Cambridge: Cambridge University Press, pp. 40–55.

2001. 'Tribadism/lesbianism and the sexualized body in medieval Arabo-Islamic narratives'. In Sautman, Francesca Canadé and Sheingorn, Pamela (eds), *Same-Sex Love and Desire among Women in the Middle Ages*. New York: Palgrave, pp. 179–98.

2004. 'Homosociality, heterosexuality, and shahrazad'. In Marzolph, Ulrich and Leeuwen, Richard van (eds), *The Arabian Nights Encyclopedia*. Santa Barbara, CA: ABC-Clio, vol. 1, pp. 38–42.

Marzolph, Ulrich (ed.) 2006. *The Arabian Nights Reader*. Detroit, MI: Wayne State University Press.

2007. 'Arabian Nights'. In Fleet, K., Krämer, G., Matringe, D., Nawas, J. and Rowson, E. (eds), *Encyclopedia of Islam*. 3rd edition. http://referenceworks.brillonline.com/browse/encyclopaedia-of-islam-3

2015. 'Sex, crime, magic, and mystery in the Thousand and One Nights'. In Tatar, Maria (ed.), *The Cambridge Companion to Fairy Tales*. Cambridge: Cambridge University Press, pp. 186–201.

Marzolph, Ulrich and Leeuwen, Richard van 2004. *The Arabian Nights Encyclopedia*. 2 vols. Santa Barbara, CA: ABC-Clio.

Ma'su'at al-qisas al-mamnu'a min alf layla wa-layla [*Encyclopedia of Forbidden Tales from The Thousand and One Nights*]. 2008. 3 vols. Al-Mansuria, Lebanon: Kitabuna.

Matarasso, Michel 1982. 'In praise of double sexuality in the Thousand and One Nights: The geste of Boudour'. *Diogenes*, 118: 12–48.

Miquel, André 1997. 'The Thousand and One Nights in Arabic literature and society'. In Hovannisian, Richard G. and Sabagh, Georges (eds), *The Thousand and One Nights in Arabic Literature and Society*. Cambridge: Cambridge University Press, pp. 6–13.

Montgomery, James E. 1994. 'Revelry and remorse: A poem of Abu Nuwas'. *Journal of Arabic Literature*, 25 (2): 116–34.

1996. 'For the love of a Christian boy: A song by Abu Nuwas'. *Journal of Arabic Literature*, 27 (2): 115–24.

Munajjid, Salah al-Din al. 1958. *Al-Hayat al-jinsiyya 'inda l-'arab* [*Sexual Life Among the Arabs*]. Beirut: Dar al-Kutub.

Murray, Jacqueline 1996a. 'Hiding behind the universal man: Male sexuality in the Middle Ages'. In Bullough, Vern L. and Brundage, James A. (eds), *Handbook of Medieval Sexuality*. New York: Garland, pp. 123–52.

1996b. 'Twice marginal and twice invisible: Lesbians in the Middle Ages'. In Bullough, Vern L. and Brundage, James A. (eds), *Handbook of Medieval Sexuality*. New York: Garland, pp. 191–222.

Murray, Stephen O. 1997. 'Woman–woman love in Islamic societies'. In Murray, Stephen O. and Roscoe, Will (eds), *Islamic Homosexualities: Culture, History, and Literature*. New York: New York University Press, pp. 97–104.

Murray, Stephen O. and Roscoe, Will 1997a. 'Conclusion'. In Murray, Stephen O. and Roscoe, Will (eds), *Islamic Homosexualities: Culture, History, and Literature*. New York: New York University Press, pp. 302–18.

(eds) 1997b. *Islamic Homosexualities: Culture, History, and Literature*. New York: New York University Press.

Musawi, Muhsin al. 1980. 'The growth of scholarly interest in the Arabian Nights'. *The Muslim World*, 70: 196–212.

2005. 'Scheherzade's nonverbal narratives'. *Journal of Arabic Literature*, 36 (3): 338–62.

2009. *The Islamic Context of the Thousand and One Nights*. New York: Columbia University Press.

Naaman, Erez 2013. 'Eating figs and pomegranates: Taboos and language in the *Thousand and One Nights*'. *Journal of Arabic Literature*, 44 (3): 335–70.

Naithani, Sadhana. 2004. 'The teacher and the taught: Structures and meaning in the Arabian Nights and the Panchatantra'. *Marvels and Tales*, 18 (2): 272–85.

Nasr al-Katib, 'Abdul Hasan 'Ali ibn 1977. *jawami' al-ladha'* [*Encyclopedia of Pleasure*], edited and translated by Salah Addin Khawwam. Toronto: Aleppo.

One Thousand and One Nights. Various e-books editions, Project Gutenberg. www. gutenberg.org/

One Thousand and One Nights. Wikipedia. https://en.wikipedia.org/wiki/One_Thousand_ and_One_Nights#Sources

Ouyang, Wen-chin 2014. 'Mujun, junun, funun'. In Talib, Adam, Hammond, Marlé, and Schippers, Arie (eds), *The Rude, the Bad and the Bawdy*. Cambridge: Gibb Memorial Trust, pp. 7–12.

Papoutsakis, Nefeli 2014. 'The ayriyat of Abu Hukayma (D.240/854): A preliminary study'. In Talib, Adam, Hammond, Marlé, and Schippers, Arie (eds), *The Rude, the Bad and the Bawdy*. Cambridge: Gibb Memorial Trust, pp. 101–22.

Payne, John 1901. *The Book of the Thousand Nights and One Nights*. 9 vols. London: Villon Society.

Pieniadz, Aneta 2009. 'Incest in early medieval society'. *Acta Poloniae Historica*, 99: 39–61.

Pierce, Leslie 2009. 'Writing the histories of sexuality in the Middle East'. *American Historical Review*, 114 (5): 1325–39.

Pinault, David 1992. *Story-Telling Technique in the Arabian Nights*. Leiden: E. J. Brill.

Qalamawi, Suhayr al. 1959. *Alf Layla wa Layla*. Cairo: Dar al-Ma'arif.

Resnick, Irven M. and Kitchell, Kenneth F. Jr. 2007. 'The sweepings of Lamia: Transformations of the myths of Lilith and Lamia'. In Cuffel, Alexandra and Britt, Brian (eds), *Religion, Gender, and Culture in the Pre-Modern World*. New York: Palgrave Macmillan, pp. 77–104.

Reynolds, Dwight F. 2006a. 'A Thousand and One Nights: A history of the text and its reception'. In Allen, Roger and Richards, D. S. (eds), *Arabic Literature in the Post-Classical Period*. Cambridge: Cambridge University Press, pp. 270–91.

   2006b. 'Popular prose in the post-classical period'. In Allen, Roger and Richards, D. S. (eds), *Arabic Literature in the Post-Classical Period*. Cambridge: Cambridge University Press, pp. 245–69.

Ringrose, Kathryn M. 2003. 'Reconfiguring the Prophet Daniel: Gender, sanctity, and castration in Byzantium'. In Farmer, Sharon and Pasternack, Carol Braun (eds), *Gender and Difference in the Middle Ages*. Minneapolis, MN: University of Minnesota Press, pp. 73–106.

Rosenthanl, Franz 1979. 'Fiction and reality: Sources for the role of sex in medieval Muslim society'. In Sayyid-Marsot, Afaf Lutfi al. (ed.), *Society and the Sexes in Medieval Islam*. Malibu, CA: Undena Publications, pp. 3–22.

   1996. 'A research note on sexuality and Muslim civilization'. In Bullough, Vern L. and Brundage, James A. (eds), *Handbook of Medieval Sexuality*. New York: Garland, pp. 319–27.

   1997. 'Male and female: Described and compared'. In Wright, J. W. Jr. and Rowson, Everett K. (eds), *Homoeroticism in Classical Arabic Literature*. New York: Columbia University Press, pp. 24–54.

Roth, Norman 1991. '"Fawn of my Delights": Boy-love in Hebrew and Arabic verse'. In Salisbury, Joyce E. (ed.), *Sex in the Middle Ages*. New York: Garland, pp. 157–72.

Rouayheb, Khaled el. 2005. *Before Homosexuality in the Arab-Islamic World, 1500–1800*. Chicago, IL: University of Chicago Press.

Rowson, Everett K. 1991. 'The categorization of gender and sexual irregularity in medieval Arabic vice lists'. In Epstein, Julia and Straub, Kristina (eds), *Body Guards: The Cultural Politics of Gender Ambiguity*. New York: Routledge, pp. 50–79.

    2003. 'Gender irregularity as entertainment: Institutionalized transvestism at the caliphal court in medieval Baghdad'. In Farmer, Sharon and Pasternack, Carol Braun (eds), *Gender and Difference in the Middle Ages*. Minneapolis, MN: University of Minnesota Press, pp. 45–72.

    2008. 'Homoerotic liaisons among the Mamluk elite in late medieval Egypt and Syria'. In Babayan, Kathryn and Najmabadi, Afsaneh (eds), *Islamicate Sexualities: Translations across Temporal Geographies of Desire*. Cambridge, MA: Harvard University Press, pp. 204–38.

Salisbury, Joyce E. 1991. 'Bestiality in the Middle Ages'. In Salisbury, Joyce E. (ed.), *Sex in the Middle Ages*. New York: Garland, pp. 173–86.

    1996. 'Gendering sexuality'. In Bullough, Vern L. and Brundage, James A. (eds), *Handbook of Medieval Sexuality*. New York: Garland, pp. 81–102.

Sautman, Francesca Canadé, and Sheingorn, Pamela (eds) 2001. *Same-Sex Love and Desire Among Women in the Middle Ages*. New York: Palgrave.

Sayyid-Marsot, Afaf Lutfi al. (ed.) 1979. *Society and the Sexes in Medieval Islam*. Malibu, CA: Undena Publications.

Schimmel, Annemarie 1979. 'Eros – heavenly and not so heavenly – in Sufi literature and life'. In Sayyid-Marsot, Afaf Lutfi al. (ed.), *Society and the Sexes in Medieval Islam*. Malibu, CA: Undena Publications, pp. 119–41.

Schulze, Reinhard 2004. 'Images of masculinity in the Arabian Nights'. In Marzolph, Ulrich and Leeuwen, Richard van (eds), *The Arabian Nights Encyclopedia*. Santa Barbara, CA: ABC-Clio, vol. 1, pp. 46–50.

Shamy, Hasan el. 2004. 'Siblings in Alf Layla wa-layla'. *Marvels and Tales: Journal of Fairy-Tale Studies*, 18 (2): 170–86.

    2006. *A Motif Index of The Thousand and One Nights*. Bloomington, IN: Indiana University Press.

Sharlet, Jocelyn 2010. 'Public displays of affection: Male homoerotic desire and sociability in medieval Arabic literature'. In Habib, Samar (ed.), *Islam and Homosexuality*. Santa Barbara, CA: Praeger, vol. 1, pp. 37–56.

Shoshan, Boaz 2004. 'Social life and popular culture'. In Marzolph, Ulrich and Leeuwen, Richard van (eds), *The Arabian Nights Encyclopedia*. Santa Barbara, CA: ABC-Clio, vol. 1, pp. 50–4.

Smoor, Pieter 2014. 'A suspicion of excessive frankness'. In Talib, Adam, Hammond, Marlé, and Schippers, Arie (eds), *The Rude, the Bad and the Bawdy*. Cambridge: Gibb Memorial Trust, pp. 24–65.

Talib, Adam, Hammond, Marlé, and Schippers, Arie (eds) 2014. *The Rude, the Bad and the Bawdy*. Cambridge: Gibb Memorial Trust.

Talmon, Adi 1999. 'Tawaddud: The story of a majlis'. In Lazarus-Yafeh Hava, Cohen, Mark R., Somekh, Sasson, and Griffith, Sidney H. (eds), *The Majlis: Interreligious Encounters in Medieval Islam*. Wiesbaden, Germany: Harrassowitz, pp. 120–7.

Tusi-al, Nasir al-Din 2014. *The Sultan's Sex Potion: Arabs Aphrodisiacs in the Middle Ages.* Edited and translated by Daniel L. Newman. London: Saqi.

Wallen, John 2014. 'The "Terminal Essay" to Burton's Arabian Nights: Tasting the forbidden fruit'. *The Victorian*, 2 (2): 1–28.

Wiet, Gaston 1971. *Baghdad: Metropolis of the Abbasid Caliphate.* Norman, OK: University of Oklahoma Press.

Wright, J. W. Jr. 1997. 'Masculine allusion and the structure of satire in early "Abbasid poetry"'. In Wright, J. W. Jr. and Rowson, Everett K. (eds), *Homoeroticism in Classical Arabic Literature.* New York: Columbia University Press, pp. 1–23.

Wright, J. W. Jr. and Rowson, Everett K. (eds) 1997. *Homoeroticism in Classical Arabic Literature.* New York: Columbia University Press.

INDEX

Abbasid, 5, 32, 125, 138, 144, 148
  Caliph, 5–6
Abbassa, caliph sister, 32
Abbott, Nabia, 3
Abyssinia, 97
Acre, 33
Africa, 36, 54
Ahwaz, 144
Alexandria, 134, 165
Alf Layla wa Layla, 1–2, 4–5, 8, 12, 23, 38,
    46, 55, 67, 69, 145, 149, 169–71.
    See Arabian Nights
  re-indigenizing, 8, 170
Amazons, 10, 83
Amer, Sahar, 1, 125, 135–7
Amin-al, caliph, 145
amrad, 6, 11, 17, 139, 141–2, 144–51, 153, 155, 168
  vs. adult men, 12, 150, 160–1
  vs. women, 6, 140, 148
Andalusia, 29
Antara, epic, 65
Arab, 3, 19, 32, 43, 54, 58, 76, 97, 131, 138, 141,
    144, 149
Arabian Nights, 1–2, 7, 40, 42, 52–3, 56, 88, 98,
    137, 140, 145–6, 149, 167–70. *See* Alf
    Layla wa Layla
  canonical literature, 5–7, 17, 125, 149, 167
  Indian ancient literature, 98
  influencing Western literature, 1–2, 170
  intellectual refinement, 4–5, 77, 167
  literary text, 1–3, 170
  orientalist enterprise, 1–2, 170
  rationale, 56, 68, 98, 112
  reflecting social environment, 3, 5–6, 77,
      167, 170
  subversive, 2–3, 170
  translation, 1–2, 7

urban culture, 4–6, 167
world literature, 1–2, 4, 170

Baghdad, 4–5, 11–13, 16, 18, 24–6, 32–4, 56, 65,
    73, 78–9, 84–6, 91–3, 103, 108, 113, 126,
    132, 134–5, 140, 144, 147–50, 156–8, 164,
    174, 180–1
Balzaretti, Ross, 151
Barmakids, 5, 32
  Ja'far, 32, 85, 94
Basra, 5, 11, 14, 18, 24–5, 53, 56, 85, 87, 95, 104–5,
    126–30, 143–4, 156, 162, 176
Bayt al-Hikma, 5
Beaumont, Daniel, 40, 43, 137
beauty, 17, 19, 24–5, 65, 88, 121, 154, 156–7,
    159–60, 162–3, 165
  androgyny, 141, 150
  contest, 39–40, 146, 163
  male, 11, 13–14, 16, 27, 39, 59, 73, 140–6,
      149–51, 153, 155, 159, 164, 168
Bedouin, 3, 34, 42, 55, 73, 81, 89, 100–1, 134
Belcher, Stephen, 36, 54
Belqis, queen, 63, 99
Bencheikh, Jamel Eddine, 4
bestiality, 43, 46–51, 134, 167
bisexuality, 128, 135
  polymorphism, 135
Boone, Joseph, 140
Borg, Gert, 47
Boswell, John, 125, 138, 141, 149
British, 171
Brundage, James, 106
Bukhara, 90
Bullough, Vern, 125, 137
Burton, Richard, 2, 43, 125, 136, 138, 141, 146
  Sotadic Zone, 138
  Terminal Essay, 138

Bushnaq, Inea, 50, 54, 55, 76, 97, 104, 107, 114
Byzantine, 106

Cairo, 5, 11, 24, 34, 48, 63, 78–80, 82, 87, 91,
    103–4, 108, 114, 134, 140, 148, 175, 179
China, 27, 34, 38, 53, 58, 60, 63, 68, 71, 78, 81–2,
    88, 119, 132–3
Christians, 16, 33, 65, 75, 78, 83, 123, 131, 142, 158
Clot, André, 4–5, 125
Colligan, Colette, 3
concubine, 32, 68, 71, 78, 84, 89, 103, 115
Crispin, Philip, 46, 50
cuckoldry, 40, 77, 80, 111–24, 168
Cuffel, Alexandra, 125, 131
culture, 1–5, 7, 17, 54, 88, 98, 106, 111, 125, 132,
    136, 138–9, 141, 144, 168–70
cunning, 3, 8, 12, 16, 24, 28, 31, 39, 44, 57, 64,
    68–9, 85, 88–9, 92, 99, 105, 111, 113,
    115–18, 121–2, 134, 168
curiosity, 10–12, 35, 44, 56–7
    forbidden doors, 11, 56–7

Damascus, 5, 16, 18, 30, 32–3, 42, 59, 82, 84, 86,
    92, 100, 102, 134, 150, 156
Damrosch, David, 3
Daniel, prophet, 94
dervish, 25, 63, 80, 83–4, 104, 109, 143, 155
drinking, 6, 65, 110, 128, 145, 156–8, 168
Dunyazad, 3
Duran, Khalid, 50

Egypt, 16, 24–5, 30, 33, 41, 70, 73, 76–7, 80,
    86, 105, 116, 120, 132, 140, 147, 156,
    158, 180
Epps, Brad, 40, 133
erotica, 5, 12, 25, 117, 152–67, 169
    literature, 6–7, 46, 125, 161, 169
eunuch, 17, 20, 73–4, 103, 107, 109, 133, 139,
    142, 163
    castration, 20, 38, 42, 107–8, 142, 163
Europe, 1–3, 7, 37, 46, 106, 151, 170

Farag, Rofail, 4
fate, 20, 23, 27, 30, 41, 50, 60, 74, 100, 103–4,
    113, 167
femicide, 8, 48, 61, 67, 95, 102–6, 115, 117,
    119, 168
Finke, Laurie, 3
folktale, 2, 7, 36, 50, 54–5, 97, 104, 107, 114
Foucault, Michel, 125
France, 1, 33, 50, 132
Fustat, 147

gender, 2–3, 7–8, 37, 40, 44, 47, 90, 99, 112, 130,
    137, 139–40, 168–70
    cryptic sign language, 28–9
    essentialization, 37, 40–3, 77, 98, 168
    hermaphrodite, 155
    mixing, 8, 10, 15–17, 80, 167
    obedience, 105, 114
    politics, 112
    segregation, 21, 23, 133, 167
    status, 20, 135, 139, 148–9, 169
    tension, 23, 27–31, 167
Genoa, 78
Gerhardt, Mia, 130
Ghazoul, Ferial, 3
Goethe, Jahann Wolfgang, 1
Greek, 54, 138, 141, 144, 148
Grossman, Judith, 4
Guthrie, Shirley, 17, 125

Habib, Samar, 125
Hajjaj-al, governor, 22, 101
Hamadan, 121
Hamah, 149
hammam, 4, 45, 56, 61, 79, 120, 134, 162
Hammond, Marlé, 6
Hanafi school, 85
harem, 8, 18, 20, 30, 67, 77, 83–5, 88, 97, 104, 112,
    115, 133–6, 168–9
Harper, April, 123
Harun al-Rashid, 5, 14, 18, 32, 62, 83–6, 94, 101,
    103, 126, 145–6, 162, 164, 174
hashish, 6, 162
Heath, Peter, 7
heterosexuality, 20, 49–50, 125, 127–31, 135,
    138–40, 148–9, 156, 168–9
Hind bint al-Nu'man, 101
Hira-al, 13
homosexuality, 2–3, 6, 126–7, 129–30, 135–6,
    139–40, 146, 155, 168–9
    homoerotic poetry, 141, 144
    homosociality, 136
    male, 132, 138–9, 147, 168–9
    simulated, 14, 134, 137, 140, 143–7, 150
honour, 29, 53, 61, 66, 70, 90, 100, 105, 136,
    153, 166
    dishonour, 21, 35, 66, 69–70, 72, 75
    shame, 66, 161
hunting, 26, 29, 34, 61, 81–2, 96, 102–3, 126
Hämeen-Anttila, Jaakko, 6, 15, 49

imagination, 14, 37, 56, 80, 129, 150, 170
incest, 40–1, 65, 71–6, 117, 136, 168

India, 24, 26, 38, 50, 58–9, 79, 81–2, 85,
        98, 132
infidelity, 40–2, 84, 88, 93, 98–111,
        133, 168
    adultery, 88–97
    femicide, 102–6
    fortune, 109–10
    punishment, 106–8
    testing fidelity, 99–102
Iraq, 13, 22, 25, 29, 96–7, 100–1, 125, 129,
        134, 164
Irwin, Robert, 1, 4–7, 18, 43–4, 48, 106, 111, 125,
        133, 137, 145, 147, 170
Isfahan, 83, 115, 120
Islam, 6, 26, 28, 33, 77, 83, 85, 131, 138, 141, 146,
        174–5, 177–8, 180
    conversion, 26, 33
    golden age, 3–4
Italy, 151

jawari, 10, 12, 17–18, 38, 59, 79, 84, 100–1, 104,
        139, 146, 149, 164, 167
    Labiba, 103
    Qut al-Qulub, 32, 84, 126
    Tawaddud, 11
Jayyusi, Salma Khadra, 77
Jerusalem, 54
Jews, 16, 20, 30, 54, 77, 81, 93, 102, 123
jinn, 11, 25–7, 30, 33, 35–6, 38–40, 42, 44,
        52–64, 68–9, 73, 106, 112–13, 126–7, 130,
        132, 142, 150, 160, 163, 167
    abduction, 58–62, 79–80, 82, 106, 112
    bad vs. good, 62–4
    demonology, 54
    exorcism, 62, 81
    ghoul, 54, 61, 80
    human love, 56–8, 99
    ifrit, 54–5, 63
    Lamia, 54
    Lilith, 54
    marid, 54, 63
    nasnas, 30
    talisman, 63, 97
Jochens, Jenny, 126, 140
Johansson, Warren and William Percy, 138
Joseph, prophet, 141

Kashmir, 24
Kassim, al, Dina, 141
Kennedy, Hugh, 5, 17, 146, 149
Kennedy, Philip, 125, 144
Khorasan, 83, 92

Kuefler, Mathew, 20
Kufa, 22, 85, 144, 164
Kugle, Scott Siraj al-Haqq, 125, 149

Lagrange, Frédéric, 138–9, 141, 144, 147
Lane, Edward William, 5, 54, 107
Lapidus, Ira, 4
Leeuwen, van Richard, 55
lesbianism, 125–31, 134–6
    dildo, 150
    sapphism, 136
    stigmatization, 130–1
    tribadism, 125, 131, 136
Levin, Eve, 106
literature, 1–2, 5–7, 17, 98, 139, 146, 149,
        169–70
    intertextuality, 1, 7, 17, 125, 167
    literary salons, 5
love, 10–11, 14, 16, 18–19, 23, 27, 29, 32–3, 39,
        42, 53–6, 58, 68, 71–3, 75, 77, 95, 99–100,
        126–7, 129, 166
    city of lovers, 17, 127
    platonic, 39, 81, 141, 144
    by a portrait, 24, 53, 58
    testing, 20, 102
    unrequited, 35, 81, 106, 130
lust, 11, 14, 22–3, 36, 59, 82, 123, 142,
        150, 152
    insatiable, 37–51, 164

Maghreb, 24, 31, 50, 77
Magian, 33
magic, 3, 29–30, 34, 53, 55, 60, 62, 78, 82, 89, 107,
        123, 132, 140
    bewitching, 33–4, 39, 43, 57, 59–61, 63, 107,
        132, 140
    magician, 26, 31, 60, 77, 83, 132
Mahdi-al, caliph, 18
Malti-Douglas, Fedwa, 1, 5, 125, 136
Ma'mun-al, caliph, 5, 15, 70, 84
marriage, 10–11, 21, 23–4, 26, 28, 31–4,
        36, 40, 68, 70–1, 73, 83, 85, 104, 112,
        121, 135
    monogamy, 24, 129
Marwan ibn al-Hakam, governor, 100
Marzolph, Ulrich, 1, 6, 49, 98
Marzolph, Ulrich and Richard van Leeuwen,
        1, 4–7, 12, 23, 43, 53, 55, 85, 122, 132–3,
        141, 145
masculinity, 37, 48, 139, 141, 167
Matarasso, Michel, 135, 137, 155
Mecca, 24, 82, 86, 109–10, 164

medieval literature
  European, 1, 37, 46, 50, 106, 123, 126, 140
  Middle Eastern, 5–7, 12, 17, 39, 41, 44, 46, 49,
      52, 106, 111, 115, 125, 139–40, 144, 146,
      149–50, 160–1, 167, 169
    Baghdadi-al, 6
    Daniyal-ibn, 6
    Fatila-ibn, 6
    Hikayat-al al-Ajiba, 6
    Jahiz-al, 41, 43, 146, 148
    Kamal Pasha-ibn, 6
    Maghribi-al al-Sanaw'al, 6
    Nadim-ibn, 6, 52
    Nafzawi-al, 6, 44, 111
    Nasr al-Katib, 6, 47, 125, 149, 161
    Qazwini-al, 6
    Rashid al-Katib, 6
    Saymari-al, 6
    Suyuti-al, 6
    Tahiri-al, 6
    Tayfur-ibn, 6
    Tifashi-al, 6
    Tusi-al, 6, 44
Medina, 100, 164
Mediterranean, 144
merchant, 16, 18–19, 21, 24, 28–9, 31–4, 63, 70,
      79, 82, 84–6, 89, 92, 97–8, 102, 113–16,
      118, 122–3, 133–4, 143, 147–8, 150,
      157–8, 164
Mesopotamia, 54
Middle Ages, 4, 38, 50, 54, 151, 170
Middle East, 2–3, 7, 50, 52, 55, 100, 104, 107, 114,
      117, 136, 138–9, 169–71
  medieval, 2, 5, 7, 122, 138, 140, 148, 169
Miquel, André, 3
Mosul, 15–16, 18, 102
Mu'awiya-al, caliph, 100
Murray, Jacqueline, 44, 126
Murray, Stephen and Will Roscoe, 139
Musawi-al, Muhsin, 4
music, 5, 15, 17–18, 126, 145
  Abi Atiq-ibn, 18, 79
  Ishaq al-Musuli, 15, 18
Mutawakkil-al, caliph, 17
mythology, 54

Naaman, Erez, 125, 158, 160
Naithani, Sadhana, 3, 56
narrative, 1, 6–7, 10, 15–16, 23, 39, 46, 49–50, 53,
      56, 64, 68, 88, 98, 107, 112, 125, 133, 139,
      149, 156, 169–70
Nile River, 103

obscenity, 3, 6, 9, 144, 168
Oman, 18, 164
orientalism, 170
otherness, 126, 169

Papoutsakis, Nefeli, 6
paradise, 14, 110, 141, 143, 145–6, 157, 164
patriarchal, 2, 13, 27, 37, 40, 44, 53, 61, 66, 90, 99,
      136–7, 139, 168
pederasty, 20, 125, 132, 138–51, 168–9
  admiring male beauty, 140–3
  anus, 148–50, 154
  homoerotic game, 144–7, 169
  pederast Abu Nuwas, 144–7
  paedophilia, 139
  sodomy, 145, 147, 150
  trade, 147–8, 168
  vs. heterosexuality, 148–9
  vs. homosexuality, 139–40, 168
  women, 149–51, 168
penis, 6, 11, 21, 38, 40, 42–5, 49, 142, 145, 148,
      152, 154–5, 157–8, 162–6
  size, 43–6, 49
Persia, 24, 26, 30, 60, 81, 95
Pinault, David, 146
poet, 3, 13–15, 18, 49, 79, 99, 128–9, 144–7,
      161, 168
  Abi'Atiq-ibn, 18
  Asadi-al Waliba, 144
  Asma'i-al, 14
  Nuwas-abu, 144–7, 168
  Rumi Jalaluddin, 49
poetry, 6, 138, 141, 144, 169
  ayriyat, 6
  contest, 14
  ghazal, 144
  khamriyyat, 145
  mudhakkarat, 144
  mujun, 138, 141, 144, 168–9
  platonic, 144
  verses, 14–15, 19, 100, 127, 143, 145, 148, 153–4,
      160–1, 165–6
pornography, 2, 6
poverty, 21, 31, 100, 121
promiscuity, 24, 40, 77–87, 129, 167
  intermediary husbands, 85–7
  multiple conjugal, 41, 80
  polyandry, 77, 85, 168
  polygamy, 24, 77, 83–5, 136, 168
  two sisters, 78
prostitution, 6, 8, 10, 17–20, 131
  brothel, 18–19, 164

qadi, 11, 21, 31, 80, 85, 91, 93, 120, 124, 146, 162
 Abu Yusuf, 85, 94
Qur'an, 3, 52, 54, 83, 141, 146

rape, 38, 47, 51, 65–71, 88–9, 127, 131, 147, 168
 politics, 65, 68–71, 168
rationality, 40, 65, 74–5, 142
religion, 31, 52–3, 74, 131, 139, 141, 146
 interfaith tension, 66, 75, 123
Resnick, Irven and Keneth Kitchell, 54
Reynolds, Dwight, 6, 52, 125
Rome, 138
Rosenthal, Franz, 149
Roth, Norman, 6, 52, 125
Rouayheb-el, Khaled, 138, 141
Rowson, Everett, 6, 125, 141, 144, 149–50

Salisbury, Joyce, 38
Samarkand, 58
San'a', 24
Scandinavia, 140
sexual
 allure, 10–22, 53, 98, 112
 aphrodisiacs, 6
 desire, 12–13, 22–3, 29, 31–3, 36, 39–41, 43, 48,
   108, 127, 138, 143, 155, 167–8
 fun, 14, 91, 117, 150, 156–8, 169
 game, 14, 134, 137, 140, 143–7, 150, 156–8, 169
 jealousy, 20, 45, 57–9, 79, 84, 97, 102
 medicine, 18
 morality, 2–3, 16, 139, 171
 nymphomania, 47–8
 objectification, 17, 20, 148
 orgy, 27, 103
 outlook, 7, 10, 12–15, 20, 35, 39, 77, 167, 169–70
 performance, 20, 37, 43, 46–8
 pleasure, 8, 17, 36, 46, 112, 148–50, 156, 169
 punishment, 45
 riddle, 11, 162
 taboos, 7, 65, 71, 158, 168–9
sexuality, 2, 5, 7, 23–36, 53, 56, 65, 68, 98, 123,
   125, 127–9, 131, 139–40, 158, 167, 169
 contrasting, 125, 139, 148–9
 demonic, 52–64, 167
 faith, 21, 89–90
 female, 12–15, 37–51, 70, 88, 167–8
 inescapable, 23–36, 112
 male, 37, 43, 88, 148, 167
 risk, 20–2
 travelling, 23–7
 violence, 58, 64–6, 68, 70–1, 102, 104–5, 117,
   127, 168

Shahrazad, 2–4, 56, 64, 68, 103, 170
Shahryar, 4, 27, 43, 61, 64, 68, 98, 102–3,
   106, 112–13
Shahzaman, 26, 61, 68, 98, 102–3
Shamy-el, Hasan, 71
Sharlet, Jocelyn, 138
Sheba, queen, 54, 84, 104
Shiraz, 30
Solomon, prophet-king, 54, 63, 78, 84, 99,
   104, 164
storyteller, 3, 52, 79
Sudan, 26
Sufism, 141, 149, 168
Syria, 30, 54, 133, 135, 148

Talmon, Adi, 5, 12
telepathy, 18
Thousand and One Nights. See Arabian Nights;
   Alf Layla wa Layla
Tigris River, 19, 94–5
trade, 4–5, 9, 93, 147–8, 167–8
transsexuality, 53, 132–3, 169
 cross-gender dressing, 125, 132–7, 169
   ghulamiyyat, 125
Tunis, 60
Turk, 91, 96

vagina, 35, 41, 47, 80, 148, 152, 157–8, 162–3
vengeance, 40, 42, 65–6, 68–70, 77, 99, 103, 107,
   112–13, 134, 168
Victorian era, 2, 171
virgin, 11, 47, 54–5, 57, 59–60, 63, 68, 81, 100,
   107, 131, 146, 156
virginity, 29, 31, 35–6, 65, 69, 136, 167
virility, 37, 43–4, 46

Western, 1–3, 170–1
women, 6, 12, 16, 23, 68, 80, 88, 96, 103, 140, 167
 agency, 4, 13, 21, 25, 57, 71–2, 88–9, 99,
   101, 111–12
 city, 107
 kidnapping, 54–5, 58–62, 127
 old, 12, 14, 16, 33, 38, 47, 61, 74–6, 83, 92, 97,
   101–2, 104, 111, 113, 115–16, 130, 133,
   156, 160–2
 self-control, 40–1, 108, 150
 suspicion, 88, 92, 95, 97, 106, 114, 117, 168
Wright, J. W., 145

Yemen, 17, 24–5, 34, 54, 63, 82, 84, 142

Zubayda, caliph wife, 32, 57, 83–4, 94, 126, 162